Nebraska Stories

Nebraska Stories

Tales of Cowboys, Ranchers, and Assorted Characters

CRAIG SAVOYE

Nobadeer Press
13331 Featherstone Drive
Saint Louis, MO 63131

Cover painting by Caitlin Heimerl:
www.caitlinheimerl.com

ISBN: 978-0-578-03277-1

Printed in the United States of America

Order this book at www.nebraskastories.com

Contents

Foreword

THERE'S a couple of things you need to know before we get started.

The Homestead Act of 1862 said a feller could get himself a hundred and sixty acres of government land for free if he settled on it for five years. A section is one square mile—six hundred and forty acres. When I say a quarter, I ain't talking about the thing jangling in your pocket. I'm talking about a quarter of a section—the hundred and sixty acres I just mentioned the government would give you title for when you're claimed up.

When settlers first come out here, weren't a tree in all the land. Prairie fires would burn them out before they ever got a chance to grow. Government wanted trees, so a way of getting a second quarter was to agree to plant trees on your claim. Called that a tree claim.

Best be straight about one thing: there are ranchers, and there are farmers. A rancher raises cattle and a farmer raises crops. Some do both, but for the most parts it's best not to be calling one the other.

About a million years ago—or maybe it was a hundred million, I ain't a geologist—this was all high, flat land out here in central Nebraska. Then it began to erode. So now you got a mess of what looks like hills and small canyons and broad river valleys and high plateaus. Most of the towns are down in the valleys and along the rivers. So when I say something like 'up on the table,' I'm usually talking about ranch land outside of town. Call it tableland, too. One you'll hear about is called Ryno Table.

You might say the geographic center of this book is Broken Bow. South of town about fifteen miles runs the South Loup River. It eroded the table there and created the Seven Valleys. Lot of folks I'll be telling you about are from the Seven Valleys— Callaway and Oconto area—along with Broken Bow and on up into the Sand Hills.

Broken Bow, the Seven Valleys—those are in the middle of about a hundred square miles of tableland and plateaus. Sometimes referred to as hard grass country.

Sand Hills are something else. They cover half the state, north central and northwestern. That's soft grass country.

A couple of other things: If I say an animal is going to town, whether it's a cow, a horse, a goat, or a sheep, it means it's being shipped for slaughter.

When I say ornery, it don't mean mean, usually. Ornery is practical joking. Mostly it's good-natured, but sometimes it's pranking with a bit of attitude.

If I say a feller left the country, it don't mean he went off to Russia. It means he left the *country* ... left central Nebraska.

All right, that should be enough to get you started.

The Horse Trader

MERLE McGee was a horse trader. Might of known horses better than anyone in Nebraska in them days. Merle called himself a religious man, but since horse auctions was always on Sundays, I don't reckon he got in much pew work. He was only about five foot seven inches and a hundred and forty pounds, but he always stood as straight as a fence post. Skin looked like an old saddle or cracked sheets of ice. Lot of horse traders are showy folk, wear a premiere Stetson or the like. Not Merle. He preferred a soiled ol' felt. Let him slip around the arena unnoticed.

Merle might of been a might short, but he had the hands of a giant. Big, powerful hands. He told stories with his hands and you found yourself watching them near as much as his eyes. There were scars all over the backs of them. Dozens. Some wounds you could tell been stitched up by country doctors. Scars looked like zippers. Some folks pull out a photo album and point to a picture and say, Remember when we was there? Merle, he could point to any of them scars and do the same remembering. Whole history of his life was gouged into the backs of his hands.

Fingers told a story, too. You couldn't help but notice them. They'd had a rough go of it. Flattened, most of them was. Over the years they'd been squashed by closing gates and trailer doors. City folk might wonder how a feller who worked around horses and cattle all his life could be so careless, but if you ever come nose-to-ass with a two-ton bull trying to back out of a trailer on you, you'd understand. It's better to get that gate closed in a hurry—and flatten a few fingers while you're at it—than save your fingers and have that bull turn you into a mattress.

Annnnnnnyway, horse auctions were held most times in a big ol' tent with a ring inside and bleachers all around and an auctioneer on a platform off to one side. There were also pens and corrals and staging areas out back. One time, Merle was at an auction over at Benkelman, in southwestern Nebraska, when a farmer come riding into the sale ring. Now, a farmer can tell you everything you'd ever want to know about tractors: induction-hardened crankshafts, spray-ready cabs, rotating drivelines, you name it. But a farmer don't typically know much about horses. Not like a rancher. And this farmer, well, this ol' boy come riding into the ring that day in Benkelman sitting in a high-back saddle—you know, a show saddle—and he was duded up in a shirt and hat. Merle was eating a sandwich while watching the action, and he about choked on his beef brisket when that farmer rode in. Spotted himself a feller he could do business with. Regular horse trader's dream.

And that poor horse, she just looked like hell. There was an old bridle on her, with rusty buckles. Cockleburs in her tail. Lead rope was gray it was so old. Mare was covered in dirt, just caked on. The hooves were in rough shape, too. They were so long they were curling up at the ends. But Merle, he seen the diamond in the rough. Little did he know.

Auctioneer usually lets a seller say a few words about the horse that's up for sale. The farmer—remember, he was all dandied up—should have been ready for his spell in the spotlight. Instead, he was dumbstruck and mumbled something about her being six years old, real gentle, name of Diamond. Ain't that perfect? Diamond. He didn't say nothing about why he let her roll around in a mud puddle before he put her up for sale.

Diamond didn't exactly create a stir among the crowd when the auctioneer started in. Who'll give me one hundred? Let me hear a hundred. One hundred.

Smoke from dozens of roll-your-owns hung from the top of the tent all the way down to the bleachers. No sound except Diamond whinnying, and no arms raised except the dandy farmer wiping sweat from his brow.

Auctioneer kept at it a spell and then started belittling the audience. Come on boys, we're looking at a fundamentally sound horse here. Good lines on this chestnut. Good carriage.

About then he run out of things to say. 'Course, all that was just to provide him a bit of cover for what come next—a price cut. Seventy-five, he said. Let me hear seventy-five dollars for this here fine animal.

Now, any auctioneer worth his chant knows who the horse traders in the audience are because that's where the action is. Auctioneer that day kept his eyes coming back to Merle about as often as he blinked. By now Merle was ready to start doing business. He raised his right index finger real slow and put it on the brim of his hat just above his ear. He run that finger forward along the brim of his felt until he got to the front edge. Then he left off the brim and let his finger fall until it was pointing direct at the auctioneer. That was his way of bidding.

Auctioneer's shoulders slumped in relief. He was happy to have a bid of any kind. Seventy-five. We got seventy-five dollars. He tried some more cajoling, done his best pitter-patter, but there was no budging the rest of that crowd. Merle's the only one seen National Velvet being led around the ring. Rest of them seen a bottle of glue. Sold!

Merle bought himself a rough-cut diamond for seventy-five dollars.

Now, most folks stay for the whole auction, even if they've done their dealing for the day, and retrieve the horse they bought when the sale is over. But Merle slipped off the side of the bleachers and headed around back to the pens. He come up on the head herdsman and asked if he could fetch Diamond so's he could take a look at her. Herdsman went and got her, and Merle led the mare over to where there was a sheep shack and a hose.

Merle set to work on Diamond. Trimmed and filed her hooves to a fine semicircular shape. He washed her down, cleaned her up, brushed her, sheared her, buzzed her mane, pulled her tail. That means shortened it. A woman at the beauty parlor don't get finer attention than a horse in Merle's hands. Spent a good three hours making that horse up to look like a thoroughbred, which, of course, was what Merle's business was all about—making a poor horse look fair, a fair horse good, and so on. Final step was to fit her with a brand-new red halter with gold buckles and tie on a shimmering white lead rope.

Merle was a showman. It wasn't the first thing you thought of when you looked at him because he wasn't much to look at, but he was a showman. Good horse trader got to have a pinch of that in him.

Merle finished up and headed straight for the consignment window. It was getting late. Said he had a horse for sale and asked if he could still sneak her in. They said sure and put his horse last on the list. Merle went to the head herdsman and told him he had a horse coming up for sale that day and asked if the herdsman could lead the mare into the ring. Save Merle from coming all the way back down there. Head herdsman knew Merle was a deck of fifty-three cards and must of figured something was up, but he agreed, and Merle give him a piece to say about the horse.

Well, near the end of the sale, head herdsman come walking into the ring leading a horse that looked like a pretty fine specimen. Beautiful shiny coat, trimmed hooves, sheared mane, groomed tail, bright red halter with shiny buckles, a white lead rope.

Auctioneer says to the head herdsman, Tell us about this here horse.

Head herdsman said, Got a six-year-old here, real gentle, good teeth, healthy coat. Name of Ruby.

Well, fall off the bleachers. Goddamn if Merle hadn't turned a Diamond into a Ruby over his lunch hour. Merle was sitting up in them stands quiet as a church mouse, no expression on his face. None. It was poker time, and cards were on the table. 'Course, his hat was so low you couldn't hardly see his baby blues in the shadow of his brim anyway, but the darkness sure made the twinkle in them eyes clear visible.

The head herdsman didn't make no claims about Ruby being a good roping horse or a cutting horse or nothing like that. He just paraded that chestnut around and let the horseflesh do the talking. Auctioneer started the bidding at a hundred fifty. *Started* it at a hundred fifty. An arm goes up right off. Merle sets back to eating the sandwich he'd started on three hours before, but I reckon it was more for cover than out of hunger. That first bite camouflaged the corners of his mouth, which were starting to creep skyward. He'd made seventy-five dollars profit before the bidding even commenced.

Who'll give me one seventy-five? Let me hear one seventy-five. One seventy-five! Thank you. Let me hear two hundred. Two hundred is still a bargain, boys. Am I offered two hundred? Two hundred! There's a man knows horses.

Bidding got real spirited. There was one feller, couldn't see him clearly, just would not be denied. Took a special shine to that horse the way buyers can. Bid Ruby up to three hundred dollars before everybody else dropped out. Auctioneer banged his gavel and then pointed it at the proud new owner of Ruby.

Merle was staring down into the ring. A bite of sandwich got lodged in his throat when the buyer appeared out of the stands to claim his horse. Merle didn't hardly panic even when he started turning blue. Looked like someone was going to have to give him the Hemlock maneuver, but the brisket finally come out on its own. Got his breath back after a few stifled coughs.

The feller who bought Ruby was the same farmer that brung Diamond in the first place.

The Walking Scale

FELLER named Judge Boblits come out from West Virginia in 1872 looking for land. Carried the flag at Antietam for Johnny Reb and got shot but lived. Settled for a spell down along Plum Creek near Lexington. Started a tannery business.

The judge rode up into these parts in the fall of '72 from the Platte River, just him and two trappers. Never saw a white man in three days, just grass all through central Nebraska. Next year and for a few years after, they run cattle up from Texas. In '76 they moved into the Seven Valleys permanent, place called Willow Ranch. That was the year his son, Jim Boblits, was born. Folks come pouring into the country after that. Judge Boblits was the first Custer County judge. He organized the county. He was about nine parts cattleman and one part judge, but everybody called him Judge.

This is about Jim Boblits, the judge's boy. Had a load of personality. Just like a barrel of honey. Smarter 'n heck. Silver tongue. Always in the center of things. By age seven or eight, they had him out on the road selling produce to farmers. That's darn near like selling snow to Eskimos. But he come away with a pile of cash every time.

Pretty soon he was buying cattle—as a kid, eleven, twelve years old. Got himself quite a few head and a pretty good bank-roll by the time he was thirteen.

One day he rode out to see a rancher about some cows, a

feller he'd never met before. Rancher takes one look at him and says, I ain't gonna sell cattle to a kid.

Jim says, My check's good.

Don't need much more than that in this country. Feller done business with him that day and for years after. Jim Boblits had three thousand head before he was twenty.

One time when he was still young, he was down to Cozad, to Hay Days. That's what they called it. Raised a lot of hay down there in the valley and had themselves a festival every year to celebrate. Jim was with his cousin, Ed Stuckey. They were the same age and always giving each other the business, but they were close.

Had a little contest going at Hay Days. There was a big ol' hog in a pen and two jars on a table. You stuffed a dollar in the first jar and stuffed your guess about that hog's weight in the second. Closest one got a prize. As they walked by, Ed tells Jim, he says, You don't know much about cattle, and you know even less about hogs, but you ought to give a donation.

Jim barely give that hog a look and says, You donate, I'll guess. Ed paid the dollar, but Jim never slowed his walking while he pulled a pen and paper from his overalls, wrote his name and a weight on it, and stuffed it in the second jar on the way past.

They gone a bit further and there was another contest. This one has five hogs of all different shapes and sizes. One was two hundred pounds or so, another maybe four hundred. Object was to guess the total weight of the five hogs. Well, some other boys was standing there scratching their heads and chewing on their pencils and figuring the average weight and adding it all up. Ol' Jim stops for about five seconds, writes his name and a number on a piece of paper, and then slips it in the jar.

Later that night a feller come over the loudspeaker and asks Mr. Jim Boblits to please report to such-and-such a place where they're doing the weight-guessing contest for that big hog. Loudspeaker goes silent for a second, and then the feller comes on again and says, Will Mr. ... Then he pauses and you hear him shuffling his papers like he got 'em mixed up, but then he goes on. Asks will Mr. Jim Boblits please report to such-and-such a place where they're doing the weight-guessing contest for them five hogs. He won both contests. Come within eight pounds on that big ol' hog and within twenty-five on the mess of them.

Later on he was known wide for that talent. One morning as he was driving past the Brighton ranch, he sees a bunch of the boys in a pasture with a pen and pulls his truck over by the fence. Them boys had weighed a bunch of big, fat cows the evening before. Two, three dozen of them. Big scales they used were sitting right there in the field next to the pen. They all knew Jim Boblits, and knew about him, and they got a mind to test him.

Got a wager for you, Jim, one of the cowhands says to him. We'll bet you a fifth of whiskey you can't pick out the fattest cow we got here. They knew, but Jim didn't, the top two weighed within five pounds of each other. That's about the same as a one-pound difference between two grown men.

A little smile come across Jim Boblits face as he pushed through a gate in the fence and crossed the pasture to the pen. Deal, he says.

It got quiet as he eyed them cows a spell. After a few minutes, he cut out two from the small herd and then looked them over for a long stretch. Finally, he says, That one on the left is the heaviest.

Well, them cowhands snickered a bit, but not much, because he was close. One of them says to him, You done all right, Jim. Them's the two fattest, sure are, but you picked the wrong one of the two. One on the right is heavier.

Jim says, Run them onto the scale.

Them boys start shaking their heads and smiling. Jim, the one says, that's the whole point. We weighed them cattle yesterday, so there ain't nothing left to know.

Real calm, without no anger or nothing, Jim Boblits says, Run them onto the scale.

Now the mood of them cowboys changes a bit. Start to get their bandanas in a twist. They ain't real happy to be challenged. It was a friendly little contest Jim had lost, but he wouldn't take losing. They got a mind to show up the famous Jim Boblits, so they done like he said. When they weighed them two cows, the one on the left that Jim Boblits said was fatter, was fatter by six pounds. Them boys at Brighton couldn't believe their eyes looking at that scale, even though they figured out right quick what had happened: the cow on the left had loaded up on hay and water overnight. But how Jim Boblits could tell that, they had no idea.

Ol' Jim just chuckled and collected his fifth. He was a walking scale is what he was.

Most everyone in this country, especially in them days, knew cattle. But Jim Boblits just seemed to know them a little better than everyone else. One time he was up in Mullen looking to buy a bunch of heifers. A rancher had driven them down from his place deep in the Sand Hills, couple of days on the trail. Ol' Jim had gotten into town just after the cattle arrived, and when he went to inspect them, they were bloated. He suspected the rancher had watered them good, trying to make them look fatter than they really were. Fatter cattle, fatter price. Rancher said they'd watered, sure enough, but he ain't overdone it.

Jim wasn't sure what had happened because the rancher didn't seem like the cheating kind. Jim Boblits looks around and sees there's a hill leading into town, and he asks the rancher if he'd walked them in or run them down that hill. Rancher says they busted loose a bit when they smelled water and come down the hill at a run, but his hands had rounded them up right quick. Jim tells the feller it ain't the water; they were bloated from breathing hard running down that hill. Rancher had never seen that before, and he'd been working cattle for fifty years. Jim seen it before. They settled on a fair price without much trouble.

Another time he was at an auction up there in Dunning, or somewheres. Some fellers was weighing cattle, and Jim Boblits moseys on over. The heifer on the scale just then come in at six hundred and thirty pounds. Now, you got to picture the scene. There's a dozen or so cattlemen, some standing around the scales, some trying to load and unload their stock off of trucks, move them, get them weighed. There's a lot of grunting and groaning and hee-yas and dust flying all around.

Folks who seen him and know him, they says hello to Jim Boblits, but for the most part, he's just standing out alone on the periphery of things, watching, taking everything in. Finally he says in a calm voice, but loud enough to be heard over the ruckus, That heifer don't weigh much more than six hundred.

Things got quiet real quick. Every set of eyes in the place turns on him and someone says, Who are you, mister?

Someone else who knows him says, That's Jim Boblits. Check the scales.

They checked them, and them scales weren't balanced proper. Heifer weighed six-o-four.

Jim Boblits got into everything he got into in a big way. He owned fifteen thousand acres at one point. 'Course, doing everything in a big way included drinking and gambling. Once, down in Oconto—place called White Hall—he got into a poker game that gone on for three straight days. It was in the '20s. They slept for a couple of hours at daybreak and then went right back to it. Lot of drink got spilled, and a lot of pride found its way onto the table. It was one of them games where all the players was real stubborn cusses. Got more serious than it should have. On the first day, Jim Boblits lost his new car. Next day another feller lost a quarter of land. When it was all over, Jim Boblits had won a dry goods store and a grocery store. Wouldn't want to be the feller that gone home and had to tell his wife he lost the family business in a card game.

Jim was a gambler through and through. In his blood. He used to wear fancy clothes around town. Tailor-made. Looked like a banker. Every time he had a suit made, he'd ask the price, and then he'd pull out a coin and say, Double or nothing? Store manager rarely bit on the offer, and Jim was probably 50-50 when it came to getting a free suit versus paying double for the one, but he always pulled out that coin.

Everybody liked Jim because he liked everybody. When ranchers would hire cowboys to round up their cattle and drive them down to the railhead, most would just pay them off at day's end and the boys would head home. Not Jim Boblits. He'd tell them cowboys to tie up their rides in the barn and feed them with his oats. Then he'd fill them cowhands full of steak, bed them down in his house for the night, and then see them off in the morning with the best wages in the Seven Valleys. Just the way he was. Done things right.

Not that Jim was any saint. In '23 he went down to Benjamin, Texas, and bought up thirteen hundred and one head of cattle. It was about the first of May. Plan was to ship them north by rail, unload down in Lexington, and then drive them north to Custer County. But first he had to get them cattle through Benjamin to the railhead. Well, it was springtime. Flowers were out in people's gardens, and town was looking as good as it ever done. But it didn't look so good after thirteen hundred and one head of cattle come through. Tore up a mess of gardens, and there was bull shit everywhere.

Some of the ladies from town caught up with Jim Boblits. One stepped forward and said, Mr. Boblits, are you the man that owns these cattle that tore up town?

He says, Yes, ma'am.

She says to him, You know, you ought to make right and clean up this mess.

Jim Boblits, setting up there in his saddle, looks around and says, Ma'am, I think it would be a might easier to move the town.

But in the end he left behind a few cowboys to put a shine back on things.

Had his own way of operating, for sure. One day he was up in one of them Sand Hills towns—Mullen, think it was—up there along the railroad. Went into a little hotel. Late afternoon after a long ride. Couldn't sleep. Damn mattress was as lumpy as bad gravy. He's two stories up, but he just opened the window, tore the sheets and blankets off, and threw the mattress right out into the street. He gone downstairs and says to the manager, Is there a furniture store in town? She says there is. He says,

Well call them up. You need a new mattress upstairs. She says, I made that bed myself this morning. He said, Well it ain't there now, and it ain't made, neither.

Feller come in just then and wanted to know whose mattress was blocking traffic out front. She give ol' Jim a look. Don't give it no never mind, he says to her. I'll be paying for the new mattress. But when I come through here next time, I want to sleep in the same room as my mattress.

Jim Boblits always wore one spur—just one. Feller asked him, Jim, why do you ride with only one spur?

Jim shrugged and said, If one side of the horse goes, the other's got to.

In the '20s, when things was roaring elsewhere in America, there was a recession out here. But Jim Boblits was doing all right in them days. Besides his ranch and cattle and store, he owned a partial share in a bank, if you could call it that. Weren't a lot of real banks in them days. Lots of folks just lended to one another. That led to Jim's downfall. Back in '29 when a feller down in southeast Nebraska couldn't pay him, there was a chain reaction and he lost nearly everything. Cattle, bank, store. Woke up one morning flat broke. That maybe ain't so bad if you didn't have much to begin with, but he'd operated big since he was a little feller. By '32 he lost his land, too. That's what hurts a feller most. Bottle got him after that. He lay drunk for years. Eight years, I think it was.

Haven't said nothing yet about Almira, Jim's wife. A woman's got to do what she got to do for her husband and family. It was unusual to see a woman in a poker game in them days, but those fellers would take anyone's money—or try to. During the Depression, when Jim was laid up with the bottle and things were real tight, she'd find a poker game when she rode into town for supplies. She was good, too. Steady hand. Kept the stakes reasonable. Usually won her a sack of flour or a load of potatoes. Family had to eat, and she was a resourceful woman.

Just before the war, about 1940, Jim hid the hooch for good. Come downstairs one morning after a bender and announced to his wife and that he was done drinking and was getting back in the cattle business. And that's what he done. His wife had kept them in groceries and made sure his insurance was paid up, so he borrowed some money from the insurance company and some relatives and leased a ranch. Place was run down—cockleburs and sunflowers everywhere, wire down on the fences. But he started making some money. Jim Boblits knew how to do that. Just had to plug the bottle. He got an option on that leased ranch in '43.

Things have a way of happening out here … can be tough on a feller. There was a time, right after Jim come off the bottle in the early '40s, when he only had about fifty head of cattle. Remember, he once owned three thousand head. There's a creek on that ranch he leased, and where it runs by the ranch house, the erosion was pretty deep. Little canyon there must be thirty or forty foot down. Well, half of Jim Boblits' cattle, about twenty-five, fell into a sink hole near there and died. He almost uncorked again. But he'd already decided to hitch up his belt and get back at it, so it didn't trip him.

Got to admire a man who starts over at sixty-five. That's how old Jim Boblits was when he put away the bottle. He made money well enough at ranching from then until the day he died at seventy-two, and he stayed dry the whole time. But the story of his life—not quite reaching his potential—played out until the end. After leasing that ranch for seven years, he was finally fixing to buy it. Like I said, owning land, owning a ranch, puts you in the game out here. Jim Boblits died a month before the papers come through.

Luckily, Almira was able to buy the place outright in '48, and it's been in the family ever since.

Nowadays at cattle sales, they got a scale built right into the floor of the auction ring. Cow come out and its weight shows up right away on the board … digital read-out come up there. Always makes me think of Jim Boblits, doing all that numbering in his head. Ain't gonna see his kind again.

Francis

JIM Boblits's daughter was Francis. She didn't have it easy growing up. When she was old enough to know her father, his glory days were behind him. He'd lost his bank and general store and ranch, and he laid drunk for a good stretch of her growing-up years. Her mother supported them with a post office job, but it didn't exactly afford a life of luxury. And when Jim Boblits did get off the bottle and gone back to work, it was on the ranch he'd lost, and for a dollar a day to start. That's tough on a man's pride, and a child can feel it. She gone off to boarding school in St. Louis and college in Colorado, but she came back to Nebraska. Married Wayne Jenkins. I'll tell you about him later. They moved onto the ranch her father first leased in '40 and her mother bought in '48.

Francis didn't really fit into this country. Had a different way about her. She was smart. She traveled. She read and could talk on any subject. Other women said things about her. Said she never knew when it was dinnertime, couldn't get a meal on the table. She belonged to ladies clubs but didn't like going because if a woman didn't show up, they'd gossip about her. Francis didn't gossip. You could tell her something and it was just like dropping it in a well. Never said a bad word about no one. She had her friends, and for them she brought 'out there' into their small-town world. She volunteered a lot. Helped out quiet, didn't make a show of things. Had a heart of gold. She could also ride a saddle horse and shoot a gun and drive a tractor if she had to. And no one ever got the last word in on Francis.

Every spring there was a roundup on most ranches out here where the cattle were branded and vaccinated. No different at the Jenkinses' place. Big noonday meal was typical on a ranch. Reward for a morning of hard work and fuel for the afternoon. Wasn't any pile of sandwiches, neither. Usually quite a spread. And that was every day. When a branding crew was there, it come close to looking like Thanksgiving with all the potatoes and rolls and gravy. 'Course, it was beef instead of turkey.

Annnnnnnyway, one spring day back in the early '60s, a branding crew of eight or nine piled into the ranch house at noon for supper. Usually neighbors helped out, but there were always some young hands—local boys—got hired for the day, too. Francis was hustling. You know how that goes. A cook wants to get the timing right so everything is out on the table at the same time, piping hot. 'Course, the boys weren't lifting a finger to help. Ol' Francis didn't expect no help neither, but a cook can get a bit steamed doing ten things at once while everyone else ain't doing nothin'.

Well, the boys started talking about shooting. Bragging, I should say. They'd shot this, and they'd shot that. They could shoot a coon at two hundred yards and a deer at four. Longer they waited on the beef, beans, and biscuits, the longer their ammunition traveled before it hit the critter they were aiming at.

Francis wiped a hand on her apron and raised a finger toward the window in the kitchen door. She pointed to a corn pile over on the side of the drive and said she'd gotten good at picking off squirrels that had a mind to climb the stack and have at the corn.

Heck, that corn pile couldn't have been more than twenty-five paces past the door, but oh, you should have heard the boys go off on that. You're telling us you could hit a squirrel way over yonder on the corn pile? they says.

Yeah, sure, I've been shooting them right off the corn pile, Francis said.

'Course, part of it may have been the Jenkinses weren't known as a big hunting family. First time Wayne's older boy was pheasant hunting, hell, he barely got to the edge of the backyard when a pheasant come up. He took a shot. Hit the broad side of the barn but didn't come near the pheasant. Except he did scare the hell out of the thing and it flew straight into the trunk of a tree. Stunned itself and fell to the ground. The boy run over and beat the durn thing to death with his shotgun. Come back into the house with that critter held high, real proud. Looked like road kill. Wayne had to explain to him which end of the gun to rely on.

Annnnnnnyway, No woman could shoot a squirrel that far away, one of the boys says. Guess them squirrels know about you all right, another one said, 'cause I don't see none of them out there right now. Pretty soon they got names for her. Dead-eye Francis. Calamity Jenkins. They were getting pretty familiar. For them boys, it was like they'd taken to bragging about how they were the best cook in them parts. This was shooting. This was *their* thing. Didn't want to hear a woman busting in talking about picking off squirrels at twenty-five yards while she was stirring the beans.

It went on and on for a good stretch of jabbering, and the boys got themselves pretty well amused about the whole thing. They'd pushed it about as far as it was proper to be pushed. Wayne was fixing to say something when a look come up in

Francis's eyes. The young hired boys didn't know she carried her rifle all over. One time she came around the side of the house with it and there was a traveling salesman on the front porch. Don't shoot! Don't shoot! I'm leaving! he says. He dropped his case and run off. Had to fetch him back in the truck. He thought Ma Kettle was going to blast him twixt the eyes and bury his body in the lower forty.

Now, Francis didn't pay no mind to the boys just setting there while she was slaving over the stove, but they'd worked her over pretty good about her shooting. She ended up as steamed as her broccoli. You never wanted to get her that way.

A couple of times while the boys were funning her, she took a look out the back window. Next thing you know, Francis drops a plate of mashed potatoes in the center of the table real hard and real unpleasant and disappears into the boot room off the kitchen. She came back holding her .22. Them boys knew they'd about toed the line in terms of riding her 'cause a couple of them slid back their chairs from the table real abrupt. Don't suspect they really thought Francis was going to plug them, but that don't mean they weren't ready to dive under the table if it come to that.

Francis moved over to the window. It was one of them new drop-down kind. By the time she got the window down, everyone around the table was leaning toward it. They could see a squirrel sitting on a branch in a big cottonwood tree out back, about fifty yards off and thirty foot up.

Francis had barely set the butt of that rifle on her shoulder—hardly sighted the thing—when she pulled the trigger. Blast rattled the plates setting on the table, not to mention a few nerves. Out in that tree, the squirrel departed this world before it ever departed the branch it was sitting on. Thing spiraled to the ground.

Francis put the rifle back and went over to the stove. Got real quiet in the dining room. Real quiet. Smell of gunpowder put a nice little exclamation point on Francis's demonstration. There was no more talk about shooting that day. Conversation drifted to other matters.

Not like Francis was a tough ol' ranch wife, though. Mostly she relied on her smarts. Like the way she handled them coon hunters. Wayne let all kind of folk use the ranch for hunting. Friends and friends of friends mostly. But one group of hunters weren't welcome. Coon hunters. Not a lot he could do about them, though. Wayne's cabbage patch stretched for a piece, and they'd sneak on after dark. They were a sorry lot, the pack of them. Weren't above picking up a stray calf while they were hunting. And of course they left gates open everywhere they went. Nothing will rile a rancher more than an open gate— except for cattle rustling itself. Open gates are to cattle what matches are to kids. Somehow the two seem to find each other, and there's a pack of trouble when they do.

The whole turkey thing didn't put them coon hunters on the right side of Wayne, neither. He and a few neighbors had come up with a plan to bring wild turkeys back to the county. State got on board, and it got done. One spot was near Wayne's ground, where Spring Creek and the South Loup come together.

Leader of them coon hunters was a man named Slick. He and his boys got to turkey poaching, and goddamn if they didn't nearly wipe out the flock by the next year. Slick couldn't keep his goddamn shotgun sight off nothing with fur or feathers.

No, it wasn't no secret who them coon hunters were. Only

ones who kept hunting dogs in the back of their trucks year round in special boxes. Wasn't no coon hunting season, of course, so there was no off season. That's why they carried them dogs all the time. They also had spotlights attached to their trucks, right up there by the side view mirror so the driver could point it and search the ground as he drove along slowly.

Them dogs of theirs got the royal treatment. They were a coon hunter's prized possessions. Fed them steaks. Some said the dogs got better treatment than the hunters' wives, but that ain't saying much. Takes years to train a good hunting dog, and they don't sell cheap. Sometimes bring as much as a horse.

Annnnnnnyway, them coon hunters would come in through a back gate and work a creek bottom or any other stretch where they'd expect to find coons. When they spotted one, they grabbed hold of the rope to the dog box and yanked her open. Them dogs would go flying out of the truck bed yapping up a storm, and most times they'd drive the coon up a tree. The coon hunters would steer their pickup over and turn the spotlight on the critter until they locked on the coon's eyes. Ain't like stalking a deer. It ain't even like hitting a deer from a blind. That coon ain't going nowhere. They'd take a last swig of liquor, put down their cigarette, drag their backside out of the truck, and drop the coon out of the tree. After the dogs mangled the body, the hunt was over. Raccoon ain't much for eating, and it ain't much for wearing. They'd sell a pelt now and then, but mostly it was just killing for killing's sake, which didn't make no sense to Wayne, especially when it was on his ground.

One night, Wayne was home and he got a call from Francis up in Broken Bow. She seen Slick's truck turning onto Ryno Table. It had taken Francis awhile to get to a phone, which meant the hunters were already on the Jenkinses' place. Wayne grabbed his coat and shotgun and jumped in his truck. At first he didn't hear any dogs yapping or see any spotlights, but then one popped on down by the creek pasture. Wayne kept his own lights off and snuck up on them. The coon hunters didn't hear Wayne's engine because of their own. He managed to get real close before he eased to a stop and got out. Wayne was like most ranchers, up before the sun and worked until she gone down, so he wasn't happy about spending middle-of-the-nights policing his pastures.

When Wayne come up on them, the coon hunters' truck was facing away, backed up to the edge of the creek. Wayne commenced firing over the top of the cab. Them coon hunters didn't pause to investigate the disturbance. They floored the accelerator. Engine of that pickup sounded like a 747 winding up for takeoff. They were in loose dirt at the edge of the creek, so them tires spun like windmills in a twister. They kicked up so much dirt they about built a dam across the stream before the rubber grabbed. Truck went flying out of there. Coon hunters got away.

This is where Francis come in. Next morning she was up early like always and making breakfast—a country breakfast—bacon, eggs, toast, the works. That's when it become clear how well them hunting dogs were treated. One after another they come out of the woods and off the pastures. Before you knew it, there were half a dozen dogs in the front yard howling for breakfast. The coon hunters had run from that buckshot so quick they'd left their prized dogs behind.

After locking the dogs in the barn with a bowl of plain old dog food, there was a family powwow. They had options. They could call the coon hunters and have them come get the dogs. They could keep them locked in the barn and torment the hunters, make them think them dogs were lost and scattered. They could call the sheriff or the game warden. Or they could shoot the dogs and hang them along the fence out front. Before breakfast was even finished, they begun seeing cars that weren't their neighbors' cruising slowly by the front of the ranch.

It was Francis come up with a plan both smart and elegant. All agreed, and she went to work on it. She wrote a story for the Saturday *Custer County Chief*, the local newspaper. She described in detail them coon hunters' trespasses, both literal and spiritual. Talked about them abusing another person's property, the wanton killing, almost getting a load of buckshot themselves, and hightailing it out of there without their dogs. She told it in a way that made them coon hunters look like the Three Stooges, but she also mentioned their dogs were safe, if maybe not as well-fed as they was used to. Francis closed by inviting the coon hunters to drop by on Sunday afternoon to retrieve their dogs. Except she left out a couple of key details— like her name and address.

In Broken Bow, Callaway, and Oconto, almost everyone reads the paper, and they read it careful. Story like that's as big as a four-alarm fire. At the coffee shop, the grocery store, the filling station—everyone was talking about them coon hunters getting theirs and wondering who the mystery writer was. Except, of course, the coon hunters. They knew exactly which ranch it was.

Family went to church on Sunday, except Wayne, who guarded the barn against a commando raid by the coon hunters. Late Sunday afternoon a pickup come up the quarter-mile driveway of Wayne's place so slow it looked like it was experiencing engine trouble or had a flat tire. Weren't neither, just good ol' fashioned hangdog.

Slick was no sooner out of his truck than Wayne was over there next to him hotter than a pistol. Been building for years. Trespassing, rustling—ain't nothing worse—and them turkeys, too. Just plain upsetting the natural order of things.

Wayne put his finger on Slick's chest and started giving him the what for. Kept poking him, and Slick kept backing up until he finally bumped into the barn.

Slick could hear them dogs in there. He was a tough feller, but he knew right from wrong, and he knew he got an earful coming.

Wayne kept his eyes on Slick but grabbed the barn door and flung it open. Having said his piece, he turned away and headed for the house while them dogs flew out of the barn. They were seeing daylight for the first time in three days, but it didn't slow them down none. Slick didn't move so slow, neither. His pickup made its way down the driveway a lot quicker than it made its way up. The Jenkinses never seen another coon hunter on the ranch.

Francis was a thinking woman, but she could be impulsive, too. The day she and Wayne moved onto the Boblits ranch in '57, there was an auction in Callaway. Somebody was selling out. Francis went in and bought some furniture for their new place. When she come back home in the car, she found out Wayne had just left in the pickup with Elmer Birnie, a neighbor friend, going to get another load of stuff from Wayne's place in Broken Bow.

Well, Francis wanted the truck in order to pick up the furniture she'd just bought. So she gone after Wayne to switch cars and caught him and Elmer on Ryno Table. It was a graded road then. Well, everyone was a little excited that day, and as Francis come up beside them boys, waving for them to pull over,

she come a little too close. The road was backsloped. She cut
Wayne off and run him clean off the gravel. Upset the pickup.
I mean the thing tumbled like a tin can on a breezy day. Wayne
don't necessarily keep a clean cab, so crap was flying all over
the place—a jack, a wrench, a tire iron—whiles he and Elmer
were going topsy-turvy, too. They were ducking them tools and
holding on for dear life at the same time.

Truck ended up upside down, along with Wayne and Elmer.
Driver's door was caved in and stuck shut. Wayne shouldered it,
managed to get it open finally, and ambled up the embankment
to the road where Francis was standing waiting for him. Behind
Wayne, the truck was on its back, looking like a dead animal,
its tires pointed to the sky and spinning slowly, a wisp of smoke
issuing forth. Elmer could be heard shoving tools aside and
trying to figure out upside from down.

What do you want? Wayne says.

I want the truck, Francis says.

Well, you can have it, Wayne says.

Francis died of cancer before her time. In an age when a
ranch wife weren't given much of a chance to leave a mark, she
left the only kind of legacy that matters—one of friendship and
goodwill.

The Kleptomaniac

RALPH was a piece of work. People checked their pockets, purses, and even the collection plate when Ralph was around. His place bordered the northwest side of the Jenkinses' land. Messiest place you ever seen. Hard to tell if it was a ranch or a junkyard.

You'd see Ralph ride into town with a tarp covering a load of shelled corn in the back of his '65 Ford pickup. Never ever did sell it. He'd come back from town with the tarp covering an even lumpier load, and you'd wonder what came home with the corn. All along his route, things would go missing. They had a way of getting lost in Ralph's corn. Big things. Little things. Many things.

For the longest spell, years in fact, folks didn't figure it out. Like the salt the Jenkinses put out for their cattle. It came in blocks. Every now and then, a few would go missing. Or a pitchfork. A feller would swear he'd left it in the hayfield, but it wasn't there, and when he got back to the barn, it wasn't there, neither. Never thought someone would *steal* your salt or your pitchfork. Didn't even occur to you.

But over the years, a lot of things gone missing. Too many things. Everyday things mostly, but every month it'd be something. The Jenkinses stored some bowling chairs in an old house they had upriver, and those come up missing. Toolboxes, shovels, tires: vanished like aliens come took them. After a while, not sure exactly when, folks begun to figure out that Ralph and all them missing things intersected.

Forced everyone in Callaway to get a bit creative. Like Wayne with his new pitchfork. Didn't feel much like hauling it back and forth just so Ralph couldn't get his hands on it, so he left it out in the field like he always done, but he wadded a bunch of tape around the handle first. Ralph never touched it. He was discriminating. Didn't care for a broken pitchfork been taped back together.

Lot of folks would go into town and get their groceries on Saturday night. You'd put the bags in the back of your pickup and maybe go over to get an ice cream or something. Got to the point where folks up and down the street would be loading them grocery bags in their truck beds with their heads on a swivel, seeing if Ralph was in town, wondering if they could get themselves an ice cream cone without losing most of their food for the week.

When Ralph's brother Floyd died, they had a sale at Floyd's place, and Wayne went up the day before with his boys to look things over. Them boys gone into the barn, and next thing you know, there's a god-awful racket—banging and smashing and things getting knocked over. Sounded like a bull got loose in there.

Right then a feller come flying out the side of the barn. Must of found a hole there, but from where Wayne was standing, at an angle where his view was blocked, it looked like the feller was shot out of a cannon and right through the barn boards. Feller run out with his arms filled to full, like he done a week's worth of shopping but didn't bother getting it bagged. He couldn't hardly see where he was going since that pile of crap was higher than his head. When he reached the bank of the creek, stumbling and bumbling the whole way, the feller tripped and tumbled head over heels. It put some separation between him and that load. He disappeared over the edge while the load of crap he was carrying sailed up in the air and hung there a country minute. Must of buried him down by the edge of the stream when man and goods reconvened. 'Course, it was Ralph. He was stealing from his dead brother. If that don't beat all.

Herb Ringenberg come up from the Platte Valley and bought Floyd's place. Wayne was standing out by the barn once, there on Floyd's old ground, and Herb says to him, Wayne, this is good cattle country up here. Mighty fine grass, but, my God, do the cows eat a lot of salt in this valley.

Wayne says, Herb, how close to the road do you throw out your blocks?

Herb says, I dump them right over the fence. You could toss a cow patty with your wrong arm and hit the road from where I drop them.

Wayne says to him, Try putting them out in the middle of the pasture. Out of sight is best. The cows won't eat them so fast out there.

Along with salt blocks, ranchers also put out protein blocks for their cattle in late fall. Wayne had a regular route where he'd start at one end of his cabbage patch and end up at the other, putting out them blocks all along the way. Once, when he come up short of blocks, he figured he'd just spread out the ones he had, so he gone back by the same route he come rather than making a big loop like he normal done. Well, when he gone back, there's ol' Ralph, loading them blocks into his truck. He's picking them up almost as fast as Wayne was setting them down.

'Course, Wayne give him holy hell. And when he saw Ralph that winter on the street in Callaway, he says, How your cattle doing? Pretty good, Ralphs says. Wayne says, Well if they ain't, I can try buying a different brand of protein blocks.

On Saturday night, a few of the fellers would sometimes hang out at Ransey's Garage. Mechanics in there would work on cars for nothing while the fellers talked. Ol' Ralph would come in, set on a workbench, visit for a spell. Then he'd get up to leave, but before he reached the door, Bill Ransey would call out, Wait a minute, Ralph.

Bill would mosey over and check him, and sure enough, Ralph had stuffed all the wrenches on the bench into his pockets. No one seen him do it, but they knew Ralph, so they didn't let him out of there until they shook him down.

Once, folks called a meeting in Callaway. Ralph been stealing more than usual, and they were all getting steamed. One feller threatened to go to the sheriff. Another one said, No, Ralph's got a problem, and we have to be understanding. Wayne says, No, *we* have a problem. He's stealing all our stuff.

'Course, Ralph ain't the only feller like that. Joe Andrews had a neighbor like Ralph near his place, up on the Niobrara River. Joe had a small apple orchard on the east end of his land, maybe seven or eight trees is all. One September a neighbor feller—nice enough but poor and a little shifty—come over and visited and said he and his wife were going to take a little vacation to see his sister in Colorado. He asked if Joe and Wilma would watch their kids. Joe said that'd be fine. And then the feller says he has fifteen milking cows. Asks could he bring them over, too. Joe says, Sure, no problem.

So all that happened, and them neighbors done their vacation and come by after and got their kids and their cows and gone home. Well, a few days later, Joe and Wilma gone down to pick them ripe apples, and they couldn't believe what they saw. Nothing! Trees had been stripped bare. Not a goddamn apple in sight. Joe come to find out his neighbor was in town a few days before his Colorado vacation selling apples on the street. So the feller left his kids to be fed and his cows to be milked at Joe's place to go on a vacation financed by stealing Joe's apples. What in tarnation.

Annnnnnnyway, it all came to a head one day with Ralph when one of Wayne's boys was going to turn some hay over on the other side of the hill. It needed turning because it was wet. If you bale wet hay, it rots, and what you got yourself then is a pile of manure without the benefit of it going through a cow first. If the hay is turned, the wind and sun dry it out, and you got yourself some good winter feed.

The tractor needed to be loaded with gas first, so Wayne and the boy got in their truck and drove on over. 'Course, it was summer, so they just left the tractor out in the field day and night. Wayne got out there, and while he was gassing her up, his boy climbs up on the tractor, and durn if the seat ain't missing. They stood there scratching their heads. Weren't tornado season, but that seat had sure enough flown off just like a bird. Just an empty ass-shaped steel platform where the seat ought to be.

Well, didn't take a whole lot of reckoning before Wayne and his boy be looking at each other, and they say at the same time, Ralph.

They got in their pickup and drove over to Ralph's place none too happy. You never seen so much junk in all your life as you seen on his ground. Started at the driveway and covered both the front and back yard. Talk about tornados. Looked like a big one had toured the state, and then, when it come over his house, just up and quit, and everything in that funnel cloud dropped into his yard. There was a tireless tractor set up on stumps, scrap wood in piles, scrap iron everywhere. You name it, it was there: a washboard, chicken cages, enough tools to open a hardware store, and as many old tires scattered round as most other people have pennies in their drawer. Maybe even a kitchen sink or two in the yard.

Annnnnnnyway, Wayne knocked on the door, and Hazel, Ralph's wife, answered. She was a beautiful woman, no question. Hard to believe a woman that kept herself so pretty could live in the middle of that junkyard. She knew what Ralph was about, but she was married to him, so she turned just enough of a blind eye to make things work.

Weren't the time for small talk. Wayne says, pretty stern, Hello, Hazel. Tell Ralph to get my tractor seat.

She don't make a face of any kind. Just turns around and yells toward the back of the house. Ralph! Did you take Wayne's tractor seat?

There's a grumble from back of the house somewheres. Nooooo.

She turns back to Wayne, and he's as stone-faced as one of them presidents' heads on Mount Rushmore. She don't even bother continuing the conversation. She just turns right back around and calls out real slow and distinct this time, Ralph! Did you take Wayne's tractor seat?"

Ralph's voice don't change at all. Same grumble, kind of bored. Nooooo.

Hazel turns back to Wayne and his boy. It wasn't like Ralph's comment needed much interpretation, but she says, Wayne, Ralph says he didn't take your tractor seat.

Well, by then the hay Wayne's boy was intending to turn

that day was on its way to mush, and Wayne had fence to fix and cattle to move. He says to Hazel, I didn't ask if he took it. I told him to go get it.

Hazel's a bit more focused now, and she shouts out, Ralph, for the last time, did you take Wayne's tractor seat?

Nooooo.

Hazel turns back toward them Jenkinses looking real pleasant, like they just handed her a hostess gift. Nice smile, no nothing else on her face. She starts to expand on Ralph's comment again, but she don't get far along.

Wayne says, interrupting, That's all right, we'll just go get the sheriff and a search warrant and see if he can find the goddamn thing.

Hazel turns and yells to the back of the house in a voice that suddenly sounds like General Patton, Ralph! Go get Wayne's tractor seat!

Wayne hears some scraping as Ralph gets himself up out of his chair. He goes out the side door and shuffles across the yard toward the barn with his head down, never looking over at Wayne.

He was about halfway there when Wayne yells out, And while you're at it, get my damn bowling chairs.

A few minutes later, sure enough, Ralph come out of the barn carrying the tractor seat and two bowling chairs. He come up to Wayne and his boy looking everywhere but their faces—at the hills, his shoes, the junk in his yard, but mostly at the heavens—and he says, Think it's going to rain, Wayne?

Wayne says, It'll be a long, dry spell if it don't.

Wayne took the tractor seat and the bowling chairs and left.

That was it, never spoke of the matter again, though Wayne

and Francis and the boys enjoyed a nice cherry pie Hazel brought by a day or so later.

Don't expect many folks ever called the sheriff on Ralph. They'd of wrung his neck first. Folks just don't like calling the sheriff when it's a neighbor. Best to handle it yourself, even though with Ralph it weren't no innocent thing. One time Wayne was on horseback, driving a few head to a pasture that bordered the back of Ralph's place. He come up over a hill, and down below was Ralph's truck, parked and loaded with all kinds of crap. Saws and chisels and blowtorches. All of it brand new. At night he'd go off and sell the stuff. Fence it. No one ever knew where. But he made some real money on that arrangement. You steal every day of the week, never pay no taxes, and you got yourself a pile before too long.

When he got older, Ralph's family put him in a rest home, but he didn't want no part of that. There were some train tracks nearby, and one day he went out and got himself in the way of a fast freight.

After he died, everyone in town went over to his old place to get their belongings. They even found a tombstone in his yard. A blank one from a monument seller up in Broken Bow. Must of been. Only place in this part of the state that sells them. Damn if he didn't manage to load that stolen tombstone in the back of his truck somehow and drive off with it. Can't recall if they used it for Ralph's grave or give it back.

Annnnnnnyway, after he died, and after Hazel went too, come to find out they left half a million dollars to the town. Half a million damn dollars. That was a lot of money back then. Hell, to this day, every kid who graduates from the high school in Callaway gets money for college courtesy of Ralph.

Wayne was sitting at the kitchen table when Francis read

the obituary to him. Went on and on about how Ralph liked children—that was news, seeing as he didn't have none of his own—how he was an upstanding citizen, generous, hard-working, beloved, and how his passing was a blow to the community. Finally it says the schools and churches and parks and Kiwanis and God knows who else were all grateful to Ralph and Hazel for their generous gift of half a million dollars.

Wayne says to Francis, They should be thanking the whole town. We all chipped in on that deal.

The War Bride

DOROTHY Miller was a war bride. She was born a Scot and a city girl. From Glasgow she was. Henry Miller met her during the war, and when it was won, she came over in '46 on a ship filled to busting with other war brides. Even in them days, though not so long ago, she was a pioneer woman of sorts. Weren't no covered wagons, of course, but it weren't like her modern house in Glasgow, neither. They were still farming with horses in Nebraska, and Dorothy's first house out here was half framed and half sod—no electricity, no running water, no indoor bathrooms.

Henry Miller was in his mid-twenties when he joined the army in '42. Trained in Texas and cooled his heels in Iceland for a spell, and then he got sent to Scotland before being shipped to England for D-Day training. Now, there's some nice gals in Nebraska, but out here in the country, there just ain't a whole lot of them. So Henry, being as old as he was, was on the prowl for a bride.

Dorothy was eighteen when Henry showed up in Glasgow one day in '43. About the only thing she knew of Yanks was they chewed gum and called every girl they saw honey. 'Course, you know what the mothers thought. There's that old saying—must of come from one of the mothers—'Them GIs are overdressed, overpaid, oversexed, and over here.'

They met at a skating rink. Dorothy was there with some

friends. First time she laid eyes on him, he was clinging to the side of the rink. As she passed him, he says to her, Wonder if you could lend me a hand. I'm just not very good at this.

Old trick, but Dorothy fell for it. Henry made a show of leaning on her for support as they did their laps. By the end of the night, though, Dorothy noticed he was one of the quickest learners ever to lace on a pair of skates. Fact, he'd become the best skater in the rink.

He wanted to see her again and asked for her address, but she wouldn't give it to him. He said he could be shipped out at any time and wanted to keep in touch. So she gave him her address. Next night she was off dancing with another feller and come home to find Henry setting in her living room, just as comfortable as could be, talking to her mother and brothers. Dorothy wasn't so sure she liked the big Yank coming around so quick, but her mother become Henry's biggest fan. He was like most folks from these parts: come right at you, not a lot of beating around the bush. Second time he come to Dorothy's house, he says, Would you have any objections, Mrs. Wallace, if I managed to talk Dorothy into going to Nebraska with me?

Just like that he'd made up his mind. Picked a bride like he was picking a yearling at auction. 'Course, there was a war on, which tends to ignite a fire under romances that have barely sparked. Dorothy figured her mother would be hesitant to see her daughter take up with an American and disappear to another continent for the rest of her life. Instead, her mother lectured her about America being the land of opportunity and such. 'Course, Dorothy's mother changed her mind some about all that when she come over on her first visit and had to use the outdoor privy.

Annnnnnnyway, Henry kept showing up at Dorothy's

house. But it wasn't long before he was shipped down to England. Wrote a steady stream of letters to Dorothy. She was able to visit him, and the romance took off. They were engaged on one of those visits. Then came the invasion. Henry went in the third day and marched across France and Germany. She didn't see him for two years.

Henry had to get permission from the army to get married. They frowned on war marriages. It was the girls they were worried about, not the GIs. Them boys all looked prosperous in their uniforms, but the army was afraid them GIs were selling the girls a bill of goods, maybe inflating their assets a might. That wasn't Henry's problem. He didn't spend a whole lot of time talking about sod houses and outdoor privies, but he was always straight with Dorothy about his prospects. Finally, a chaplain took up their cause, and permission come through. They were married in Glasgow in the summer of '45, just after the war in Europe ended but before the Japanese surrendered. Henry was sent back to the States alone, in case he had to be shipped to the Pacific.

Army promised to send the wives over later. And there was a passel of them. Army was good as its word, but it wasn't until March of '46 it kept it. Dorothy came over on a troop ship with five or six hundred other war brides. Slept on a bunk. Mice and rats running here and there. Can't quite imagine being the captain of that tug. The girls were from all over Europe: French, Scottish, Irish, Belgian, Norwegian, English. Dorothy had to wear a big sign around her neck that give all her particulars. Some of the gals couldn't speak a lick of English, which is why they had them signs. The women were delighted to board that ship, figuring they were in for American food after four years of rations. They were right, but the food come up almost as soon as it went down. Rough winter passage. Took nine days instead of five.

Henry was from Gothenburg, Nebraska. The ship of war brides put in at New York. Dorothy took a train to Chicago and then boarded another one headed for the Great Plains. Henry was the oldest of eight children. When Dorothy stepped onto that platform in Gothenburg, they were all there to meet her: Henry and his six big, strapping brothers, his sister, and his parents. They were a good family to join, took her right in. Just about swallowed her up. No time to be lonely or homesick.

She come in on a Sunday. Henry took her over to see the place he had just bought lock, stock, and barrel: pastures, farmhouse, cattle, horses, hogs, chickens, and a few other animals. His parents' place was only one spread over, but to drive there, you had to go half a mile around. They did that, and as they come up on his folks' place in the twilight, they were hit with the headlights from dozens of cars lining the highway. This was pretty far out in the country, not much around there. Having been in Nebraska only a few hours, it put a fear in Dorothy. Henry told her it was a shivaree bunch. Dorothy had never heard of that tribe before but calculated well enough it must be an Indian attack. By the time she pulled into her in-laws' driveway, she realized they were just people welcoming her. They come to see what color she was. Scotland was a ways yonder in those days, and there weren't many folks moving to Gothenburg from Glasgow.

A shivaree is nothing much planned. Just put the word out, and a shivaree bunch sort of forms up to welcome a new couple. Set a time, and folks come from miles around. That day Dorothy and Henry stood in the front hall of his parents' house, and the shivaree folks come in the front door one by one, shook the hands of the bride and groom, and then filed right out the back door. Don't know what shivaree means, exactly, but it ain't French for wedding shower. Had a bit more of an edge to it than that most times. Friends of the newlyweds would sneak onto their place at night with their headlights off and start firing off shotguns, lighting firecrackers, blowing horns, and generally raising Cain until the couple come out and invited everyone in for treats.

Along with the treats, there was some tricks. Them shivarees could be anywheres from a couple of dozen folks to a hundred. Get that many people together and throw in some drink, and the pranks sometimes escalated. Groom usually got thrown in the horse tank, among other indignities. Bedroom drawers got emptied. They'd hide things, too. Folks would find their undergarments in their chandeliers years later. A shivaree bunch would take the labels off of canned goods so newlyweds would never know what they were going to eat until they opened the can. Sometimes they'd hoist one of the bunch up the chimney, unbeknownst to the young couple, and he'd put a wet gunny-sack over the top. When the bride fired up the woodstove the next morning, the couple would get smoked out.

'Course, newlyweds knew the shivaree bunches were coming, just didn't know when. But who's going to stay up every night waiting? So most times couples got caught, but plenty slept with one eye open and got away. One time a shivaree come on a house and surrounded it and raised a ruckus, but no one came out. The bunch went inside and into the bedroom. It was clear the couple had gotten away just a short spell before. Well, they searched here, there, and everywhere inside the house, outside the house, under the house, in the barn. Left disappointed. Turns out they searched low but didn't search high.

Come to find out later the newlyweds were no more than thirty feet away watching it all and trying not to bust a gut from not laughing. Just about every house had a windmill for drawing water in those days, and the couple had scrambled up it when they heard cars coming up the drive. They sat on a small platform in the dark above the car lights and enjoyed the show.

Annnnnnnyway, it took a city girl like Dorothy a spell to get used to country life. First day walking into her house, she gone straight into the kitchen. Two rooms were sod and three rooms were framed. The kitchen was in the sod part. Had a hand pump in the middle of the sink to draw water. She looks over and says, What's that monstrosity? Something that looked like a beached battleship was setting right there in the corner of the kitchen.

That's your stove, Henry says. Stoves were big in those days.

Dorothy slid over to it. Where's the buttons, she says. How do I turn it on?

Henry scratched his head and picked up a corncob. Ain't no buttons, he says. These are the only buttons they got.

If you kept hogs, you used corncobs to fire your stove. Had to take the stove tops off, load them from the corncob pile outside, put a little kerosene in, and light them up. They burned real good. Dorothy was getting an inkling about her new life about then.

Soddies and city girls reminds me of a story from the Sand Hills. Thedford or Mullen, one of them towns. Late August a young feller was scheduled to go pick up a new arriving teacher from the east and fetch her back to the ranch next door, where she was going to board while teaching in a sod schoolhouse. She was fresh out of high school. Eighteen-year-old city girl from

Omaha or Lincoln or somewheres. Got her teaching certificate over the summer. Word was she was a pretty one.

This feller going to meet her had made a deal with a neighbor about his age to swap a draft horse for a saddle horse. Neighbor lived on the way to town, so the two of them boys hatched a plan. Decided to do their business and give the new teacher a welcoming party at the same time.

Well, the feller picked up that new teacher at the train station in town, and sure enough, she was as cute as a spotted pup in a little red wagon. He was just getting to know her on their buggy ride across them barren Sand Hills when a lone rider pounded up from behind. He was wearing a bandana over his nose and mouth and kept looking behind him. He drew on them and demanded their horse. Said he was a wanted man, a renegade, with a posse after him, and he needed a fresh horse. The bad hombre started unhitching the horse from the wagon at gunpoint but paused to admire the pretty young girl. Made some rather familiar remarks. The other feller moved over to shield her. He looks right down the barrel of that gun but don't quaver a bit, and he says real forceful, You go on now and take the horse and get on down the road.

The other feller saddled up and rode off. Teach's eyes were as wide as a heifer's dropping her first calf. She clutched that feller's arm and hid her face in his shoulder, amazed that he'd stood up to an armed desperado. She wanted to wait for the posse and tell them what had happened, but the feller convinced her they were lucky to be alive and have a horse, and rather than tempt fate, they should hitch up that horse and get on out of there before he came back for her.

Teach sure had quite a welcome. When they got her home

to the place where she was going to board, they had to pry her hands off the rails of that buggy seat.

Don't know how long it took her to figure out the last bandit roaming them parts probably disappeared about the same time as the last grizzly bear. She might of put it all together at her wedding when, after a whirlwind romance, she married the man that fetched her back from the train station that day … and the best man sounded a lot like the masked man that attacked them.

Annnnnnnyway, back to Dorothy. She wasn't as lonely as you might think. When you live out here, the land shrinks. Somebody lives over a hill a mile away, they're your neighbor. In fact, Dorothy talks about the neighborhood back in those days. Six or seven families there were in their neighborhood. Well, that doesn't mean it's one house after another on a shaded street in town. That means six or seven ranch houses within two or three miles of one another. Those houses were down in the valleys and hollows. Couldn't even see them from her place, but they were there. That's a neighborhood in these parts.

'Course, it still took Dorothy a while to adjust to things, especially remembering all the names. One time a couple, name of Green, come out to visit. In them days the women usually congregated inside and the men outside. So Mrs. Green come inside, and she and Dorothy were talking in there. Mrs. Green says, How do you like your new house?

Well, between the sod and the snakes in the sink and the corncob stove, Dorothy says, I'm afraid I can't say too much good about this house.

Mrs. Green says, It's not so bad. A little paint and paper would make a big difference.

Dorothy says, It would, but we don't have the money.

Mrs. Green says, The landlord will do that for you, won't he?

Dorothy says, No, he's tighter than a rusted screw.

Well, maybe she don't say that, because she's from Scotland, but something like it.

Mrs. Green don't say much after that, but she don't need to because that's when the men come in from outside and Henry introduced Dorothy to Mr. Green, their landlord.

Maybe the biggest thing took getting used to for Dorothy was the phone. Weren't any individual phones back then, they were all party lines. That meant the Millers' phone was connected to eighteen other houses. Anyone could hear anyone else's conversation. Way it worked was there were eighteen different rings. You were only supposed to pick up when you heard your ring. But people are people, you know. They're curious.

Dorothy's brother came over from Scotland not long after her and settled in Toronto. He'd call Dorothy regular. One time he was getting a lot of background noise on the phone, and he says, I can't hear you, Dorothy. Are Agnes and Nona and Edna all on the line, too? Real quick, Agnes and Nona and Edna all say, Yes, we're here! And they said it just as happy as can be. Dorothy's brother was just tickled by that, but it took Dorothy some getting used to. All that background noise her brother heard were the dishes clanking, chairs scuffing, and kids screaming in three different houses.

Thing was, no one was real embarrassed about being caught listening in. Just something you did. Not a lot of secrets out here. But it wasn't just the listening. One time Dorothy was talking to her brother, and they'd been going on awhile about family and such, and Dorothy doesn't know if anyone else is listening and ain't really thinking on it. Her brother says one of his kids has got a cold he can't shake. Well, ol' Agnes suddenly pops in on the conversation and recommends chicken soup with a pinch of zinc. Next thing you know, Nona is recommending gargling with salt water. Then Edna advocates plenty of bed rest. Dorothy was taken aback, but that was just the start. Agnes, Nona, and Edna commence arguing about the best remedy for a cold, and Dorothy can't get a word in edgewise with her brother, who's laughing and having a jolly time.

Some folks didn't just listen in, they figured it was their sacred right to. A neighbor of Lester Miles practically spent her life on the phone either talking to friends or listening to strangers. One time she told Lester to tell a couple of German fellers working for him to stop talking in German all the time. Lester says, Why's that? She says, 'Cause when they're on the phone, they could be talking about someone I know, and I don't understand them.

Using the GI bill, Henry and Dorothy bought a place near Callaway. Real house—wood frame, with running water, bathrooms, and a gas stove. Mostly pastureland, but some farmland, too. Henry did both farming and ranching all his life. Had four kids. Henry died pretty young, of cancer, in '77. After a few years, Dorothy moved into town. Family still owns the old place, and her youngest son lives on it. Dorothy's been widowed nearly thirty years, but it hasn't hurt her disposition none. One of the friendliest people you're ever going to meet.

The Flying Cowboy

THERE'S lots of fellers out here who know cattle and could have done well in the business—or did do well in the business—but their lives got hijacked by the bottle. None, though, was a finer cattleman or drank more than Davey Davis. Story of Davey is funny, sad, and uplifting all at the same time. He definitely seen some living in his seventy years.

Davey come from a cattle family. His granddad, Lon, used to drive cows up to Montana in the late 1800s, back when it was all open range. But one bad deal broke him. Bought a trainload of cattle up in the Sand Hills for eight cents a head and shipped them to Chicago. All he could get was three cents a head. After that he moved into Broken Bow, got a little house, and eventually opened up a Rexall drug store and became a country doctor. He'd make his calls in a horse and buggy. Delivered a bunch of babies all up and down the South Loup.

Davey's Dad, Albert, got back into the cattle business. He was a sharp one. Real sharp. Knew cattle and knew how to deal. Davey was born in Loup City. His mother died in childbirth when he was two. His dad remarried. The ranch Davey grew up on was thirteen hundred acres, about two miles south of Broken Bow. They run eight hundred, maybe a thousand yearlings. Take them to grass. Contract them. Sell them in the fall.

Albert was also a brand inspector for quite a spell. Ranchers would unload their cattle for auction, and he'd check the brand, make sure everything was legitimate. But he'd also get to talking to the ranchers as them cows come off the truck and ask them what they thought their load would bring that day. They'd say, Well, I'm hoping they'll bring two hundred dollars a head. If Albert thought that was a reasonable price, he'd wish them well, inspect the brand, and move on. But if he thought they were underestimating the total weight of them cattle and under-pricing them, he'd jump in and say, Hell, I'm looking to buy today, and that's a fair price. I'll give you that for them right now.

Rancher don't want to mess with an auction if he can get the price he been thinking on for a few days, so he'd say, By God, you can just have them. Rancher would sell his load on the spot. Albert would turn around and resell them cattle that same day in the sale barn. Maybe get two hundred ten a head. Them ranchers were already halfway home in their rigs about the time Albert was filling his pockets with the cash they'd left on the auction ring floor. He done it sale after sale.

Davey wanted to go to med school after college, but his dad had a heart attack. He lived, but Davey come home—suppos-edly for one year—to help out. His dad died when Davey was twenty-six, so Davey ended up staying put. He became a fine cattleman. He'd buy and sell cows from here to Iowa. Has a silver tongue and a way with folks. Opened a sale barn even-tually. Natural born auctioneer. Made a lot of money. Lot of money. But there was always the drinking.

The money would come in hand-over-fist, but it would go out just as quick. He was running bar tabs of over five hundred dollars a week, a tidy sum back in the '60s. People would call the bars in Broken Bow and ask if Davey was there. Bartender would say, Yeah, he's here. You want to talk to him? No, they didn't want to talk to him. They'd hang up real quick and rush over because they knew they'd be drinking all night for free. Davey picked up the tab. 'Set everybody up.' Them words must of come out of Davey's mouth about every night back in them days.

There's just nobody in a bar like Davey. To this day he can take out a newspaper and just start reading a story and make up voices and characters and pretend he's them and twist the words all around. Have the whole place howling just by reading from the durn paper. He done some crazy things in bars. One time he was headed over to the York Legion Club dressed in his usual cowboy gear. That morning in the newspaper he read where Sean Davis, the famous bronc rider, was going to be inducted into the hall of fame over the weekend at the Ak-Sar-Ben Rodeo in Omaha. But he wasn't going to be able to ride because he'd had a back injury. Well, after a few hours at the Legion Club bar, Davey got up slowly, stooped over from drink. A couple come up to him and they says, We think we know who you are. Davey says, Really? They says, What's your last name? Davey says, Davis. Uh-huh, they says, injured back. We knew it. You're Sean Davis the bronc rider, ain't cha? You're going to get inducted into the hall of fame down there in Omaha.

Hot dang, says Davey. How did you know all that? I try to keep a low profile. They says, Don't go nowheres.

They gone home and got their kids and brung them down so they could get pictures of the family with Sean Davis in front of the Legion Club. Right after the pictures, Davey notices the Ladies Auxiliary is having a cake sale that night. Them cakes usually brung five or ten bucks. Now, remember the sale barn. Davey's an auctioneer by trade, not a world-famous bronc rider. So he tells the ladies he'll auction the cakes for them. He says to the crowd, I'm starting them all at fifty, and I want you tight-wads to give it up for a good cause. Well, folks only bid them up to fifty-one or fifty-two bucks, but ol' Davey sold every last one of them cakes.

By then the family that got their picture taken with Davey was spreading the word about Sean Davis. One thing led to another, and soon Davey's autographing drink napkins all around. Everyone's whooping and hollering, and people are thrilled that Sean Davis is drinking with them in their little ol' club. All of a sudden the country-and-western band stops playing, and a feller gets up on stage and makes an announce-ment. He says, Folks, we just can't keep the secret any longer. We have a celebrity in our midst tonight, and we'd like him to come up here. The auctioneer you just had, well, that's none other than the world champion saddle bronc rider from White Falls, Montana, Mr. Sean Davis.

Crowd was beside itself. Men's chests swoll up with pride by association while the womenfolk clutched them new-bought cakes to their chests like they were flowers from a favorite suitor. Davey got up there and says, Well, folks, I've never seen so much hospitality in my life, and if you ever get to Montana with the family, come on by and we'll put you up in the bunkhouse and let you borrow some trout rods. And he went on and on like only Davey can. Then he looks down, and sitting right there in the front row are three big cattle feeders Davey done business with nearly every week. They were laughing so hard nothing was coming out of their mouths and tears were streaming down their faces.

Them boys never give Davey up that night. Folks in York didn't figure out which Davis was which 'til about a decade later. Not long ago, one of the ladies from the auxiliary—must be eighty-five now—she run into Davey's wife and told her in the thirty-odd years since, they ain't never come close to raising the kind of money at their annual cake sale as they raised the night Davey served as auctioneer.

Davey was merciless when it come to being ornery. One time he had a feller named Floyd—an old-timer from up there by Taylor—working for him at the sale barn sorting cattle. Well, Floyd was deathly afraid of mice. Davey was in the office once with some fellers and spotted a nest of baby mice. He got one and stuck it inside a box of wooden matches along with some coins. Floyd was across the room, and Davey shakes that matchbox with them coins in it and says, Floyd, how about going across the street to the restaurant and getting us some Cokes. On me. And he flips that matchbox to Floyd.

There was a screen door on the restaurant. Floyd opened it, went in, got them Cokes and brung them to the counter to pay. When he opened that matchbox and seen the bald baby mouse, he threw that box and that mouse and them coins up in the air, and coins and critters and boxes were bouncing off the ceiling and walls. Floyd took off and run smack-dab through that screen door like he's in a TV cartoon.

Floyd was so damn mad when he got back across the street, it looked like he was going to burst. He stormed down to the end of the pens at Davey's place. Had his prod pole with him, and he was banging it on the corrals and the ground and the cows and muttering about quitting and killing that son of a bitch Davey Davis. But Davey really needed Floyd that day. They were trying to sell twenty-five hundred head of cattle. This is how silver Davey's tongue is. It took him forty-five minutes, but he talked Floyd into not quitting and not beating him to death.

There was a similar incident, only a week or so later, with the Rittenhouse boys. They're twins. Davey decided to poke at their phobia, too—which was snakes. Must have been his success with Floyd that inspired Davey. He found a little snake, not even a foot long, and put it in his shirt pocket and went into a bar in Broken Bow. Snake just curled up in that pocket and stayed put, nice and warm in there. Davey ordered a drink and decided to do a little test before the command performance for the Rittenhouse boys.

Bartender was Dorothy. Come time to pay the tab, Davey pushes his chest out to her and says, My money is in my pocket there, Dorothy, but I pulled my shoulder yesterday down at the sale barn.

So Dorothy reaches in and pulls out that snake. She about wet herself. She screams bloody murder while throwing up her arms and leaping backwards. Her daughter was walking behind her carrying two pitchers of beer on a tray. Her, the pitchers, the beer, and the tray all went flying. Both women were mad as hell. Davey ended up buying everyone drinks and talking himself blue for half an hour apologizing and promising to mend his ways.

Well, that last part didn't go on long. Few days later Davey was in that bar again, and them Rittenhouse boys were in a booth. Davey got the same snake curled up in his shirt pocket. Davey known them fellers pretty well, and he bought them a round. Davey gets up to leave and, on his way out, passes their booth. They thank him for the drinks, and without stopping, Davey says, Sure boys, and have a snake on me. He tosses that snake in the middle of their table. Quicker than a switch can light a room, them brothers gone vertical. But there ain't much space in them booths, so in getting up real fast, they smacked each other flush in the head. Knocked one of them cold. Laid him out flat. At first everyone was too concerned about filling the conked-out brother with blackberry brandy and getting him revived to be mad at Davey. But when the brother starts coming to, muttering something about the short, sad life of Davey Davis, all eyes in the place turned on Davey. He got out of there quick. Ended up driving to their ranch the next day and found a way to spare his life, again.

Davey's orneriness got a long history. In college he saw the movie *Rear Window* and took a shine to it. So he and a friend bribed a security guard and got one of them starter pistols used in track meets, and Davey got himself a wheelchair. They gone down to the Strand, the movie theater in Lincoln, and when the show lets out, Davey—president of his class—rolls up on the sidewalk in the wheelchair to within a few feet of his roommate, and he says, You'll never step out with my wife again, you rotten little bastard—and blazes away with the gun. Bam! Bam! Bam! The roommate spins before he falls, turning so his chest, red with ketchup, is facing the crowd coming out of the movie house. In the dark, you couldn't see the barrel had no muzzle, but you could sure see the smoke and fire coming out of it. Folks that didn't scatter in every direction were hitting the deck. There was mayhem for a few seconds until Davey got out of the chair and his roommate got up off the pavement and they ran for it. Didn't get far, though. Both got fined fifty bucks for disturbing the peace.

Contrary to what you might expect, things started to go down for Davey instead of up when he bought a helicopter in a bar one night. He was heading to Iowa to see some Holsteins, but instead he found himself in a club along the way with a go-go dancer on a barstool on his right and a helicopter salesman on his left. Davey's buying the dancer drinks and jawing with the salesman, and he ends up buying the copter, mostly to impress the girl. Didn't know how to fly, of course. That was a problem and it wasn't. It wasn't because the salesman was a pilot, and he give Davey ten hours of lessons free, and then Davey soloed. After that you're supposed to take another thirty hours of lessons and then take a bunch of tests and get your license. Well, that's where the problem come in. Davey never bothered with them thirty other hours or the testing—or the license, neither. He just flew the durn thing. Just flew it. And drunk, usually.

'Course, the copter was practical in some ways. Davey owned the sale barn then, so instead of driving up to them huge ranches in the Sand Hills, looking at cattle to buy, bouncing around pastures at ten miles an hour, and opening and closing a hundred gates on every ranch, he'd fly and save a mess of time. And there was a bonus. Cattle are curious critters. He'd land that thing near a ranch house, and them cattle would come from miles around to stare at the blade spinning on idle. He'd count them up and judge their weight without ever moving more than fifty yards from his chopper.

But Davey couldn't just fly the thing. No, that ain't Davey. One time he seen a friend of his out in his combine in the fields, and Davey come down real slow behind the feller and just hovered there, following a few feet behind and a few feet above. Next thing you know, the farmer jumps off that rig while it's still going and runs like a headless chicken, falling and stumbling and tripping through the cornfield while that combine keeps on chugging along without him. Davey lands and can hardly stand up he's laughing so hard, and he asks the farmer why he jumped ship. The feller, not appreciating the humor near as much as Davey, says, All of a sudden there was a helluva noise everywhere, and the stalks was flattening all around the combine, and I thought for sure either my rig was going to blow or an alien was landing.

Speaking of hovering, back when Davey was getting them ten hours in, the salesman took him up for a lesson—learning how to hover. Guess hovering is easy unless you're the feller learning it. You got two different sticks to control this and that, and you have to move them just right so this tilts this way and that banks that way.

Annnnnnnyway, ol' Davey's hovering lesson was on a Sunday morning. He got a notion as to where his stationary flight plan ought to be. Afterward, he landed in a feed lot on the edge of town and come down to the house. Asked his mother how church went.

She was a staunch old Presbyterian—and a disgusted one that day. There was some helipeter thing, she says.

Helipeter thing, Mother?

You know, one of them whirlybirds. I don't know what he was doing, but he was right above our church the whole hour. I never heard a word of the service. It wasn't until a few weeks later that Mrs. Davis learned her son owned a helicopter.

Kind of ironic Davey was giving them churchgoers the business that day because the Lord done some hovering Himself back then—watching out for Davey, I mean. One time for sure He saved him for another day.

Davey lived in a real nice house in Broken Bow, built by a doctor originally. Big two-story house on a large lot. One time, after he'd had a pint of schnapps or more somewhere else in the state, Davey was flying home and says to himself, Hell, I'm not going to land at the airport and drive home when I'm this tired. I'll just land behind the house. It was a dark night, and of

course he'd never landed behind his house before, so he forgot
there was a radio tower back there with guy wires all around and
big power lines feeding into it. But, don't matter. He just landed
right there in the middle of all that. He goes into the house and
sleeps it off. Comes out the next morning and just about faints
where he's standing. Looking out at the parked helicopter, he
sees both ends of his resting main rotor are only a couple of
inches away from guy wires on either side. He'd landed in an
opening between wires that was barely wider than the rotor
blade itself. He doubted a stone-cold sober professional pilot
given ten tries in broad daylight could have landed where he did
… not that any would try it. In fact, Davey had to rent a flatbed
with a winch and haul the chopper out of there. Wasn't no way
he could fly it out.

Another time, over drinks I'll bet, Davey and his buddies
decided the chopper might prove to be an aid when it come
to duck hunting. They all gone out to the river. Davey got the
chopper up and headed downstream. He got a flock in the
air and tried to herd them over the blind where his buddies
were sitting. But it was like herding cats, and I don't think they
bagged a one that day except for a mallard that flew up into the
rotor. Davey got a call from the game warden. Said he'd fine
him big if he ever caught him hazing the ducks again. Davey
started to protest it weren't him, but the warden cut him off
and says, There's only one feller in the state—maybe even in the
whole world—would try to herd ducks with a helicopter.

But it wasn't where Davey flew the thing, it was where he
landed it that caused most of the trouble. Landed it in the main
street of Brewster once so he could get himself a six-pack in
the general store there. He blew gravel all over the street and
cars and buildings and put a scare in the women and children

and stray dogs. When he come out with his six, an ol' pug was standing there and he says, Goddang you, Davey. You stripped the damn paint off my building. You're going to pay for that. Davey says, Oh, bullshit. I'll buy you a drink, though. Feller moaned and groaned until Davey got a few in him.

One time, years after his helicopter phase, a woman come up to him and says, Davey, you remember the time you blew our hogs through the barn? He shook his head, trying to remember, because everything from them days was fuzzy from the flavored vodka. Then he remembered. He was flying up there around Halsey and got thirsty, so he decides to land in a large hog pen by the edge of town so he can visit a bar there. As he starts to land that big, loud, dirt-tossing chopper, couple of sows, fat for processing, got themselves all confounded and started *woof woof woof*ing. Stampeded for a lean-to shed at the edge of the pen and crashed plum through it like they just learned they were going to town. Davey got his drinks all right, but he ended up writing a check that day for the busted shed.

One time Davey flew into Omaha airport and called a feller he knew who runs a helicopter service and told him he was in town. The feller says, What did you drive down? Davey says, I come in my chopper. I thought you didn't have no license, the feller says. I don't. Well, the feller about flipped out. You can't do that, he says. Didn't they talk to you on the radio as you come in? Remember, Davey never took them extra thirty hours of lessons where they explained all that radio stuff. Davey says to the feller, Yeah, they were talking to me, but I didn't understand any of that shit, so I just shut it off. I think the FAA's still looking for Davey.

Since everybody liked Davey so much, he was able to juggle his life and the bottle for the longest spell. Once, he went off to

truck driver's school and came back and got a job out of Clay
Center. Vale was the name of the feller that owned the trucking
company. He must of fired Davey a dozen times. I can't put up
with this shit no more, he'd say. You're supposed to be in Des
Moines, and you're in a bar in Omaha. The last time he got
fired, Davey took a detour through Columbus and got a dozen
roses, and then he stopped at Vale's house.

His wife came to the door, and like everybody else, she'd
taken a shine to Davey, had him over to dinner a bunch of
times, treated him real good. Davey has his Stetson in one hand
and the flowers in the other and says to her, You know, Lois, I
just wanted to say good-bye. Ol' Vale has fired me, and I feel so
bad because we were just like family. And then Davey give her
the dozen roses.

Tears were streaming down her face. He is *not* going to fire
you! she says. Well, Davey drops off his truck in Clay Center,
picks up his last check, and heads to the bar. Vale calls him
there. Davey, what you doing? Get your ass over here to the
office. You and I need to talk. So Davey gone over there. You
son of a bitch, says Vale, and he starts laughing. I've had all
kinds work here, but none of them ever brung my wife flowers.
You knew damn well that was going to save your ass. And it did.
He not only hired him back, Vale took him out to the Legion
Club for dinner that night with Lois.

One time Davey took his mother's new Cadillac down to a
party in Lexington. Beautiful car. A doctor had owned it before,
but that was back in the days when well-to-do folks got a new
car every year, and Davey's mom got this one from the doctor
with only twelve thousand miles on it. Gorgeous camel hair
seats.

Annnnnnnyway, one thing led to another, and Davey

bought a mule from the owner of the spread where the party was at. Figured he could sell that mule at auction and make a little money off him. Only problem was he didn't have a trailer. So Davey loaded that mule into the back seat of his mother's new Caddie and rolled down the windows. Davey was so drunk it's a wonder he made it home, but he pulled into the driveway of his mother's house and went in to sleep it off.

There's a man named Harold worked for the Davises, along with his brother. Next morning, the brothers are sitting at the breakfast table when Davey's mother come in. She tells them she's going to go get her hair done and walks out. Harold says to his brother, I hear if you drink enough, you start seeing things. By God, I got to cut back. I went out to milk the cows about six this morning, and I could have sworn I seen a donkey sticking its head out of Mrs. Davis's car.

Davey stumbles down the stairs with a hangover right about then and walks into the kitchen. He says, What was you saying about seeing things? Harold says, I thought I seen a donkey in your mother's car. Davey's head cleared real fast. Just then, from out in the driveway, he hears, Davey!

Davey rushed outside with Harold and his brother trailing behind. They drug that donkey out of the car and looked inside. There was donkey crap all over everything, especially them camel hair seats. There was a series of high-pitched conversations about the matter over the next few days. Davey ended up trading in the Caddie for a brand new Mercury Marquis with them push-button shifts.

First time Davey went to rehab was '69. He was heading to Montana to buy cattle but rolled his car near Dunning, only an hour out of Broken Bow. He still made it up to Montana and managed to buy some cattle. But then he ended up in Reno on that same trip, where he went off on a bender. It's a long story. His family flew him straight to a treatment center in Minnesota. He walks into the dining room there at the center and sees a rancher from Valentine he'd been drinking with not two weeks before. Davey says, Jerry, what're you doing up here?

Jerry says, My wife made me come. I drove. But I had a few before I left home and forgot the horse trailer was hitched on with a pair of horses inside. Now they're charging me ten bucks a bale per day to feed the horses, and them mares ain't happy about living in the parking lot. Had to fly his hired man up there to haul the horses home.

Here's how Davey's life was going back then. His wife at the time was a former beauty queen, Miss Nebraska. Not that Davey wasn't responsible for his own actions, but she sure wasn't the antidote. When he come back from rehab, she threw him a huge open-bar coming home party to celebrate. Thanks, honey. He was fine that night, but after about six months, he'd tumbled off the wagon.

As it gone along, his wife announced she was leaving. Davey was so mad—probably at himself if the truth be known—he just up and took off. Left town in a truck. Left Nebraska. Left behind his sale barn. Headed west at first, landed in Colorado Springs for a spell. Met a feller there in the air force who had all kinds of different outfits and uniforms. Davey and him would dress up as doctors in surgery clothes and use a spray bottle with red die to stain their scrubs and wrap clear plastic around their shoes and walk into a bar. The bartender would hail them and say, How's it going, doc?

Davey would shake his head and say, God, that was a helluva surgery. Them brachiolysis-hysterochdemy-dorsi ain't easy when you *haven't* sprained your right wrist. I had to do that baby left-handed today.

The girls would swoon, and Davey and the feller would get free drinks from a grateful public. Sometimes this feller Davey met would call ahead to the bar and ask the bartender, Is Davey Davis there? *Captain* Davey Davis?

The bartender would put his hand over the phone and holler, Is there a Captain Davey Davis in here?

No Davey Davis. So the caller says, If you see him come in with the co-pilot—they're both wearing Hawaiian shirts—tell them our flight to Rio de Janeiro has been postponed and we have to lay over another night.

By the time Davey and his buddy got to the bar in their Hawaiian shirts, the story had made the rounds, and the girls flocked to them flyboys.

Davey ended up in Cleveland somehow. Hit bottom there. Lived in a Goodwill box for a spell. Once, about three o'clock in the morning, a feller come by to dump his old clothes. The little door on the Goodwill box ain't more than a foot by a foot—a pull-out/drop-down kind of thing—but the Goodwill box itself be maybe six foot square. Annnnnnnyway, this feller come by in the middle of the night and drops his clothes right on Davey's head. Voice come out of that dark box, What the hell you doing! Can't a feller get some sleep around here? In the streetlight, Davey could see the feller's eyes get as big as country moons.

Worked for a spell as a garbage man, but he never stopped being Davey. Ended up getting to know the fellers he worked with and went to a bar with them called the Hobby Horse. Four hundred or so people about every night. Bar was all black folks and Davey. They took him right in. He got to telling his stories, and they all know in short order he's a cowboy from Nebraska.

So, next thing you know, he gets some chaps and a holster and cap gun from the Goodwill store next to the box where he lives. At the Hobby Horse, he gets up on the pool table and pretends he's two black guys jawing and cussing one another. Remember, a speeding bullet ain't no match for Davey's tongue. He jabbered away, mixing a cowboy drawl with black street talk, both dialects wrapped around each other like the cords of a thick rope. He'd lasso the patrons, whoop it up, draw his cap gun, and have the two black guys shoot each other, and then he'd fall off the pool table dead. The whole bar'd be in hysterics. It become a regular floor show for several weeks. Got him a helluva lot of free drinks. Turned himself into the black drunken Will Rogers of Cleveland. Only Davey.

Making light of things here and I shouldn't. When Davey was in Cleveland, he was in tough country. A feller sitting next to him was blown off a barstool with a .357 Magnum. Davey finally got himself together enough to hitchhike home. Showed back up in town one day, '74, I think it was. Been gone four years. Started to get himself straightened out but still struggled with the bottle for quite a spell. Met a nice gal, LaDonna. She had her own problems with pills and booze, but she give it all up in 1980. Made it easier on both of them to have each other. Davey finally took his last drink February 23, 1981.

You can imagine Davey's finances got all wrapped around a wagon wheel back then. A lawyer told him it'd be best to declare bankruptcy, but he wouldn't do it. After a few years back in Broken Bow, he finally called a friend and told him he was ready to pay off a debt with interest from the '60s. Feller said he always knew he'd get that call from Davey one day. Davey wrote a check for $56,216 and a few cents.

That was Davey, see. Even in his drinking days when he done some crazy things, he never cheated a man. Weren't none of that. Everybody knows that when Davey tells you a thing, that's the way it is. Which is how he could come back to town and get himself on his feet again. Does real estate now. Part of some national firm. He's their best producer in something like nineteen states.

Couple of years ago, Davey won an award from the Elks for citizen of the year in Broken Bow. Deserved it. Come a long way back from living in a Goodwill box in Cleveland.

Horatio of the Heartland

RAY Brown come from nothing. I mean nothing. He was born up on the table south of Broken Bow. His mother come up from Kansas, his father come out of Indiana. His dad was a laborer. Changed jobs quite a bit. Family moved a fair amount, too. They lived in a soddy for a while and then come into town when Ray's father got a job working at Walt Harris's scrap yard. But then come '29.

Fellers like Ray's father were hit hardest by the Depression. Not like it was easy on the farmers or ranchers. Plenty of them packed up and left the country, but if you had land you maybe could scrape by growing your own food. But day labor work, all them jobs just dried up and blew away. Ray's father been making ten cents an hour when he was let go. They lost the house they'd bought a few years before for $170. Couldn't afford the four dollars a month in mortgage payments. All through the '30s they had no regular money coming in.

Ray's father was a good shot, and there was still plenty of game around here back then, so Ray would go out with his father most days and hunt everything from raccoons and skunks to coyote and badger. To this day Ray can call out the price for them pelts: coyote bring you four bucks, badger bring as much as six or six fifty, coons were about four bucks and a half, muskrat about ninety cents, skunk would get you two fifty. Hell, two and a half bucks would buy groceries for a week for a family of five. But that's in winter time. Can't sell furs in the summer.

Family never bought any meat. Only meat they ate was what they shot. They got tired of eating cottontail several times a week. Ray's mother and father talked on it awhile and come up with a plan. They chopped up three or four pounds of rabbit meat and three or four pounds of sausage, mixed it all together, and created rabbit burgers. Guess they're pretty good with beans and cornbread.

The Browns' first house in Broken Bow was near the railroad tracks. Had two bedrooms and a porch around it. Ray had five sisters, no brothers. His folks got one bedroom, a couple of sisters got the other bedroom, and the rest of them sisters got the living room. That meant Ray slept out on the porch, summer and winter. Wintertime, he'd get in his makeshift bed out there, and his sisters would pile blankets on high as a haystack.

Short time later, the family moved across the tracks into a different rented house, but it didn't have any electricity or water. Quarter mile away from the house was a park. Ray was about eleven or twelve then. When the family needed water, he'd take his wagon over to the park where there was a hydrant. In the wintertime the hydrant froze solid, so he'd have to build a fire and wait for the ice to melt before he could draw any water.

Ain't like Ray is one for self-pity. When he tells stories about growing up, he's the first to say they had plenty of neighbors had as tough a go of things as the Browns.

Ray never made it past the eighth grade. Well, that ain't exactly right. He went to high school for six weeks. One thing he's good at is math. He's a whiz is what he is. Not long after the school year begun, he had a test in algebra class. Sixty problems. Aced the test. The teacher was outraged and accused him of cheating, saying there was no way anyone could do so well without cheating. To prove his point, the teacher called Ray up front and made the thirteen-year-old face the class while the teacher wrote a new set of ten problems on the board.

The teacher spun Ray around and handed him the chalk and told 'smart boy' to solve them. Ray did, like they were one plus one equals two. He was just that good at math. Teacher took and erased them problems and answers and accused him of cheating again, I guess by magic this time rather than somehow stealing the answer sheet. Teacher grabbed him by the strap of his overalls and hauled him down to the principal's office.

Ray admits to maybe getting under the teacher's skin before that by raising his hand on occasion in class and correcting him, but that ain't no excuse for what the teacher done. Got him expelled for the rest of the semester. Weren't no appeals or challenging authority in them days. Ray never went back after that. He ain't a bitter man, but all that don't set well with him to this day.

Started working construction. Wasn't a lot happening in '36 and '37, but he got some work digging footings with a shovel, mixing cement by hand and pouring it, tending the bricklayer, tarring roofs. Learned the business from the ground up, literally. Then the WPA come into being, and there was money to build schoolhouses and whatnot. That's about when he started getting construction in his blood.

Ray got married in '38 at age sixteen. His bride was seventeen. In them days, small towns without no movie house would show a film for free outdoors against the side of a building. Ray met his wife Dorothy while watching a free movie shown against a hardware store. They was married for sixty-three years before she passed.

Ray was in the service during the war. Had two kids by then, but he enlisted in the navy anyway. At gunnery school in Virginia, he stepped out and says, Anyone here from Nebraska? Feller by the name of Don Denesia raised his hand. He was from Wayne, in the northeastern part of the state. Later, by chance, they were assigned to the same ship. Ended up island hopping in the Pacific—Guam, Saipan. Ray was a gunner's mate on an amphibious landing craft; Don was a fire control officer.

Okinawa is the last island before mainland Japan. That's where Ray was, getting ready for the invasion of Japan, when the atomic bombs were dropped and the war ended.

Ray and Don talked about what they'd do after the war. Don wasn't sure. Ray was. He was going into the construction business. They decided to form a partnership and thought about setting up shop around Dallas, but when they come home, there was so much work in Nebraska, they just stayed put. Their first nursing home job was in Osceola, Nebraska, in 1961. Ray didn't even know what they were at first. Thought they were a home for retired nurses. The one in Osceola might have been the first free-standing dedicated nursing home that wasn't in a large city. It filled up quick, and they built a slew of them over the next few years.

In '65, Ray and Don built a nursing home in Franklin Groves, Illinois. Little town of about six hundred. Filled right up. Their local partner says, You know, half these people don't need to be here, but they got nowhere else to go. Solution seemed obvious. They added another wing and another kitchen and put all them people in there didn't need all that nursing. Within two months, both wings were filled. That was one of the first assisted-living centers in the country.

One time Ray was on one of his job sites. Wasn't no smoking

allowed, but Ray come upon a feller digging a hole as he was puffing away.

Ray says, Ain't no smoking on the site. How come you're smoking?

Feller says, I'll smoke if I want.

Ray says, You're fired.

Feller gets out of the hole a bit dejected, goes down to Ray's trailer, collects his wages, and heads off.

Next day Ray is back on the site, and there's the same feller in the same hole, smoking and digging.

Ray says, What are you doing back here? I fired you yesterday.

Fellers says, I know, but I've never worked for you. I work for the telephone company.

Ray had a scare back in 2002 when a doctor told him he had a certain type of fast-spreading, inoperable cancer and had three months to live. He went to another hospital, and they confirmed it was pancreatic cancer. He got his affairs in order, a will and all. Arranged for his own funeral and sold a bunch of properties. An accountant told him to liquidate everything, but something told him not to.

He went to more doctors and got himself a shock, a good one. The cancer really turned out to be carcinoid syndrome of the pancreas, whatever the hell that is. It's a long way of saying he has a benign tumor that don't really bother him none. That only happens to three people in a million. I always said Ray was one in a million, but I guess three is pretty close.

Annnnnnnyway, by the time he got the good news, he was supposedly down to only a few weeks to live. You can imagine his relief. Well, Ray didn't get where he is in business by being loose with his money. He marched right down to that funeral home and got a refund for not dying. Got his money back for the service not rendered. He's still going strong today. His business been going for sixty years.

All told, Ray's built over four hundred buildings, most of them nursing homes, but there were also quite a few assisted-living facilities and retirement centers and a handful of apartments, clinics, hospitals, schools, and churches. The boy who grew up on the wrong side of the tracks in a house without water or power and sold skunk pelts in order to buy groceries also owns a fair share of the buildings in his hometown of Broken Bow.

Ray been all over the country, of course. Used to fly his own twin-engine plane to job sites. Was an industry big shot in Washington for a long spell. Folks ask him why he's stayed in little ol' Broken Bow and didn't move to Los Angeles or New York. Lot of folks in them places kind of snicker at the thought of living in the middle of nowhere. But Ray says them people never seen Broken Bow. But I seen New York and LA, he says, and he don't say no more.

One time I asked Ray about the secret of his success. He said, Luck. I pressed him some more, and he said, Timing. I wouldn't let it go, and he said, Business model. Now, Ray. I continued to press.

Specialized knowledge, he said.

I says to him, Come on now, Ray, that ain't all of it. He turned to me and he got a little steel in him now, and I swear I seen that frozen hydrant in the park flash in his eyes, and he says in a low, hard voice, I just decided I would never be poor again. Never.

The Buffalo Cowboy

FRANK Stefka is a younger feller than most I been telling you about. He was born and raised in Comstock, and to this day he lives within two miles of where he was born. Only time he been away was to a two-year college, but that only lasted about six months. Funny thing around here versus other places. Most everywhere else kids leave for college thinking their parents don't know nothing about nothing. Frank left college knowing his father was the only one could teach him everything he wanted to know—about farming and ranching.

Family done both. Frank's father and uncles had a partnership for a while, run close to seven hundred head of cattle. Later, Frank's father developed a quarter, put in a pivot. Grew alfalfa. So Frank done a little of everything. When he got going on his own, he turned his land into a haying operation. Come last cutting in the fall, he was done, so he went to work for other fellers until May, when he started haying again. Over the years he worked for and with an interesting assortment of ranchers and cowboys.

Calving season is one of the most important times of year out here. Most cows can deliver their calves without any help, but maybe one time out of a couple dozen, they need a hand. Call it pulling a calf. Every rancher out here can tell stories about pulling calves, but ol' Frank had an epic battle with a pregnant cow not many fellers can top. It was a Salers cow.

Breed come from France, or somewheres. Very athletic. They can jump right into the bed of a pickup—and sometimes they do.

It was the first of April, maybe late March. Bad blizzard was just ending. From the ranch house, Frank could hear a heifer bawling and knew she was having trouble calving. It was just getting dark as Frank saddled up. The herd was coming in to water at the tanks on the outside of the corral as he rode out. A ways off there was a big snowdrift right in the middle of the pasture, past where he'd bulldozed out a mess of plum bushes just a few weeks before. That's where the heifer was. One of the calf's hooves was hanging out her back end. When Frank come up on her, she spun around and went the other way. He tried to circle around the drift, but when she seen him coming, she spun around again. Went on that way for a while. Frank was trying to get her in the corral where he could work on her.

She finally stopped underneath a tree and stood still for him. Frank come up behind her, still on horseback. He reached down and started working on that hoof. When you wiggle a leg like that, it can feel like a contraction, and the heifer will usually push. But not this heifer. She weren't of a mind to cooperate, but Frank didn't know that yet.

If you throw a lasso and dally the rope, it means you wind it around the saddle horn. Don't mean you tie on. Friction alone will keep the rope snug. So Frank grabbed his calf-pulling chain, dallied it, and wrapped the other end around the calf's leg and pulled it a bit. Too much leg come out. That's a bad sign. Means the calf's head is down. Head should come out with the leg. Means once you got the heifer on the ground, you have to reach your hand in, drop down underneath, and pull the calf's head up. All the time, that heifer's pushing and hunched over against you. And that's on a good cow. This was a Salers.

Annnnnnnyway, the heifer decides she don't like the situation that's developing and starts to lope off. Frank thought fast. He knew in a deal like that, with the leg chained, if the heifer starts walking, you can pull kind of circularwise. Usually that will lay her right down because with the calf's head pushed down in her pelvis, it kind of paralyzes the cow's spine, and she gets floppy-legged. But the heifer was right where Frank had bulldozed them plum bushes. Snow had mixed with the dirt there and created a mud pond a foot thick. Frank dismounted. Decided to walk along behind the cow, holding on to that chain until she had cleared the muddy area, and then try to flop her down.

That Salers had another notion. She bolted for a second, jerking Frank off his feet and into the mud. His wide-brimmed hat went flying. She hop-flipped around and clobbered that hat—probably thinking Frank's head was still in it.

Meanwhile, Frank is on his hands and knees half-buried in brown quicksand. When he looks up, he's nose-to-nose with the Salers. She let him have it. Butted him square in the face. Flipped him clean over onto his back. He was lucky she didn't have any traction in that slop. He was wearing buckle boots with nothing but barefeet underneath. One of them flew clean off.

Now she come at him with both front feet. He pulled his legs up and give her a mule kick in the head, but she kept coming. Rammed him in the ass and flipped him over again backwards. That made for a full three hundred and sixty degrees she had rotated him. Now he's back where he started, on his hands and knees, nose-to-nose with her.

She stumbled over some of them plum bushes, which give him a moment to get to his feet. But like I said, if cows were athletes, them Salers would be Olympians. She recovered quick, and while Frank was making a strategic retreat, she give him another boot in the butt with her head for good measure. Sent him sprawling chest-first in the mud again.

He was near an old thrashing machine rusting out in the yard. He scrambled underneath it as she come after him again. The Salers hammered that thrasher for quite a spell before Frank managed to crawl out the other side and run like hell.

His horse was just standing there spectating. Frank slowed to a walk as he reached the critter. He'd put a bit of distance between him and that Salers. He was tired, cold, wet, beat-up, worried about that heifer, and pissed off at her too. Right then he stepped into a hole where one of them plum bushes had been and fell into thirty-two-and-a-half-degree mud right up to his knee.

He didn't know until later what he looked like, but when he got to the house and stepped inside, he was covered in mud and bleeding from the nose, mouth, and eye. His wife was shocked and asked him what had happened. He don't normal order his wife around, and she don't normal take orders so well neither, but he wasn't about chatting right then, and he says, Don't matter! Get me a dry pair of socks and my other boots right now!

She jumped up and run off and done like he said. Shortly, he was back in the saddle, but it was pitch-black, and he couldn't find that durn cow nowhere. He give up on the horse and went back for his truck. Finally found that heifer lying flat on the ground trying to calf. Sometimes when that happens, you can drive up fairly close, leave the lights on, and get out and circle around behind them. They're blinded by the light, and by the time they figure out where you're at, they resign themselves to the intrusion, and you can pull the calf without a fuss.

Not this Salers. When she heard that truck door open, she was on her feet in a second, and in two, she had rammed the door shut. Frank was barely able to dive out of the way. He found himself crawling backwards through some more snow and mud while he watched her go to work on his grill. She charged it again and again. By the time she was done sending him a message about his midwifing services, she'd caved in most of the front end of his pickup and smashed a headlight. That ended the night's activities for Frank.

Next morning he learned how bad the blizzard was. His father lived only a couple of miles away, but he couldn't make it over, even with a tractor, the roads had drifted so bad. Finally, his brother-in-law made it over to his father's. They got a 'dozer blade on the tractor and put chains on the tires. You can get through most drifts with that getup. The two of them threw a bale in the back and headed for Frank's place.

His father drove right into the corral, cleared a spot in the snow, and dropped that bale of hay in the middle of it. Herd come right in. The Salers had worked up a hunger, too, beating up on Frank, and she come in with the herd. Frank roped her from the top of the 'dozer.

Most of the stuffing been knocked out of her by then, but she still put up a bit of a fuss. Frank's father drove over the rope, on purpose, which made her choke down finally. She squatted. Frank grabbed her tail and rolled her over so he could work on her. He reached in and that calf was about as constricted as a calf can get. Been that way too long.

He and his dad and brother-in-law agreed to take her to the

vet, which meant finding a way to get a horse trailer through the snow and mud and backed up to the corral—and then get the Salers loaded on. Took half an hour, but they done it. They went back to the house, got the trailer, hooked it to the tractor, and started pushing back in toward the corral.

This story don't end happily ever after. But I guess in any epic battle there's going to be death. Frank come around the back corner of that trailer and the Salers was on her feet. Or on three of them anyway. One of her forelegs had snapped. Frank figured he must of broke it when he rolled her over. After all that, they had to put her down. Not to make light of it, but Frank wondered if it wouldn't have been easier to have just shot her the night before.

Actually, it was tough on Frank. Cows out here ain't pets. They're raised for slaughter and they're raised for cash, but that don't mean fellers like Frank don't love calving time. Hell, if seeing something being born don't put a bit of wonder in you, you ought to check your pulse. But every now and then you lose one.

Annnnnnnyway, whole point is to tell you about Frank and buffalo, not Frank and cattle. He started working for a feller had upwards of fifteen hundred head of cattle, maybe three hundred horses, and a herd of buffalo about two hundred and fifty strong. Kind of an experimental thing. See, price of buffalo was high for a while. But there's all kinds of problems getting into buffalo ranching. Infrastructure, you might call it. Feed lots ain't set up for buffalo—neither are cowboys when it come down to it—and the packing plants are a problem, too.

They're funny animals. They can be gentle and agreeable one day and a wild beast the next. Herd that Frank worked, there was several would come right up to him and eat cotton cake—protein cubes—out of his hand. He could whistle, and they'd come running like cattle to the silage he was spreading. One time he was parked in a pickup out in the pasture, looking over to the right, when next thing he knew, something was leaning through the window licking him in the ear. When he looked around to see what done it, hell, that head might as well been an alien in a bad movie it was so big and hairy and ugly and close.

One time a feller was building a hunting lodge up in the Sand Hills and wanted to buy part of the herd. Can't understand the idea of hunting buffalo. Don't see the sport there. Couldn't hardly be a challenge if you can whistle and they come running right up to you.

Annnnnnnyway, like I say, they can be gentle, but pity the man who don't treat cattle and buffalo different. Cattle can get ornery, but for the most part they know who's boss. But with buffalo, if a man thinks he's boss, he can get himself in a pack of trouble in a short spell. When you're separating cattle in a pen—at least calves and heifers and steers—you can be right down there in the pen in between them. Like with fat cattle, if some are ready for market and some ain't and you want to sort them, maybe you run them down an alleyway in a pen, and you stand in a spot blocking their way. They'll turn and head through one gate, or you can shift position and they'll veer away from you and go through a different gate.

Man wouldn't try that with buffalo. Least not a man got anything working underneath his hat. You just don't test a buffalo. If you do, be prepared not to pass. What Frank and them boys done is tied ropes to the gates, and when a buffalo come along, they'd yank on that rope and steer the critter where they wanted it to go from a safe distance.

Same kind of thing with horses. Cowboy on his horse herding cattle is as old as the west. But with buffalo, keep them horses in the barn. Reason is, if them buffalo ever got mad at a horse and turned on him, the buffalo could run him down. Same with a working dog, like a border collie. If a buffalo gets tired of having its heels nipped, it'll flat run down a dog and kill it. And they can run forever. Hell, if you're chasing them in a four-wheeler and they have a mind to run ahead of the wind, good luck keeping up.

They can be testy, make no mistake. For a while, until they found a market for them, the feller Frank worked for had several buffalo bulls in the same feed lot. They'd get to running, and they'd run and run in big looping circles. They grunt like hogs, only it's an eerie sound. They also charge each other. If one of them is hurt, hell, they'll run him to death. They smell blood. If they get one on the ground, they'll gore him and stomp him to death. Don't pay to be weak if you're a buffalo.

Got to watch the horns. A regular old cow will put its nose down and butt with its forehead. But a buffalo rolls his nose down between his front legs and jump-steps to charge, which means his short horns are shooting straight ahead like daggers. If them horns hit home, he'll jerk that huge head and gut a rival bull—or a cowboy. Frank seen a big ol' bull lift another one clean off the ground with its head and then toss it.

Annnnnnnnyway, one time Frank was running the feed wagon out to the buffalo herd. They had electric wire up, and it worked as well for the buffalo as it did for the yearlings because it was real powerful. Knock a man flat. When Frank went to open a pen, he noticed the hot wire wasn't working. He looks around and sees why the fence shorted out. Down in a corner of the pasture, the electric string is looped over the barbed wire.

So he grabs a stick and walks down there. He notices a big ol' buffalo bull lying up on the hill but don't give him much thought. That hot wire got a way of focusing a man's mind.

Well, that wire was a bit tricky to get untangled. After he done it, Frank looks around and sees the buffalo bull has gotten to his feet and is headed his way down the hill. Wasn't charging or stampeding or nothing, just moving a bit faster than normal, coming right at him on a line so straight it would make a ruler jealous.

Frank took one look at the feed wagon and knew there was no way he could beat the buffalo to it. Normally, for cattle, you have three strings of barbed wire, but this fence had five for buffalo, and they were strung tighter than a fiddle. Weren't no way ol' Frank was getting through there. So he starts jogging along the fence line. He takes a quick look back at that bull. Buffalo is trotting now, easy but intent, and he ain't heading to where Frank *was*, he's heading to where Frank *is*. All Frank can think of is what them buffalo bulls do to each other when they smell blood.

Fear is an amazing motivator. To this day, Frank don't know how he done it, but one moment he was on one side of the fence, and the next moment he was on the other. Pretty sure he went through that tight wire rather than over it. Ended up down in a creek bed on the other side, checking himself and wondering if he was going to fall apart like one of them cartoon characters gone through an egg slicer, but he was in one piece. Not to say he wasn't a bloody mess, and his overalls looked like they been in a knife fight, but he was all right.

He climbed up out of the creek bed with his head down, dusting himself off. When he stopped and looked up, he was right in front of the fence. On the other side, not five foot away, that buffalo bull was standing still, breathing hard, right where Frank had been. He was big enough that man and beast were eye-to-eye with one another. Frank swears it's the only time he ever seen a buffalo smile.

They're amazing beasts, no question. Cattle out in the field tend to wander off. They'll usually stay within sight of each other, but for the most part they'll scatter pretty wide. Not buffalo. Herd sticks together, moves together. Out in an open field, on the run, when one turns, the whole herd turns in unison. Like a big flock of birds but on the ground.

Jack Longfellow, the vet in town—I'll tell you more about him in a minute—bought a couple of buffalo about eight years ago. A while back there was a two-day blizzard. Jack got a pretty small herd of cattle on his place relative to the full-time ranchers around here, but he was worried well enough because they were spread out all over his ground and stranded by the storm. Well, by the time he got his driveway pushed out, and got the bulk of his herd pushed out, and got grassland pushed out so the cattle could feed, a week had gone by, and he was still missing five expensive Angus bulls out on the range. Just as he was fixing to go after them, his bull buffalo, named Samson, come over the hill. He was walking slow, taking a step or two at a time, then stopping and lowering his massive head and sweeping it side to side. He pushed the two foot of snow on the ground out of his way and then took another step and done the same thing again. Right behind him were those five Angus bulls. Samson cleared a yard-wide path all the way to the corral.

One time Frank was in his truck with a feller named Don, and he come up on the buffalo herd and they were going nuts, running up the hills and down them, full tilt, dust cloud trailing behind. Didn't look right somehow. Frank come up over a rise in that truck and stopped as the buffalo run past, and he says, Don, I believe there's an emu in our buffalo herd.

There was an old cowboy out here I'll tell you about later, Martin Armstrong, and he got himself several emus he eventually turned out. Annnnnnnyway, one of them emus ended up in the middle of the buffalo herd. Buffalo about went crazy. They were racing around the hills this way and that. The emu was smack in the middle of them, his neck and head sticking up above the herd, fitting right in but inciting a riot, too. Looked like that Pamplona thing, but instead of people running with the bulls, it was that emu running with the buffalo. Sight it was, way Frank tells it—just that scrawny neck and head rising up above the hairy, brown, running herd.

Didn't end well for the emu. Don says, Got your rifle?

Frank says, Yeah.

Don says, Go get it.

When Frank got his rifle, they watched the buffalo do another lap at full tilt before Don tugged on the brim of his Stetson and said, Shoot it.

Frank says, The emu? I don't want to shoot that bird.

Don says, You want to fix fence for a week and round up buffalo for two?

Was a tough shot, but Frank ended the great emu adventure rather abruptly.

Them buffalo are majestic animals, no question. With cattle, pretty typical in ice and snow to see them slip and go down when you're chasing them across a pasture or moving them around a frozen pen in a feed lot. In five years of running buffalo, Frank never seen a single one slip and fall. He says when he'd go out in the feed wagon and call them and they'd come thundering down the hills with a snow cloud billowing up behind them, the earth beneath the wagon would rumble like an earthquake and his insides would shake right down to his soul. Except for the fence all around, he says he'd swear it was two hundred years ago.

The Country Doctor

ONE of the biggest characters to ever leave his mark on the Seven Valleys was Doc Chaloupka. When he walked into a room, he about filled it to the brim. I suppose nowadays they'd say ol' Doc lived large. He was a helluva doctor and also done his share of drinking and hopping neighbors' back fences, if you know what I mean. He was arrogant, egotistical, larger than life, and had to be the center of attention. Big heart, big mouth, big gut. He was darn likable when he wanted to be, but he could also just plow you under. He tore up hotel rooms like a rock star and was banned from high school basketball games for yelling at the referees. He just about owned the town—and I don't mean real estate–wise.

Doc was born and raised in Omaha, but he set up shop in Callaway. He was your typical country doctor. Made house calls. Hell, to him, driving fifteen miles to a ranch was like going down the hall in the hospital to a city doctor. If you lived outside town and called Doc, he'd get in that Cadillac of his, drive like a spooked mare, and that big ol' shadow of his would be filling your front doorway in ten minutes. Can't hardly guess how many babies he delivered along the South Loup.

Doc always drove a black Cadillac. Living in a small town, he didn't want folks thinking he was charging too much for his services. So he got a new car every year, but he always got the same model of Cadillac, and it was always black. That way he could have a new car, but folks would never know. It looked like he was driving the same car year after year. It just happened to stay real shiny and new.

He was in more car accidents than the insurance company could count. Had a limp for a long spell because of one. Some of the accidents were drink related, some speed, but most were both. With party lines, word would get around quick, even after midnight, that Doc was in a ditch or a snowbank off the road from Broken Bow. A few fellers would go out there with their trucks and chains and drag him out. Haul his car to the garage and him home. Most times he'd be up early the next morning ready for doctoring or even surgery.

Doc just went like a bat out of hell, period. All the time. Everywhere. Lived his life like that. Folks said Doc was a manic-depressive. Don't really know about that condition, but I suspect for most folks them two balance each other out—you're manic sometimes and depressed the rest. Not Doc. Any given month, he was manic thirty days and depressed one. And if there was only thirty days in the month, hell, he'd skip the depression altogether. Too busy.

Like I said, Doc done his carrying on, but he was one of the best doctors you're ever going to meet, and in a lot of different ways. One time in the winter, a woman gone into labor in the middle of a blizzard. She lived on a ranch northwest of Callaway. It was one of them blizzards where you couldn't hardly see the front of your car from the driver's seat, but it wouldn't have mattered if you could, since there were hardly any plows in them days and the roads were impassable. Woman couldn't get into town, and Doc couldn't get out to her. She was getting panicky on the phone, and Doc was beside himself because he couldn't do nothing about it. Well, he's racking his brain and finally remembers a railroad spur line run right by her place. So he gets a couple of fellers in town and they mount a handcar—one of them things with a handle like a teeter-totter—on the tracks. Ol' Doc in his tie and overcoat and black bag gets on the handcar and pumps his way up to the ranch, trudges through a couple foot of snow from the tracks to the woman's door, and delivers her baby.

He done something like that another time when a woman gone into labor on a ranch maybe twenty-five miles outside of town. It was way out on a dirt road and too muddy for a car, so folks set up sort of a Pony Express, only it was with wagons instead of mounts, and it was Doc rather than mail they were trying to get through. Someone in town loaded up Doc and run his team hard, as fast as the horses could go. They got to a ranch five miles outside of town, and Doc switched to another rancher's wagon. They done that four or five times, relayed him all the way to the ranch where the pregnant woman was. Delivered her baby without a hitch.

He'd do anything for his patients. And they loved him for it. There was another delivery, this time at the hospital in Callaway. Young woman give birth and then starts bleeding. She bled and bled, and Doc couldn't stop it. Tried everything, but she still went into shock. It didn't look good. They decided they had to get her in an ambulance and down to Kearney as fast as possible, but it's an hour-and-a-half drive, and she was losing way too much blood. Doc knew he was the same blood type as the woman, so he lay down in the ambulance next to her, stuck a needle and a line in him and hooked the other end directly to her. Continuously fed her blood the whole trip. She lived.

He felt personal for his patients. One time a feller with eight

kids was in a car wreck that crushed his chest. At the hospital
Doc rigged him up with safety pins and God knows what else
to keep his broken ribs from puncturing his lungs. Doc was
trying to keep the feller alive, hoping he might stabilize so they
could move him to Omaha. Doc stayed with him all day and
all night and all the next day and all the next night. Morning
of the third day, Doc dozed off and the feller died. Doc went
into another patient's room and cried his eyes out for twenty
minutes, blaming himself. 'Course, there weren't nothing he
could have done.

He was a good doctor, but he was practical too. Knew
people and knew the way of the world. One time Ray Brown
come to him complaining about migraine headaches he'd been
getting. Instead of a pill, Doc orders him to write down everything he done all day every day for one month. Especially when
he got a headache. Where he was, what he was doing.

Ray done it. When he come back, Doc sits him down across
his desk and goes through them notes, and finally he says, By
God, it's as plain as the nose on your face. Every time you travel
with this feller so-and-so, you get a migraine. Who is he? Stop
traveling with him.

Well, ol' Ray knew exactly who it was. It was a feller always
trying to shake him down. He worked for a church group
that was sponsoring nursing homes Ray was building at the
time, and he was the go-between for new business. The feller
wanted kickbacks and threatened to give the church's business
to someone else. Ray wouldn't pay. Instead, after seeing Doc,
he went to the feller's boss and said, I can't travel with him no
more. The feller was relieved from duty, and Ray has never had
even so much as a small headache since, much less a migraine.
Been over twenty-five years.

Doc would work Saturdays. Waiting room would be jammed. None of the other doctors would work weekends. Understandable, but this was a small town. In big-city hospitals, there are so many doctors they're all rotating their schedules, and someone's on duty twenty-four hours. Out here, if a doctor takes off, there ain't no doctor. Folks would call at Doc's house at all hours, too. Once a doc from Omaha come to Callaway and took over Doc's practice for a week and also lived in his house. Late one night there was a ruckus at the front door. The visiting doc, waking up in bed, hears the door open. No one locks their doors out here. Scared the hell out of him and his wife. He put on a bathrobe to investigate, and when he stepped out of the bedroom, down the hall come a whole family brung their father who had chest pains and needed fixing up. Not exactly your regular-type house call.

Now, I ain't saying Doc was Mother Teresa. Ohhhhh, no. Davey Davis would call Doc and say, Hey, I got some schnapps. And Doc would say, Come on by. We'll go out to my place, and I'll show you my bulls. So Davey would pull up to the back door of the clinic. There'd be a dozen people in the waiting room. Doc would slip out and get in Davey's car. While the nurse is explaining that Doc had been called out on an emergency, he and Davey would be at Doc's place drinking schnapps and wandering the pasture looking at Doc's bulls. But mostly they'd be drinking schnapps. An hour later, they were heading back to town. Doc would smoke a cigar and chew on a pack of Certs. Davey would drop Doc off at the back door of the clinic, and he'd return to treating all them folks been waiting in the waiting room.

When Loren Jacobsen, who eventually became Doc's partner, was completing his internship, he got a call from Doc.

Doc says he wants Loren to maybe come work with him in Callaway, says he's going on a short trip soon, and maybe Loren could cover for him. Test of sorts. Just a day or two. See how things went.

Loren been through all his schooling by then, and like I said, his internship, but he hadn't done his residency yet. Up until then, any time he been with patients, supervisors were watching him pretty close. What I'm saying is, Loren ain't been by himself in an office, flying solo. So he's a bit skittish going in that first day. When he gets to the office, Doc is decked out in his cowboy gear—hat, boots, jeans, big buckle—and says he's headed to Texas to buy a prize beefmaster bull.

Jacobsen didn't see him again for thirteen days.

First day alone, Loren seen thirty-five patients. Hell, about needed a doc himself by the time the sun dropped. Apparently, Doc had done this before with other young doctors he was thinking about partnering with. Pattern was pretty much the same. First day the new doc would see thirty-five or forty folks, whatever was on Chaloupka's schedule. By the second day, word was already getting around town that Doc was away, and maybe only twenty or so patients come in. By the fourth day, it'd be down to a trickle, maybe half a dozen, and they only come in because they were really sick. By the time Doc got back from whatever trip he was on, his office would look like a ghost town—and Doc would still be looking for a partner.

Happened with Jacobsen at first. Number of patients ebbed. But he was real good with them. About the fifth day, they started to flow again. The number of folks coming in begun to creep back up. And it kept creeping.

The day Doc got back, Jacobsen saw over thirty patients. Doc didn't say nothing about how his 'day or two' trip turned into thirteen, but he did offer to partner with Loren. Can't say for sure whether all that was Doc's plan from the start or if he was just off carousing for thirteen days. With Doc you never knew.

Like I said, Doc made himself available, but he didn't like his availability being taken advantage of, neither. One time a rancher busted up his hand and called Doc at home pretty late, maybe ten or after. Doc's days were pretty long, and he was tired that night, but the way the feller described it, Doc said, You better come on by the house. So the feller comes in and Doc takes a look at his hand, and it's busted up all right, but it don't look like a fresh wound. As Doc is walking over to his desk, he asks the feller when it happened. Feller says, Oh, I don't know, three or four days ago, can't really remember.

That lit Doc's fuse, and it weren't never a very long one. He yells at the feller, Why didn't you come in business hours any of them three or four days? Then he picked up the phone, jerked it out of the wall, and threw it at the rancher. He missed, but the phone went through a window. Doc calmed down, fixed the feller up, and didn't bill him. He usually didn't bill you if he threw something at you. It was after midnight when Doc got to bed, him having to nail up the plywood and all. Neighbors driving by the next few days seen that plywood and knew Doc was heaving stuff through his windows again.

Oh, he had a volcanic temper all right. Legendary. But everything with him was on the surface; he didn't harbor nothing. One time, he was watching TV at home. It was a bad combination when his team wasn't playing well and he had too much to drink. Shot a hole in his TV. One time, late in his doctoring career, when he'd moved up to Broken Bow to a remodeled clinic with several nurses and staff and whatnot,

something set him off. He come out of his office one morning
and heaved a clipboard like a baseball down the length of the
hall. He stormed back in his office and slammed the door, and
all was quiet. There might have been a nurse in the way of the
clipboard, but if there was, he missed her.

Annnnnnnyway, the clipboard sat in the same place on the
floor all day. If that's where Doc put it, none of them nurses
was going to touch it. Patients come in all day long, and they
were stepping over the clipboard, and when they did, they'd
look at the nurse with them, expecting her to pick it up, but the
nurse would look off into space, not seeing no clipboard. Next
morning when they come in, the clipboard was gone, and Doc
took the whole clinic out to lunch.

Another time at the clinic in Broken Bow, he wanted some
lab work. It wasn't done. He started getting madder and madder
until that temper of his fired off like Krakatoa. He stormed
down the hall and kicked the wall. He was a big man with a
big boot. Put a hole clean through it. Next day was his day
off. Weekday, but it was his day off. In the morning, he shows
up with a bucket of plaster and water and a trowel, and all
morning he was on his hands and knees fixing that hole. Day
before, everyone was treading lightly. But now Doc's laughing
and funning with the nurses. Who's the son of a bitch putting
holes in these walls? We spent a lot of money to fix this place
up, he says.

One time, he got cockeyed at the country club and kicked
up a ruckus, and they asked him to leave. He picked up the
jukebox and tossed it across the room. Jukebox ain't light. Doc
gone out to his truck, pulled out his shotgun, and peppered the
weathervane on top of the country club roof, got it spinning
pretty good. He paid for the jukebox and all of them records,

too. Weathervane never worked so well after that. Couldn't hardly turn in a breeze with all them holes in it.

Feller like Doc, with his big appetites and gambling and free-spending ways, you might think he'd be greedy, too, or at least trying to stockpile cash in a big way. But he just wasn't like that. One time there was a rheumatoid feller, froze up so bad he could hardly walk. He come in to see Doc and got regular treatments, but then all of a sudden he stops showing up. Four or five months later, he finally come by and seen Doc, and Doc says, You feeling better? That why I ain't been seeing you?

Feller hems and haws, and finally he says, No, feel as bad as ever, but I owe you so much money and I can't pay, so I didn't feel like I should come in.

Doc says, What are you talking about? Let me get my ledger. So Doc goes and gets his ledger, brings it over to the desk, and opens it. There's two pages of single-line entries, all recording visits by this feller. Doc takes a pen, and he run a red line through the first entry. Then he done it to the second and the third. Fact, he gone through the first page and the second, and he left only the last entry unmarked. Then Doc says, Says here you owe seventy-five dollars. That ain't too much, is it?

Think Doc thought it was fair if the feller paid for *one* visit out of thirty, but Doc had his pen poised above the last entry, ready to scratch that one, too, if it come to it. Feller always said after that, Doc saved my life.

Doc had a wife of fifty years and a new girlfriend every couple of months. Hell, he'd sometimes have them over to the house, set with his wife. Don't see that much. Rhoda was a saint. Everyone will tell you that. Got to wonder about it, though. Doc was climbing over every back fence in Custer County and drinking like parched prairie, and setting at home is the nicest woman you ever want to meet. She put up with more bullcrap from him than any other ten women put up with from their husbands.

There's not much of a social hierarchy out here—everyone's a rancher, a farmer, or a ranch hand or they work in town. But a feller like Doc was an exception. He was an eight-hundred-pound gorilla in Callaway, so his wife could have put on airs, but that wasn't Rhoda's way. She was as nice as a sunny day in spring. Lived her life as straight as his was crooked.

Rhoda's first husband died in the war. She never forgive him for that. He was out of Montana and a smart feller. Had a master's degree in animal science. When he enlisted in the war, they told him he wouldn't be sent overseas because they needed fellers like him in the states to help feed the troops. But he wanted to see action. Got himself on a PT boat and was killed in battle. Rhoda was a schoolteacher during the war. They come to tell her at school. Lot of kids in that class are still around. They'll never forget that day as long as they live. Life can turn on a dime. It sure can. After that, Rhoda met Doc and got pregnant by him, so they got married under less than ideal circumstances.

One time, Rhoda called down to the clinic and wanted the Cadillac. Their house was only a few blocks away. Doc was busy and didn't really answer her. She called again, and he was even busier, and he didn't do nothing. She called a third time, and Doc lost it. He gets in that Caddie and roars home. There's two big trees in their front yard, and he drives on the grass and lines that Cadillac up between them. Then he rams his foot into the gas pedal, and the car leaps forward, smacks one of them trees and smashes in the front end. Then he puts it in reverse and floors it and smashes the back end. He done forward and reverse two more times each, like he's practicing to be the world's worst parallel parker. By then, the radiator gets punctured. Doc gets out and stalks back to the clinic, leaving that crumpled Cadillac smoking and hissing in their front yard.

Doc loved to gamble, but he was terrible at poker. Couldn't hide nothing. A crazed mule could bluff better than he could. Lost and then lost some more, but he had more money than most, so he always seemed to stay ahead of the game. He used to fly to Las Vegas on them three-day–two-night things, except Doc wouldn't get a hotel. He'd stay up sixty or seventy hours straight. Always go alone, although I don't think he was alone much. One time he was having so much fun he missed his flight from Vegas to Denver. Got on the next one, but by the time he got to Denver, he missed the last connecting flight that day to North Platte. Not much ever stood in Doc's way. He had pressing business at the hospital, so he went out to the taxi stand and told the driver he wanted a ride to Callaway, Nebraska. Taxi driver was dozing, but that woke him up. It was a six-hour cab ride one way in those days.

Doc was one of them fellers attracts a lot of friends, and a lot of them were just like him. One was a doctor down there in Kearney named Bob Sydner. I know the feller that had him as his surgery resident. He laughed when he said Sydner was absolutely worthless. Wouldn't do a durn thing he was told. But he was also brilliant. He had a bit of the devil in him, though. Liked to tweak the system on occasion. He and Chaloupka were big buddies. I suspect they raised more hell than any other two doctors on the plains. One time Sydner went up to the Mayo Clinic for two weeks of training. This is back when the Mayo Clinic was floating on a white cloud. World known. Prestigious. As part of orientation, they'd tell them docs about the esteemed history of the place and made it clear them boys was there to bring honor to the Mayo Clinic, and they weren't to do nothing to soil the name of the great institution.

I'm glad they didn't invite Chaloupka. But they did get Sydner. After a week of classroom work, they gave the docs the weekend off. The county fair was going on. A demolition derby was part of it. Well, wouldn't you know it, that weekend, along with Buck's Barber Shop, Ernie's Garage, and Elmer's Dry Goods, the famed Mayo Clinic had an entry. Ol' Bob Sydner went and got him a junker, painted it about a dozen colors, and scrawled Mayo Clinic as big as day all over it. He even came up with a logo—a diseased cell. Sydner did the driving, of course. They say it did a lot for the Mayo Clinic's public relations among regular folks, seeing the diseased cell car right in the middle of it all, smashing into the barber shop, the garage, and the dry goods store. The Mayo Clinic didn't quite see it that way.

Word about the derby got back to the authorities there, and Bob got a stern lecture. They wouldn't give him his seminar certificate, neither. All's fair, I guess. Sydner wouldn't give them the first place trophy from the derby. He never got invited back to the Mayo Clinic, but the county fair folks up there called him every summer for years.

Doc had a way of making even enemies his friends. He was in the air force early in his career. Even though he was a doctor, he was low on the totem pole, since he was so young. Based at Offutt Air Force Base near Omaha, which is headquarters for the Strategic Air Command. Them's the B-52s that carried nuclear bombs. If there was a war against the Russians, the bombers would have taken off from Offutt.

The commander of the base at the time was General Curtis

Lemay. He may have been the most feared man on earth. After the Cold War was over, found out the Russians were scared stiff of him. Lemay is the one that bombed the hell out of Japan during World War II. They say them raids of his did more damage than the atomic bombs they dropped later. The Russians were afraid they might get Lemayed.

Annnnnnnyway, Lemay apparently didn't hardly visit the officers' club on base. 'Course, Chaloupka did. Pretty much every night, and sometimes all night. He'd drive around the lot looking for a place to park, and every night he'd see Lemay's reserved spot, right there by the door, setting empty. Well, one night when Doc was on call at the base hospital, he pops over to the officers' club. He's driving around the parking lot, and he sees Lemay's empty slot like he always done, and he says, Hell, just this once. He goes ahead and parks there.

Well, sure enough, Doc is inside the club only a few minutes when Lemay comes storming in like it's D-Day and the club is Normandy Beach. He demands to know who's parked in his reserved spot. When he found out, he dressed down Doc something fierce and just about court-martialed him on the spot. They say it was one of the few times Doc was ever at a loss for words—or maybe he was just smart enough to keep quiet. Annnnnnnyway, Lemay calmed down a bit, gave him a reprieve, and Doc headed back to the base hospital in the offending car with his tail between his legs.

Lo and behold, about three in the morning, the general's wife gets sick, and Lemay calls the hospital. Well, the doctor on call was Chaloupka. They say that when Lemay answered his front door and saw Doc, he just about had a stroke. Doc had brought along a corpsman. They took a blood sample, and Doc sent the corpsman back to the hospital to have it tested.

That meant Doc and the general had to sit in the living room together for a couple of hours before the results came back. Wouldn't you know it, they found out they were birds of a feather. Talked all night. They became fast friends and stayed in touch for years. Lemay come out to the Seven Valleys and gone hunting with Doc quite a few times.

Doc died in April 1983. He was having a heart bypass and died right on the table. Not sure what the bottom line is on Doc's life. Done a lot of good, done some harm, too, was friend to a lot of folks, saved a lot of lives. His own mother may have had the last word—at his funeral. She was very elderly by then, of course. When all the Bible reading and praying was done, someone in the crowd spoke out. They said, Doc is in heaven now. Or headed there, or some such. Doc's mother was heard to mutter, I doubt it.

Vicky

THERE aren't a lot of symphonies and ballets and Broadway plays to go to in central Nebraska. No professional ball teams. Opera ain't big. Have to drive a spell just to get to a movie house. Not much organized entertainment of any sort. That's maybe why there's a lot of practical jokers. Liven things up. Francis Gschwind is one of them.

His grandparents were Swiss, come to America in the late 1860s and settled for a spell in Ohio. They had some kids while they were still in Europe and a passel more when they got to Cincinnati. There were nine surviving children in all by the time they come out here homesteading in 1882. A few members of the family—a couple of Francis's grandfather's brothers—had already moved out this way.

The Gschwinds got a rude greeting when they arrived. Their quarter was about six miles northwest of Callaway. Weren't any buildings on the property, of course, so the Gschwinds stayed with a German family by the name of Schreier, on the next farm over, that come from Ohio shortly before. The Schreiers were among the first homesteaders up here. On the other side of the Gschwinds was a homesteader by the name of Nelson, a Danish feller.

In them days, there was a place called the Brighton ranch just down the valley from where the Gschwind's were home-steading, and the boys working it were a wild bunch. They raised more hell in those days than the famous Olive gang ever did. They shot and killed a homesteader name of Province right there on his farm.

Folks don't generally know that a fair number of cowboys in those days were kids off the streets of Chicago or Omaha. Couldn't find a job in the city, so they come out here on the railroad. A rancher would hire them, teach them to ride, hand them a six-shooter, and not care much what they done when they weren't working his cattle.

Annnnnnnyway, one day them boys from the Brighton ranch run a bunch of horses up through Nelson's corn. Out of spite. No other reason. Ruined the crop. Nelson reported them to the foreman at the Brighton ranch, who was a tough guy, and the foreman chewed them boys out pretty good and said he was going to dock their pay for the corn they ruined.

Day later, Nelson come over to the Schreiers' to visit and meet the Gschwinds. Well, here come them cowboys, four of them, from the Brighton ranch. They went over to Nelson's place, didn't find him there, and tracked him to Schreier's. Their plan was to shoot him. Francis's grandmother and the nine Gschwind kids, along with a mess of Schreier offspring, ran inside and dove under what beds there were. Well, a scuffle broke out, and one of the cowboys drew his gun. When it went off, the bullet grazed Schreier in the side. Ripped his shirt and took off a layer of skin, but mostly missed him. That put a fear in them cowboys, who maybe weren't as tough as advertised, and the homesteaders run them off. Fact, them boys didn't even head back to the Brighton place, just vamoosed out of Nebraska entirely. Hopped a train and headed to Wyoming, last anyone heard.

Any man come out here to homestead had to be pretty

tough, but these fellers were just farmers and family men. Still, they were awful proud of themselves, taking on them hombres the way they done. Fact, because of the ruckus, they named their little community up there Triumph, and it's officially Triumph Township to this day. 'Course, Francis's grandmother had a different view of the incident. When she come out from under that bed, she was ready to pack up and not only go home to Ohio, hell, she was ready to head clear back to Switzerland. But they got her calmed down, and them Gschwinds have stayed a hundred and twenty-five years.

The Schreiers, of course, had a sod house—no frame houses in those days—and I reckon more kids than a man has fingers. Throw the nine Gschwind children in that soddy, and a feller can only imagine the clatter inside those five hundred square feet on a rainy day. Might be why it only took a few weeks for the Gschwinds to fashion themselves a home for the winter. Wasn't as nice as the sod place the Schreiers had. It was a dugout. Two, in fact. They dug a hole in the bank of a dry creek bed, put a roof over it, and dropped a curtain or two across the front. They built a second dugout on the north side of the creek and put the livestock in there. The first dugout, on the south bank, is where the family lived.

Remember, these are folks that lived a settled life in a frame house in the Old Country. They didn't know much about dugouts or prevailing winds, although they ended up with all winter to think on it. While the horses and chickens and pigs were relatively warm in the dugout on the north bank, frosty winds out of Canada whistled right through those curtains fronting the family dugout on the south bank and made for an unpleasant season. Grandma Gschwind made mention of Switzerland more than a few times that winter.

Family suffered a tragedy only a couple of years later. Francis'
grandfather was helping to build a sod schoolhouse when he fell
off the roof and was hurt bad. No hospital anywhere nearby,
so it took a couple of days to haul him by team and wagon
down to Plum Creek, which is now Lexington. Must be close
to fifty miles on rough road. He didn't make it. Imagine his
widow. Out here, in a sod house by then, but with nine kids,
and she's got to make it on her own. Well, not entirely. Folks
rallied around, like they do, and the oldest boy was of age by
then, so the family pulled through.

Francis's father and mother got married in '09 and moved
onto a ranch just a few miles outside of Callaway. Francis was
born in the house they built on the ground in '20. He's lived in
that house all of his life. Still does to this day. Past eighty years.

Annnnnnnyway, Francis was a practical joker going way
back. Friend of his is a lumber broker by the name of Earl
Peyton, from Oregon, who came down every summer to a place
he had here in Callaway. Another friend of Francis's is a feller
name of Lane Brabham, a World War II navy vet, who still lives
in town.

This'll give you a good idea of how little we got going on
around here. One Sunday afternoon Lane and Francis went
over to visit with Earl at his place in Callaway, right in town.
This is before Earl's wife come out from Oregon for the season.
They were sitting in the kitchen with the door open, except
for a screen. The neighbors two doors down were visiting the
neighbors right next door, setting out on the front lawn in the
shade in folding chairs.

Earl didn't hear so well, so Francis and Lane's conversation with him was just this side of a screaming match. Francis
happened to glance out the screen door and could see the folks

next door had turned into an audience, listening to every word coming from Earl's kitchen. It was a bit dark in there and bright outside, and throw in the screen door, and Francis could see out but them folks next door couldn't see in.

Francis decided to give them something to listen to. He whispers to Lane what he's got in mind and then practically has to crawl in Earl's ear canal to let him in on it. But when it finally sunk in with Earl, he was all game.

Now, when Francis and Lane were talking to Earl, they were loud to get themselves heard. When Earl was talking to *them*, well, hell, if Giddeon wanted to tumble down the walls of Jericho, he wouldn't of needed no trumpet if he could of brung Earl along. Annnnnnnnyway, Earl blurts out, real loud, No! Not in here! Keep your britches on! What's the matter with you, girl?

Francis is watching them neighbors the whole time. They were looking out toward the street, but their heads were cocked towards Earl Peyton's place like a particular strong and steady wind come up out of the east.

Earl was quiet a spell. Then he says, Lane Brabham, don't your dare touch her! This is my home. You too, Gschwind. Keep them hands of yours off her!

By then them folks next door were practically tipping over their chairs they were stretching so far to listen. It went on like that for a few minutes. Earl was getting into it now. Big, huge smile come over his face just before he jumped up, ran over to a kitchen drawer, and grabbed a dish towel. He ripped it in two and let out a dainty cry. One of the fellers next door stood clean up, like he'd sat on a cattle prod.

Francis had to leave. For real. He told Earl to think of

something good. Earl says, "Francis! That just ain't natural. Get out of here. Go on. Get out of my house. Now!"

Francis pretended he was angry and burst out of the house, slamming the screen door behind him. I was just having some fun, he yells back at Earl. He squealed out of the driveway in his car, throwing gravel like buckshot. When he got home, the phone was ringing off the hook. Earl and Lane were laughing so hard on the other end, Francis couldn't understand them. After Francis left, the neighbors went inside. One of the women was holding her face in both hands, and the other one was fanning herself and had to be helped as she walked.

Next day Earl called Francis back and says, Come on over, we need to talk.

When he gets there, Earl says the wife next door come over later in the evening and says, Earl, what you have going on over here today? Earl says, Gschwind brought this cute gal over, and we had a few drinks, except she had too many. She used to be a go-go dancer, and next thing you know, she wants to go-go all over the kitchen table.

The wife next door says, She was taking her clothes off right in your kitchen?

We could barely stop her.

Earl Peyton, what would Kate say! That's Earl's wife, who was still up in Oregon.

It weren't me, says Earl. It was Gschwind and Brabham and the bottle. You wouldn't go and tell Kate now, would you?

She shook her head, but she wasn't answering his question when she done it, she was just disapproving. Mighty disapproving. She says, That ain't like you, Earl. You shouldn't be doing that. Right here in your kitchen. You ought to be ashamed.

Well, ol' Earl, he was indeed ashamed. Never seen a man more ashamed. She walked off shaking her head some more. About five minutes later, her husband come over, walking real quick, looking back over his shoulder, and he was grinning from ear to ear. Earl, what in tarnation?

Earl explains it—not for real, but like he told the feller's wife—and says, You should of dropped over.

Pshaw, he says. My wife ain't in Oregon, you ol' dog.

'Course, word was all over town by the next afternoon. Heard what happened over at Peyton's place on Sunday? Didja?

Annnnnnnyway, that weren't enough for Francis and Earl. No, sir. They got to plotting, and the following Friday in the weekly paper, a small classified ad appeared. It said, *E. P., when do I get paid for services rendered at your house last Sunday? Vicky.*

Francis just pulled that name Vicky out of a hat. Didn't know no Vicky.

Well, folks around here read the classifieds like they read the grass in early spring, which is to say, real close. If someone's selling this or someone's selling that, you get a little peek into their lives, you see.

Like I said, ad was small, buried somewheres between a tractor for sale and a lost cat, but a stampede of wild horses couldn't have caused more commotion in Callaway. All folks could talk about was what the hell went on at Peyton's place on Sunday. And everyone's talking about Vicky like she grown up in town and they'd sat next to her in fourth grade.

Next week another ad appears: *L. B.—E. P. is paid up, now it's your turn. Else I'll talk. Vicky.*

That got the twister to spinning even faster. Town's in a

ruckus now. 'Course, just then is when Kate arrived from Oregon.

Next day Francis Gschwind is pulling into the parking lot of the grocery store, and Earl come up alongside him. Earl had a huge shiner. Prize-fight big. The mother of all black eyes. Francis says, You have too much to drink and run into a door? Earl just kind of lowered his head and says, Kate's back in town.

Francis says, Hell, go on now, what are you trying to pull, Earl? I'm in on this joke, remember?

Earl laughed and as they parked and walked into the store, he says he got a bug bite that started to swell up. Well, his nephew's wife was a makeup artist, so he let her and Kate in on the joke, and his nephew's wife give him a Hollywood shiner.

When they got into the store and were checking out, the grocer says, God's name, Earl, what happened to you?

Earl just kind of mumbles, Had a little trouble at the house.

'Course, the grocer knows all about Vicky. His eyes get as big as dinner plates and he just blurts out, Did Kate sock you because of that prostitute Vicky being at your house a few Sundays back?

Francis jumps right in and starts scolding the grocer, Don't you call Vicky a prostitute! She's a professional dancer. She may be a might quick to get out of her clothes, but she's a nice gal. She ain't no prostitute.

Earl steps in between them, to hold Francis at bay, making sure he keeps his back to the grocer so the grocer don't see him cracking up.

Francis snatched his change and stormed out, leaving the grocer with his jaw running along that little conveyer belt they got there at the checkout stand.

Francis and Earl walked right from the market to a bar in town, although it must of looked like they were coming out of one, since they were laughing so hard they could barely walk.

The feller that owned the bar, his sister-in-law was tending it that day. She and her husband, Ray, were both from Kentucky. Ray was one of the few that Francis and Earl had let in on the secret.

Well, Francis and Earl are in there and going on about Vicky and the black eye and Kate's right hook and all while Ray's wife is wiping down the bar. She ain't buying it. She says in the high, squeaky voice she had, Ain't no prostitute going to put an ad in the paper like that.

Right on cue, her husband, Ray, walked in the back door of the bar, sees Francis and Earl and the black eye, and without missing a beat, he says, I just saw Vicky up north a ways and give her a lift downtown. She's an awfully friendly gal.

That set off Ray's wife. She was madder than a wet cat. If fingernails scraped against a chalkboard could talk, that's what she sounded like. What are you doing picking up strange women and giving them rides? I don't want you anywhere near that Vicky! Where did you drive her to? You leave that woman be!

They had to scrape Francis and Earl off the floor.

That might have been the end of it, but the thing had taken on a life of its own, so it's only right the story had another chapter. A few days later, the newspaperman in Callaway run up to Arnold. He got a few classifieds from up there every week. He stopped off for a refresher, and a couple fellers come over to him. They were telling him a young couple had moved into town there, into Arnold, not long before, and if you drove around town early in the morning, you might see the wife's car parked in a variety of driveways, none of which were hers.

So help me God, her name was Vicky. Them boys had heard she was down in Callaway causing a commotion around there, too!

The newspaperman come back to Callaway blabbering all about it, and tongues were wagging for another few weeks. Most folks in Callaway eventually got wind of the joke, but I'm not so sure Francis ever got that genie all the way back in the bottle.

The Newcomer

I'M telling you about families been around here as long as the hills—grew up in sod houses and all—but that ain't everyone. There's some newcomers, and them greenhorns have got stories to tell. Like Mike Cox. Got a place in the North Loup River valley outside of Burwell. Mike's father was a hired man on a farm in Iowa. Mike grew up pretty poor. Back then, a rich feller bought up a bunch of farms around Ames. He hired a man for each farm, let him live with his family in the farmhouse on the land, and did a 60–40 split on the crop.

Mike's father got one of the farms. Pretty normal arrangement in these parts. Only problem with being a tenant farmer is them crops hardly ever throw off enough cash for a feller to get ahead, and if you don't own the land, you don't have no leverage, no fallback. So you're always on a treadmill, worrying about making it from season to season.

Farm itself they lived on in Iowa was big, three or four thousand acres. Mike's father raised hybrid seed corn. They only got two acres out front between the house and the road for themselves, to raise a few animals and chickens and whatnot to help them get by. Mike and his brothers went to school in a small country town, but it wasn't much for learning. About the seventh or eighth grade, their dad figured if his sons were going to get educated, they'd have to move into Ames. And that's what they done.

Mike's father ended up with a long commute out to the farm, but the overall plan worked. Mike got his education. Went on to Iowa State. He was a good football player and got drafted by the Kansas City Chiefs. Played two years for them. Was on the opening-day roster both years but then dropped down to the taxi squad, where he was only making a hundred and fifty dollars a week. Had a wife and baby by then, so he pulled the plug on that and went to work for AT&T. He was with them for twenty-five years. Moved him to thirteen different cities. Ended up in Chicago the last five years. They lived way out in the suburbs, but the office was downtown. That commute about killed the country boy in him.

Five years before he hung up his white collar, Mike's wife's uncle called and told him about a hundred acres of good farmland for sale that wasn't selling. Uncle said he'd work the ground if Mike would buy it. They'd split the crop. Mike and his wife done it, and the deal worked pretty well. So then, couple of years later, five hundred and fifty acres come up for sale near Burwell. Full farm with house and barns and pens. Mike bought that for an investment, too.

That deal also gone along fine for a couple of years. Then one day Mike's boss in Chicago comes in and tells him AT&T is consolidating divisions, and they're going to move him to Basking Ridge, New Jersey. Sounds like a nice sunny place on a hill, but Mike said, I don't think so. Chicago was one thing, but New Jersey was another planet. Just so happened AT&T was offering an early buy-out right then, so Mike says, Instead of New Jersey, I'll take the early retirement.

The deal was supposed to be for sixty-year-olds that had burned the wick down to near nothing, not folks in mid-career, but they gave it to him anyways. Mike and his wife moved out to the five-hundred-and-fifty-acre place, and they been there ever since. Added near another five hundred acres along the way. Got a nice piece of ground now.

Even though Mike grew up on that farm in Iowa until he was twelve or thirteen, that was more in the nature of doing chores, maybe tending a milk cow or a couple of sheep or some chickens. Wasn't like he was out with his dad plowing and seeding—or calving. So when he come out here, after twenty-five years of occupying a desk for AT&T, he was one part farmer and nine parts phone company executive.

Kind of showed early on. Every spring you walk your fence all around, make sure your wire is up and tight and the posts are in good shape, too. On some spreads out here, it can take from sunup to sundown to walk your whole fence line. First spring out here, Mike had no idea how long it would take to walk his fence. He started out in the pasture early one afternoon. Well, a lot of ranches, in addition to the border fence, have a mess of cross fences to separate pastures and paddocks. Mike was following his border fence but also hopping cross fences. It was starting to get dark when he come up to where his true border fence turned at a right angle, only he thought it was another cross fence. So he kept going. Next thing you know, it ain't getting dark, it *is* dark, and he's lost. Ends up down by a gravel pit about five miles from his house. He manages to find his way out to the highway. A neighbor come by he hadn't even met yet. She stopped and offered him a ride. He was obliged, got in, and told her he was new in them parts, had just bought the old Gonkle place. She says, I know who you are. Then she says, What you doing way down here? He says, Lost heifer. A little smile come over her face, and she says, Didn't find her, huh? And hell if that story didn't echo around the general store in

Burwell for weeks after—the new city-feller farmer that got lost walking his own fence.

It wasn't pretty the first couple of years. Usually, it's livestock that gets the newcomers. Breeding and all that. When Mike was growing up, you turned a bull loose in a pen of heifers, and that was your breeding. Ain't the way it works no more. Not by a stretch. When Mike started with cows, he didn't have none of his own. He took a feller's cows on shares, meaning he fed them and calved them out. Mike got 60 percent of the calves, and the partner got 40 percent. Well, the first year he gone out one morning and sees a pregnant cow, about a month before she's ready to drop her calf, with something coming out her back end, and it ain't no calf. Had no idea what it was. Well, a pregnant cow can get so swolled up her uterus starts to come out. That ain't good for a lot of reasons, not the least of which is you can't hardly get it back in if it freezes up in cold weather.

Annnnnnnyway, Mike takes her into the vet and what the vet does is he pulls the outer skin back tight and puts a stitch in there to hold it closed. Now, this is a big ol' cow, so that stitch ain't like the thread you use to put a button back on your shirt. This thing is more like a cord. Vet says, I tied the right end of the cord in a slipknot, and when she starts to deliver, you need to pull the short string, which'll untie the cord. She'll open back up, and the calf will come right out. But the vet warns Mike, he says, Just loosen it, don't pull it out, because after she gets the calf out, you have to tie her back up so her uterus don't spill out entirely.

Mike kept her in a corral close to the house. About a month later, in the middle of the night—always happens at night—she starts bawling, and Mike come out to check on her. She's lying on the ground, and there's two feet coming out her back end.

Mike knows this is it. Except by now that cord is all covered in manure, and it's dark outside, and it's as cold as the North Pole because Mike calves early, in mid-January. And now he can't remember if he's supposed to pull the short string or the long one and whether it's tied on the right side or the left side, but it don't matter much because he can't see a durn thing anyway. He gets down on the ground behind her in the muck and the cold, and it don't smell so great there. He crooks a flashlight between his cheek and shoulder. He's straining so hard his neck starts cramping up, and then it cramps so bad he's afraid his head might end up permanently tilted at a forty-five-degree angle.

He reaches in and finds the cord. Well, sure enough, he not only pulls on the wrong end of the cord, he puts a knot in it. So now the mother's bawling to beat the band. The calf's hooves are sticking out, the cord is knotted, Mike is covered in manure, his hands are near froze, and his head is angled like the RCA dog.

Finally he manages to loosen the cord. The calf come out pretty quick after that. But as soon as it's out, the heifer decides she's had enough of the whole operation. She jumps up and starts running around the corral. Mike is on his feet, too, chasing after her and her flopping uterus, stumbling, walking on his knees, reaching out, trying to retie that cord. All the while his flashlight's bobbing and his head is cramped to his shoulder. He finally run out of gas and let her be. All worked out, though. Calf was fine, and the vet come out and got the mother's uterus back in. Just put his fist right in the center of it and rammed 'er home.

One time early on, Mike and his wife decided they were going to raise some chickens. So Mike ordered a hundred broilers. Those are the chickens that fatten up real quick. And twenty-five layers. Them's laying hens. They came in the mail, believe it or not. The chicks are only two days old, and they ain't much bigger than an egg. The box they come in is sectioned off in little squares. Now, you got to dip their little beaks in water so they know how to drink. If a setting hen hatches out her own chicks, she'll go over to a water source, dip her beak and drink, and the chicks see that and learn from it. But without a mother, if you don't dip their beaks, they'll never drink.

A friend of Mike's named Ray was out to the ranch the day the box of chicks come. Ray's a stutterer, bless his heart. Mike says, We just got these chicks, Ray. Need to take each one of them out, dip their beaks, and we'll count them at the same time. Ray says he'll do the dipping and the counting and Mike can record the numbers. Well, they set to. Got a lot of chicks to count. A lot. Ray takes the first one out, dips his beak in the dish of water, and says, Www-www-www-www-one. Mike makes a mark on the page but immediately gets concerned about the pace of things. Ray takes the second chick out, dips its beak, and says, Ta-ta-ta-ta-two.

Mike says, You know what, Ray, I think I'll just count them later.

One time Mike had a bull got sick with pneumonia late in the year. Had him in the barn. Mike went in, and the bull was lying on the ground. Needed to get him up to give him a shot, but the bull wouldn't budge. So Mike says, Well, buddy, looks like you're going to get it right here. So he stuck the needle up his butt. Bull wasn't too pleased. He was on his feet in a second and turned on Mike. He was snorting and stamping and generally pissed off. Had Mike pinned up against a wall with nowhere to go. Bull up and come at Mike, charging hard. Only thing Mike could do was jump up and grab hold of a big rafter. He chinned himself up and swung his legs forward like he was on a jungle gym, until his knees were about hitting his stomach. Bull passed underneath him. Only problem was, when the bull come back around, Mike had relaxed a tad and his ass was hanging level with that Angus's forehead. Bull rammed him in the rump. Force of the blow swung Mike up, over, and on top of the rafter. He ends up draped across that rafter like a cougar napping on a high branch, except his heart is pumping like a piston. Bull had his mean on for quite a spell, just stood underneath Mike, watching him and snorting. Finally Mike tossed his hat in one direction and dropped down and ran in the other.

One problem you run into a lot out here in summertime is pinkeye. Starts with the cows brushing up against cedar trees or knocking into a thistle while they're grazing and getting poked in the eye or getting a laceration near it. Usually it's the calves. The older cows tend to figure it out. Sometimes it's so bad you have to sew the calves' eyes shut for a spell, but most times you can just glue on a patch. Well, one summer it got pretty bad. Mike had half a dozen calves with pinkeye. He calls the vet out to his ranch. Deal is vet shoots the calf with a tranquilizer, it gets drowsy, and then Mike sets on it while the vet gives it a shot and affixes the patch. They done that to a couple of calves, but then they come on one with pinkeye that was just standing there real docile. Mike says he'll lasso it, no need to dart it. So he puts a patch in his hand, face down with the glue side up, and throws his lasso. The rope slings over the calf's head well enough, but as Mike goes to cinch it, the critter jumps through the loop with its front legs, and the rope tightens around its belly. The calf is spooked and bolts. Yanks Mike right off his feet.

The calf starts dragging Mike across the pasture on his stomach. He holds on to the rope with one hand while raising the other arm like the Statue of Liberty, except instead of a torch, Mike's holding up that patch with the glue on it. The calf runs past the pickup. Mike manages to rotate his body and get his boots out front. He uses his heels as brakes, which gets him slowed so he can loop the rope over the truck's trailer hitch. When the calf hits the end of the rope, it can't go no farther. But it *can* change its direction and start going around the truck.

Mike made the mistake of getting between the rope and the truck, and after the calf gone around that truck one and a half times, Mike was pinned up against his Ford like Captain Ahab against the *Pequod*. After a spell, he managed to get loose and wrassle that calf to the ground with his one free hand. They rolled over each other several times before Mike secured him and got the patch on. Barely. Calf ended up peeking out at him. Glue had spread to both of Mike's hands. By the time it was all over, Mike was sprawled on the ground and over the calf and got one hand plastered to the critter's shank and the other glued to the truck's fender. The vet looked on in a state of wonder.

Mike tells them stories on himself. Had a lot of learning to do when he first come out here, but he's been at it now more than fifteen years. He's as good as any rancher been out here a lot longer. The real greenhorns are the relatives who come out from the city with their minds set on becoming instant ranch hands.

One time, Mike's wife's sister visited with her boyfriend plus a brother-in-law and his nephew. Summertime. Hotter than hell. Mike had about six hundred square bales of hay out in the field needed to be picked up and trucked to the barn. Had a tractor pulling a flatbed trailer to do the hauling. Them three visitors were eager to get started. Wanted to do some ranch work. Well, they got themselves out to the field, next to the first group of bales, and the boyfriend announces he can't really lift nothing because his belly button is sore that day.

Mike never heard nothing like it, but he chose not to inquire further. Instead, Mike says, Well, okay then, we need a driver for the tractor, and it looks like it's going to be you. Meanwhile, the nephew strips off his shirt and says he's going to get a suntan while he works. Mike says, You best put your shirt on or you'll get more than a tan. But there was no dissuading the nephew. Couldn't tell him nothing. The nephew reaches down, lifts up the first bale, and rakes a half dozen square feet of stiff and tight-packed straw up his stomach and chest, leaving a wide, red mark. He cries out in pain but manages to steady the bail in his arms. Meanwhile, Belly Button, trying to be helpful—they all are—drives that trailer over as close to the nephew as possible, but Lord if he don't run the wheels of that flatbed right over the kid's feet. The nephew drops the bail, cries out in pain, and starts hopping around because his feet hurt and rubbing his stomach because that don't feel so good, neither.

That was the one and only bale the nephew accounted for. He limped down to the house and called it a day. The third feller, Mike's brother-in-law, was a bit better. He managed to help load the first trailer's worth, about a hundred bales. But after they come down to the barn and started unloading, Mike looks over and sees the brother-in-law sitting under a shade tree, sweating like a racehorse, near collapsed from heat exhaustion. He was a gamer and tried to help with the next load, but he only made five or six bales before he redded up like a tomato and Mike had to get him back to the house. Kind of typical with visitors from the city. Started the day fresh with four hands, but by midmorning he was back down to just himself. Plus Belly Button driving.

The nephew's name was Rueben. He come back for more on another occasion. Mike needed some barbed wire rolled up. Rueben was eager to comply. Mike pointed to a big wooden spool on the ground—about thigh-high it stood—and asked Rueben to roll up fifty yards of wire that was laid across a pasture that went up over a hill. Mike went into the barn for something, and when he come out, instead of rolling the spool on the ground, Rueben had that big ol' spool lifted over his head and, with considerable effort, was winding the wire up as he climbed that hill.

Mike moseyed over and begun telling Rueben about the invention of the wheel five thousand years before by the Sumerians. The kid wasn't catching Mike's drift. He still had that spool over his head and was huffing and puffing up the hill. Sure enough, he'd also sliced himself on the arm with that wire flying all over the place. Breathless, Rueben asked Mike if he could get tetanus from rusty old wire. Mike said he didn't know about tetanus, but a farmer up the valley cut himself like that and got syphilis from it.

Rueben froze and started to lose color in his face and blood to his extremities. He dropped the spool backward over his head and it rolled all the way down the hill, unwinding all the wire he'd just collected. Never heard if the sight of it give Rueben a clue about the proper operation of a spool.

Speaking of adverse reactions, there was another time Belly Button and Rueben come out to help with spring roundup. Remember, that's where you brand the calves, give them their shots, and castrate the baby bulls. Mike had a three-man operation set up that day. After the cattle were herded through a chute, one feller would get the calf in a head catch, another would cut them, and a third would give them their shots. Well, that day Rueben was doing the shots, so he had a long needle in each of his hands. In his left hand was the needle that give the tetanus shot, and in his right was a needle with a combination of vaccines. Belly Button was responsible for getting the bull calves in the head catch.

Annnnnnnyway, they got to going, and of course about half the calf herd got past Belly Button. He's fussing and fighting with them and having a devil of a time. Still, they get it down to a system of sorts: Belly Button wrestles them into the head catch, Mike cuts them, and Rueben steps forward and sticks one needle in the calf and then the other. The calf is released and scampers off. Well, one time a calf was getting the better of Belly Button. It's close quarters in the corral there, and when that calf balks, Belly Button stumbles backwards and takes one of Rueben's needles right in the ass. He sets to whooping and hollering like he got the knife rather than the needle.

Mike got him calmed down, but Belly Button was worried about the shot and if he's going to have some sort of reaction. Concern was etched across Mike's face when he stepped over to Rueben and asked him which needle stabbed Belly Button. Rueben says it was the penicillin needle. Mike gasped. Made a face like the end of the world was coming—or at least the end of Belly Button—and he tells him, You ain't going die, but your testicles are going to swell up either to the size of a baseball or a soccer ball, depending on how much juice you took. Well, Belly Button starts to dance around in circles. He's hunched over holding his privates and crying about his fate, and then he begs Mike or Rueben to suck the drug out of the wound—like he seen in the movies, where they done it for venom from a rattlesnake bite. Considering the location of the wound, weren't

no takers. Didn't matter no how because Mike couldn't contain
himself no longer and busted out laughing.

Mike must be over sixty now, but he don't hardly look like a
man past his mid-forties. Don't know what he looked like when
he was wearing a coat and tie and riding that train into Chicago
every morning, but today, ain't a man looks more at home on a
Nebraska ranch.

The Big-Time Rancher

MOST ranchers in Nebraska would grow their ground if they could. But land don't come up for sale much, and when it does, not like everyone's got cash lying round so they can buy it. And a lot of them fellers that ain't grown inherited their ground to begin with, so they should have an advantage.

Then there's Ted Hanich. Started with nothing but caught a fast train and never slowed down. At his peak, Ted must of had a hundred thousand acres and ten thousand head of cattle all told, including two thousand cows. If you don't know, those are big numbers. Two thousand cows will drop a million dollars worth of calves a year.

Ted's father was a wheat farmer south of Paxton. Large operator for a time. Run them ol' ten-bottom plows. But the '30s didn't spare many folks. Drought come first, and then prices for everything broke, including wheat. Ted's father went under. Things got tough. Ted and his brother Bob run around barefoot in summer because the family couldn't afford shoes. Ted and Bob slept in a loft in the barn because there was only room in the house for his parents and two sisters.

His father got going again on rented land just as Ted headed off to the war. He was an aviation engineer for four years, chasing the American advance, building landing fields for fighter planes from Australia to New Guinea to the Philippines and some of them smaller islands before ending up in Japan at the end. But he was always a country boy. There's that song about how you're going to keep them down on the farm after they seen Paris. Weren't a worry with Ted. He couldn't wait to get back to Nebraska after he seen most of the South Pacific. After the war, he partnered up with his brother. They farmed for about eight years, from '45 to '53. Every time they got a spare nickel, they bought more land. But Ted had ranching in his blood.

When Ted come home from the war, a friend of the family, Harvey Applegate, he said, Ted, I want to get you started in the Angus business. Come on over to my ranch, and pick you out a hundred of my best heifers. Ted went over to Harvey's place near Sutherland and chose him a hundred Angus calves. Paid a hundred and two dollars each. Harvey wrote it all down on a piece of newspaper, had Ted sign it, and stuffed the paper in a pocket of his overalls.

Ted and Bob leased a ranch and grew the herd, but by '55 Ted was hankering for his own place. Took two years to find the right spot, but Ted bought his first ten thousand acres in '57, and it's the same spread he's on to this day near Dunning, up in the Sand Hills. Called the place Four Corners because it's near the junction of four counties. If you never been out, it's a sight. All dirt roads, fence lines, and cattle. Ted lives at the end of an eight-mile gravel road. The ranch sets in a broad valley, rimmed by low rolling hills. Along the road in, there's no buildings or structures of any sort and almost no trees as far as the eye can see, which is four or five miles to the ridgelines all around. Just a few windmills pumping water. Imagine the moon with grass. When you get to the ranch house, there's a few more trees—they serve as a wind break—but the ranch house and outbuildings are pretty modest for a feller with as many zeros in his bank account as Ted got.

Annnnnnnyway, Ted and Bob got themselves a pretty fool-proof system. Bob the farmer raised the feed, Ted the rancher raised the cattle, and they fattened them cattle on the feed. Ted was off and running.

Some say Ted was ruthless. When he took over a ranch, they say he was quick to send most of the ranch hands packing. Or if you owed him money on a place, he'd foreclose rather than stretch the due date. Usually ain't the way out here, but others might call it being a smart businessman. Don't know enough about the particulars to judge. Maybe not being able to afford shoes as a kid leaves a mark on a young buck. Maybe made him want to make sure that didn't never happen again. They say it's all about the money with Ted, but he and Bob run off the same checkbook for over fifty years and never had a word between them. Maybe that's just family, but don't know that family has ever been much of an antidote for greed.

Ted had ways of making money even when he didn't make money his first priority. Early on, three brothers called and offered Ted some two-year-old steers. Them boys didn't want the money upfront, they always wanted to get paid the next winter for tax reasons. The brothers said they'd driven them steers down to Coker station, and they were in pens there if Ted and Bob wanted to take a look. Coker station was the railhead for a Union Pacific spur line. Had some scales there. You could weigh fifteen to twenty head there in drafts.

Ted says, What about the weight?

When it comes to buying and selling cattle, it all comes down to weight.

One of the brothers says, Check the gate. Then he hung up.

So Ted and Bob drove down, and there were them steers in corrals. They checked the gate, and scrawled in pencil on it was the weight of them cattle. That was the bill of sale, some penciling on a gate. With the scales right there, Ted and Bob weighed them steers again. The three brothers had weighed the cows heavy by thirty-five or forty pounds a head.

Bob was madder than a snake got stepped on. He wanted to give them boys the what for, but Ted calmed him down, said they ought to try the deal. So they bought them steers for twenty-two cents a pound in the fall, give them a hundred-and-twenty-day feed, and sold them for twenty-six cents fat. Made money that was worth their while, even buying them heavy to start, and they didn't even have to pay for them until after they'd sold them.

Same thing happened the next year. Went down to Coker station to look at a hundred steers offered up by the brothers. Total weight was written on the fence gate. Weighed heavy again. Bob fumed. Ted bought. Sold them fat and made some money. Went on like that for years. Not only made Ted and Bob a pocketful of jingle, but they shipped some of them steers to Kansas City, and the processor there thought they were so good-looking, he put their picture on his calendar. Headline under the June snapshot said, 'The Hanich Brothers, Some of the Fattest, Prettiest Black Angus Cattle You'll Ever See.'

That's just the way it went for Ted, year after year, deal after deal. Don't know if it was skill, luck, or the Lord. Ted'll tell you it was all three. But after he started building the herd on the Four Corners ranch, his wallet started getting as fat as his cattle. And he put it to use. Some fellers buy seed, raise a corn crop, and sell feed. Others buy and sell cattle. Ted did all that and bought and sold feed lots, too. But mostly he was about ranches. Born dealmaker. Buy a ranch, hold on to it for five years or so, and then sell it. Ain't only the city where land prices are going up. Since '57, he must of bought and sold a dozen, maybe fourteen ranches. Only bought big ranches. Reason was less competition. Fewer people bidding for really big spreads, so he always got a better deal.

This is how it'd typically go for Ted. Back in the mid-1990s, he heard about a ranch come on the market north of Taylor in the Sand Hills. Owned by the son of a famous Hereford man in these parts. Twenty sections, so we're talking close to thirteen thousand acres. Asking price was $135 an acre. Owner turned down an offer for $130 an acre in the fall. Went over until spring. Nobody bought it. Story was feller who owned it lived in Omaha and was rich from computers, and he was buying land right and left all over the Sand Hills. But then, all of a sudden, things turned for him, and he was selling. Ted drove down to Omaha in the spring and offered $125 an acre. Agent chuckled and told him the feller had already turned down $130 in the fall. Ted told him to make the offer. Agent come back and said, I can't believe it. He'll take the $125 an acre. Cash. Ted only bought with cash. Ol' Ted got a deal that time. Like he seemed to done every time. He run cattle on it for about five years, making money off of *them*, and then he sold the ranch for nearly two hundred dollars an acre. You do the figuring.

But it ain't like no rain fell in his life. Fact, fate took a pretty nasty turn on him. He was out in a hay field one day when a storm blew up. His first wife was home in their house, which was just over a rise from where Ted was working. A bolt of lightning struck the house. Ted saw the roof blow off, and he raced back on his horse. They figured out later there was a leak in a propane tank under the house. Weren't much of a problem until it was hit by lightning and exploded. When Ted got back to the ranch house, he found his wife dead.

Ted eventually remarried, and he and his second wife been together now for decades. Ted's a religious feller. Talks about it a lot, but you can't hardly say it ain't working for him. Hell, one time down in Leoti, Kansas, he got his dealmaking and the Lord all mixed together in one big pot, but it sure come out right on both ends. He and his wife saw an ad in the paper for fifteen quarters of wheat land. That's about twenty-five hundred acres. Like I said, Ted's the rancher and Bob's the farmer, but Ted figured he'd take a look at it anyway. Leoti is smack dab in the middle of the wheat belt. It was dry land, flat as a board, brand-new house on the property. A woman in her eighties who owned it wanted to cash out. Ted didn't really want to farm, but he called on the Lord and the Lord give him the terms of the deal. He bought the farm and planted twelve hundred acres of wheat. After a spell, he and his wife were pretty much living down there, and they become part of the community.

They started attending the Assembly of God church in Leoti and didn't like the fact that there were only thirty-five members in a town of twenty-six hundred. Part of the problem was they needed a real church. They had an opportunity to buy a Baptist church for eighty thousand dollars, with a down payment of thirty thousand. This here is Ted's golden touch. Feller ain't even a farmer, he's a rancher, and he ain't even from Kansas, he's from Nebraska, but his wheat crop come in bumper that year and his tithe off the profits was thirty thousand dollars— almost to the zero. Bought out the Baptists. Short time later, the church bought an old school bus and put a new set of tires on it, and within a year they were ferrying a hundred kids to Sunday school and back home. Then the parents started coming.

Two ladies come out from Washington State, evangelists. They been going church to church preaching, and by the time they got to Leoti, they were plum wore out. Ted invited them to stay on his farm and rest up a spell. One morning at the breakfast table, one of the women suddenly threw up her hands like she was getting a communication from upstairs—and I don't mean upstairs in the house—and she says, Hanichs, pack your bags. You'll be home within a year.

Ted and his wife didn't know what to make of that until a feller come down from South Dakota within a year and offered to buy the wheat farm. It wasn't even on the market. Ted sold it and made $330,000 profit on the land after owning the place barely five years. And this was back in the early '80s. Ted says he figures the Lord was just using him down there, and when His work was done, He got Ted out of there. Don't know that the Lord dabbles in the land brokerage business much, but it's hard to figure how He weren't in the middle of that deal somewheres.

Like I said, Ted just got the golden touch. Ain't done bad for a feller only finished eighth grade. One of his biggest deals was back in the mid-'90s. He bought a ranch near Hobbs, New Mexico. Hundred sections. That's about sixty-five thousand acres. He kept living in Nebraska, but he and his wife would go to Mexico—old Mexico—and buy a few thousand yearlings and stock the New Mexico ranch with them. Ranch threw off some cash, but he had trouble running the place. Couldn't seem to get good help. He also bought a feed lot near Clovis and run into some trouble with that. He didn't have any insurance, and a bad storm come through. The cattle all huddled up against the steel-pipe fence. Lightning strike electrocuted a bunch of steers. Killed sixty-five head in all. About seventy thousand bucks, gone in a few seconds.

After five years, he got a call from a feller who wanted to buy the ranch. Even with the troubles down there, Ted told him he didn't want to sell. Feller explained he owned a big feed lot in Kansas and needed to supply it. Feller asked directions to the ranch, wanted to see it. Ted give him directions to the northeast corner. Ted says, Just follow the fence line around a hundred sections, and you'll see more of the place than I ever seen. Well, the feller weren't in a car. He flew over it in a plane. Without ever setting foot on the ground, he called Ted and said, Put a price on it. Ted did. Cleared another million bucks after owning it only five years.

But even Ted's slowing up now. He's eighty-three. Back in the day, everybody in the Sand Hills knew if you had a big ranch and you wanted to sell, you called Ted first. If he liked it, you got cash. He's still getting calls every morning, but he ain't buying like he used to. He got a call the other day from a feller who just got back from Argentina—down there in the pampas, they call it. He says, Ted, you want to buy a big ranch? Twenty thousand acres for twenty-five cents an acre. Ted's hand went inching toward his checkbook, like a gunslinger been challenged, but in the end, he bucked the urge. His glory days of buying and selling may be over, but he's still ranching at Four Corners every day. Still living the life.

The Country Vet

I have to tell you about one of the nicest fellers you're ever going meet—and maybe the most discombobulated one. Jack Longfellow talks slow and funny, like his tongue is swoll up in his mouth. Big feller, big belly. Got small legs, waist hidden up under there somewheres. Jolly feller. Dressed in a white beard and red suit, he'd make a great Santa for the kids at Christmas. But he'll fool you. Looks like a country bumpkin, but he's sneaky smart when he gets his thoughts together and heading in the same general direction. He done pretty well by himself for a feller lucky to get his breeches put on frontways every morning.

Jack's a veterinarian, owns the Grassland Hospital in Broken Bow. Oldest haul-in vet hospital in the state. Don't matter he got the clinic; Jack's out doing barn calls all the time. Once, a feller calls Jack and says he got a cow ain't feeling so well and could Jack come over. He says he don't have any money, but maybe he could give Jack a calf that don't see so well as payment. Jack gone over there and heads out to the pasture. There's musk thistle everywhere. State says you're supposed to spray it, but when you ain't got money, you ain't got money.

Annnnnnnyway, this farmer was raising hogs as well as fat cattle. Nice feller, but his bulb was flickering a bit, if you know what I mean. Didn't have any pens or nothing, so the cattle had got into the hog feed. Jack pulls into the yard and sees a twelve-hundred-pound steer down from overload. He'd gotten into the hog self-feeder, and that stuff is too high in protein for cattle.

Steer was in bad shape, and Jack says to the feller, This steer ain't going to get up, and it ain't going to live. We got to do something fast.

Jack told the farmer he could put it out of its misery, and then the farmer could hang it up and butcher it.

He says, Will you do that, Doc?

So Jack put the steer to sleep and slit its throat and told the feller to go get his tractor so they could hang the cow up and bleed him good.

The feller says okay.

Well, without any pens, them dadgum hogs smelled the blood and run over. Looked like a herd of razorbacks coming at him. They went wild. Had a mind to make a meal of that steer and Jack both. Didn't discriminate between the two. They were every size, shape, age, and gender. Mongrel herd, none of the males been castrated. Jack starts kicking at them while they're grunting and going nuts over that blood from the steer and nearly knocking Jack over.

Finally, the feller comes over in the tractor, but it doesn't fit through the gate. He backs it up and tries again, but it's just plain too big. That doesn't stop him from backing up and trying it again, though.

Jack says, You can't get an elephant through the eye of a needle, and you ain't going to get that tractor through the gate!

There's another tractor nearby, so the farmer abandons the first one and runs toward the smaller one. Meanwhile, that herd of hogs is starting to gnaw on Jack's ankles. He looks up, and the feller is on the second tractor, but he can't get it started.

He jumps off, runs into the house, and come out with a cup of water.

At that point Jack's life begun flashing before his eyes. Cup of water? he mutters. The feller runs over to the pump jack in the yard and pours the water down the top to prime it.

Jack calls over, What in tarnation are you doing? I'm being eaten alive over here!

Farmer says, Can't afford antifreeze for the big tractor, so I drained the antifreeze out of the small tractor and put it in the big one. So now I'm getting water for the small tract—

Save your breath and pump the water! Jack says.

Feller got the water and run over and poured it in the radiator while Jack keeps dancing and booting pigs in the snout. He looks up to see the farmer got the small tractor started and moving. He come through the gate—glory hallelujah—and stops in front of Jack. Feller brought along a log chain with a hook on one end. Jack wrapped the free end of the chain around the teeth on the loader and attached the hook to the hind legs of the steer. Now they could raise the critter clear of them hogs and butcher it. Jack says, All right, raise the loader.

Feller tried it, but it wouldn't budge. Tried it again. No nothing. Didn't have any hydraulics. The oil! he says. I drained the oil and put it in the big tractor like I done with the antifreeze. Feller jumped off the second tractor and runs toward the first one.

Jack begun to whimper now. More hogs everywhere. They were coming over the horizon and then diving under what fences there were in the yard. Sows, boar hogs—herd of biblical proportions.

Finally, the farmer got the oil out of the old tractor and into the new one. He lifted that loader, and the steer started rising up. It got pretty high, but the feller didn't have enough oil to top off, so the loader only gone up so far. Still had to kick the hogs away. But at least the steer was up high enough to work on.

After all that, the farmer says, Doc, I could butcher this thing myself, but that's an awful sharp knife you have there.

Jack's a vet, not a butcher. He stood there exhausted and suffering from various flesh wounds about his feet and lower legs, but he just didn't have the heart to say, I have to leave now.

So the feller got a barrel, and Jack got up on it. Farmer took his turn doing crowd control with the hogs. Jack got the steer skinned down and was ready to tie off the rectum. Didn't want any fecal matter contaminating the meat when he split the pelvis. Jack asked if the feller had any twine.

He run off, and Jack could hear tools clanking around in the barn. Farmer comes back and holds up a piece of twine not much longer than your index finger and covered in grease. All black. Jack, up on the barrel, was so shocked to see that greasy little sprig of twine that his arm fell forward, and he run the steer's gut through with his knife.

That eliminated the need for twine.

Jack quickly split the belly and dropped the entrails. When they hit the ground, them hogs took it up a notch from wild to frenzied. Had to back the tractor up to get the beef out of the way, and then they laid the carcass out in the bed of the feller's pickup. He was thanking Jack up and down. Meanwhile, guts is everywhere. Filthy hogs is everywhere. Excrement is everywhere. The farmer's hands were covered in all that plus oil. He says, I can't pay you right now, but would you like a sandwich?

Jack about barfed. Instead, he politely declined the hospitality and left rather hurriedly.

Jack was back to the same farmer's place a few months later, doctoring another critter, and the feller still don't have no money, of course. He says, Jack, I want to pay you by giving you a calf that don't see so well.

Farmer says he's going to ride up and drive his calves down through a wash, and Jack can rope the one that don't see so well. Pretty soon the calves are trotting by Jack. Now, Jack ain't never been comfortable asking for bill payment even when it's owed him, so he didn't say nothing when the calf that didn't see so well come running by and it's plain it don't see *at all*. Thing was blind and a runt: it can't see what it ain't eating. It was stumbling and bumbling into the other calves while they were on the run. Jack knew the calf wouldn't come close to paying for the half dozen visits he'd made to the feller's place, but he figured a regular calf would do it. So as those calves run by, he aimed at a healthy one just ahead of the blind, sickly one. If Jack roped a healthy calf 'by accident,' weren't likely the feller would say nothing about it. But it's just Jack's luck with money that the loop missed the good calf and dropped perfect over the blind runt. Ended up costing Jack more to doctor that sickly thing and feed it for six months than he sold it for.

Jack was born and raised on a farm in Iowa. Went to Northwest Missouri State University on both football and academic scholarships. He still had to count every penny in them days and had trouble putting meat on the table. One weekend he had off, so he went home to Iowa. Shot seventy-two rabbits in two days. He was a crack shot. He dressed all those rabbits, ground up the meat, and made rabbit meatloaf, rabbit pizza, rabbit burger, rabbit stuffed with rice and tomatoes, stewed rabbit, fried rabbit. Froze it all and had rabbit dishes for weeks.

Jack come out with a degree in mathematics and physics and a minor in general science. He taught at Northwest Missouri for a while—physics and computer programming—and then started pursuing a doctorate in physics. Like I said, he only *looks* like a country bumpkin. He was also accepted to be a pilot in the air force and was offered a job as a programmer for McDonnell Aircraft company back when a computer filled a whole room. But he was also accepted at vet school.

To say veterinary science runs in Jack's family is understating things a might. His wife is a veterinarian. His brother is a veterinarian. His father-in-law is a veterinarian. His two sons are veterinarians. One of their girlfriends is a veterinarian. His daughter-in-law is a veterinarian. And Jack had wanted to be a vet since he was eleven or twelve. So he gone to vet school in Missouri. Met his wife Diane there. To put himself through, he drove a semi cross-country for a while. Forty-three states in all. Never stopped hardly. Made eighteen thousand dollars back in the '70s driving for only three and a half months. He once fell asleep face down in a pizza at a truck stop. Another time, in Washington State, they had to wake him up to order, wake him up to eat his burger, wake him up to pay, and wake him up to leave.

He come out to Broken Bow while a student to get some vet practice—month or so, back in '73—at Grassland Hospital. He liked it and moved to Broken Bow and Grassland after he graduated. They offered him a full-time salary of twelve thousand dollars a year.

It's rare out here anyone gets by doing just one thing. Same with Jack. He's a rancher and a farmer—done some construction, too—as well as being a vet. It ain't talked about much out here, but everyone knows that most folks in Nebraska inherited all or most of their ranch. Jack is one didn't have no land to start with, but he managed to put a ranch together. He's living on a piece of ground I'll tell you about later on the edge of town. He's bought a number of other small parcels over the years. But he rolled the dice in '85 when the economy was as bad in ranch country as its been since the '30s.

Feller with a last name of Fred had three sons. They put the Four Freds ranch up for auction—3,105 acres on the road to Sargent. Folks was watching land sales like that with a sharp eye. Bankers thought it would go for $220 an acre. Jack had bid $140 on it the previous fall. It'd been appraised at $400 per acre three years earlier. At auction, Jack got the ground at $115 per acre. Gamble paid off. Worth quite a bit more than that now. Quite a bit.

Let me tell you about Jack's home place. I ain't saying it's messy or nothing, it's just heavy lived in. It's kind of old and been added on to a bunch of different times. Behind the house, there's all kinds of critters in a paddock that stretches up over a hill. There's a couple of buffalo mixed in with some cattle. There's goats and chickens. Lot of stuff hanging around the yard—vehicles, equipment, stuff no one ever seen before in their life. In the kitchen, every flat surface is piled with dishes or stacks of yellowing papers and other crud *several foot high*. Weren't that different from other ranch kitchens, but it could maybe use some paint or new wallpaper or a bulldozer. Probably ain't been updated in half a century.

To top it all off, there's a big feed lot just across the road to the west. Feed lot is where they stuff a mess of cattle in a bunch of pens and feed them like hell, fatten them up for market. But when you feed, you get the residue, too, so to speak. So when the wind come out of the west, and you're inside Jack's house, it smells like there's been a death in the basement that ain't been tended to. I ain't saying there's anything Jack could do about it—a feed lot's a feed lot—I'm just telling you is all.

One time I been over there and we were talking in the kitchen, and the prettiest young gal, maybe eighteen, come around the corner from down the hall. She was clean and well-dressed, cultured and mannered and all, and when she says hello, it's in the sweetest, soft-spokenest voice you ever heard—and with a charming French accent. I thought she was an apparition. Jack introduced her as a foreign exchange student from Paris. I about fell out my chair. Between Jack, the kitchen that looked like a recycling center, the critters, the equipment in the yard, and the feed lot upwind, she must of thought she'd landed on Mars.

Last time I been over, I drove up to the house, and right next to it in the yard—not ten foot away—was a big ol' church. That's what I said. Jack's house sits up on a small rise. The dirt along the south side of that little hill been shaved away, and there's the church—big as a church—propped up on a mess of railroads ties, snug against the little cliff, creating a breezy, twelve-foot basement underneath the floor of the edifice.

Jack, ain't that a church? What's it doing here, next to your house, out in the country, near a feed lot?

He says, They were going to burn it down, so I bought it for a writing and sculpture studio. Them two don't seem to go together—Jack and sculpturing, I mean. I ain't saying Jack can't make pretty sculptures, but when you look at Jack, the first thing that come to mind ain't art. And it ain't the ninety-ninth thing, neither. He's going to put a four-car garage underneath the church for all the equipment he's got sitting out in the yard, and he's going to connect it to the cellar in his house by an underground tunnel.

The feller that moved the church from up north a ways is getting older, and he and Jack worked hard and close together to get that church moved, and when it was all done, the feller offered to sell the business to him. Not much more than a couple of semis with flatbeds, bunch of hydraulic jacks and steel beams. But Jack seen *Mega Movers* on the History Channel a few weeks before and took a shine to the whole idea of moving things that's large. Thought hard about buying the business, but cooler heads prevailed—or maybe it was his wife's head that prevailed.

Annnnnnnyway, Jack works about eighteen hours a day. He says he's got to work that hard to pay for everything needs paying for, so I don't know when he's going to find time for writing and sculpturing. Like when I gone over and seen the church there. Night before, he was going to fix his pivot. Pivots are them big, tall, long sprinkler rigs you see in farm country. They can be upwards of a quarter-mile long, built up above the crop on wheels. They roll across the field around a center hub. Water is pumped from the aquifer sitting underneath Nebraska. Cost comes from the electricity running the pump. It ain't cheap, so most farmers run the pivot at night when the rates are about one-third what they are in the daytime.

So when it come to fixing the pivot, Jack does it at night. Well, he didn't finished his other work and chores until about one in the morning. He gone out and sat down on a bench outside the back of his kitchen, preparing himself mentally for heading out to fix the pivot the rest of the night. But then he looked up and seen the stars. The stars in Nebraska ain't like none other. He laid down on that bench to see the stars better, and next thing you know, he'd slept there all night. Which means fixing the pivot'll take up most of the *next* night. That's the kind of schedule he keeps.

But Jack is mostly running in place because he works so hard, yet he don't send out any bills. He don't like to. Don't like taking the time, and he's too nice, too. Thinks it's impolite to ask for money, even when it's owed him. Usually, he only sends bills out when folks he owes money to come calling and they need to get paid. That happened a while back. Jack needed cash flow, and some folks that had calf doctoring done by him five years before finally got a bill for services rendered. Just the other day, Jack managed to collect a bunch of checks, eighty-five hundred dollars in all, and stuck them in his billfold. He was going to put them in the bank one of these days, but before he could do that, he washed his pants with the billfold in it. Wiped out most of them checks, except he was able to save some in the middle of the stack. So then he had a littler group of checks stuffed in his billfold. But he gone and washed his pants again a couple of weeks later with the billfold still in them, so he ended up losing that whole wad of checks he started with.

Jack gets all kinds coming into the vet clinic. There was a feller lived in the hills about forty miles out of town. Very remote. Lived like a hillbilly. Didn't come to town hardly never—just once every few months for supplies—so it was something of a surprise when he shuffled in through the front door of the clinic one day holding his hands in front of him at his waist. With his head mostly down, he says real slow, Would Doctor Jack happen to be here?

They gone and fetched Jack, and he come out to the front there. The feller reaches out his hands and, real slow again, says,

Is there any way you could fix this little duck's leg? And he opened his hands, and he was holding a fuzzy little baby duck dragging one leg. Feller was about seventy-five years old, but he had a heart as big as a washtub. He never went nowheres, but he drove eighty miles to see if he could fix up that baby duck. Jack worked on that duck a spell, managed to fix him with a tiny splint, and sent the feller on his way.

Heck, Jack's worked on everything: cattle, horses, goats, hogs, buffalo, snakes, parakeets, even an elephant that come through in the circus. His wife even did a Cesarean on a pregnant mouse having complications. Kid's pet. Jack give his wife two buffalo once for her birthday. She turned around and give him two pygmy goats for his birthday. After that, they quit giving each other critters for presents.

One time, Jack got a call on a winter evening just as he was closing the clinic. About twenty-five below that night. Call came from right across the street. Feller and his two boys that run a ranch had a cow down. She was weak from the weather. Jack gone over, and they tied her hind legs and then turned back her head and tied it to her back legs. Jack was going to give her an IV.

All that tying up immobilized the cow and give Jack a clear spot to stick in the IV. Jack done it, give her the IV, but she doesn't respond right away. He told the boys to spread some hay around her head in case she stayed down a spell longer. But as they were getting ready to undo all the ropes, Jack also says, Careful now, sometimes when you pull the needle and unhitch the ropes, they can hop right up and take you.

That's just what she done. When they pulled the IV, untied her hind legs, and jerked the rope off her head, that fifteen-hundred-pound Hereford come up angered and spoiling for a fight. She charged them straightaway.

Jack took off running like a scalded dog. Runs for his life with that cow snorting and stampeding right behind him. He heads in the general direction of his truck. One of the brothers is right in front of him and not moving as fast as the situation called for. Jack is looking at him and watching that their feet don't get tangled, and also turning his head to track that cow gaining on them, but none of that helps much. Jack is tripping and slipping and running up the one brother's back. He loses track of the second brother as he reaches the passenger side of the pickup. The mad Hereford is still hot on their tail.

Jack and the first brother turn the corner by the fender and cross in front of the truck, bumping into each other as they go. The cow makes the turn with them. The brother takes a right turn and heads across the pasture. Jack turns left and keeps going around the truck, passing down the driver's side now. The Hereford stays with Jack.

Jack gets a bright idea and jerks open the driver's door of the pickup. That's when he finds the other brother, sitting in the driver's seat. They look each other over a split second before the brother pulls the door closed right quick. Message was clear without no words. *This spot is taken.* Even though it weren't his truck or his seat.

Jack keeps them short legs of his moving, hooks an arm in the crook of the truck bed, and whips around the back of the pickup, along the drop-gate side. Meantime the cow is raking its head all along the metal body on the driver's side and then whooshes past him. Jack done another half lap, jumps into the passenger seat, and slams the door shut. Safe. Sudden quiet.

Jack looks at the brother in the driver's seat, but the feller ain't looking his way. He's checking the weather outside. And he don't make any conversation about leaving Jack outside to get run over by that Hereford. That's just the way it is in ranch country: all's fair in love and cow evasion.

One time, Jack was working cattle down south of Callaway. He was dehorning longhorns, not a breed you see a lot of in these parts. The dehorner is a mean-looking cutter with big, long handles. It's like a guillotine. You put it over the horn and pull them handles together, and the guillotine slices off the horn. With them longhorns having a three-inch base, it takes some muscle to do the job. After you cut the horns, the wound bleeds, but you cap it quick.

Annnnnnnyway, the owner of the ranch sends out a feller to help Jack. He's a big, rugged cowboy, but a nice feller. He was supposed to hold the tool in place at the base of the horn while Jack did the actual dehorning. They cut a few, but the feller looks away each time, which means the dehorner ain't held on right and they ain't getting a clean cut. Turns out that big tough cowboy can't stand the sight of blood. But Jack don't know that then, and while he's capping a horn, he finally says to the feller, If you don't start holding it on better, you're liable to miss a thumb. Jack turned and picked up that long-handled dehorner off the ground, and when he turned back, the feller was gone. Well, he wasn't gone exactly, he was laid out on the ground. Passed out, just like that. Ended up being a long day of dehorning.

One time Jack was back in the corral next to the clinic, and there's a greenhorn there just started working for him. Jack was supposed to do a fertility test on a big ol' bull. Idea was to run the bull into a dead-end alley and then crank his tail or put a post behind him so he can't back out. Then Jack would come in from behind and do the doctoring. But when they run the bull into the alley, the kid would jump up on the fence and whoop and holler. Don't know what he was thinking except maybe he was going to run that bull further down the alley. But somebody must of told him to do it without explaining the concept, because when he'd jump up on that fence he was in *front* of the bull. Consequently, he torqued the critter, spooked him so he backed out.

Kid did it once and then twice. Bull torqued each time and got himself more and more rattled. Finally, Jack says, Son, you do that one more time and you're going to get that bull to where no one's going to get him in.

Well, sure enough, kid done it one more time, and that bull spooked. He come after Jack and hit him a glancing blow. Spun him. Jack starts running for the side of the corral. He don't make it. Bull hits him square in the ass and knocks him ten foot in the air. Ten foot! Arced him clean out of the corral. Fact, if there was a basketball hoop there, Jack might have scored. Jack kind of landed on all fours, but the top of his head kept going and smacked hard into the ground. Opened up a gusher.

To give you a feel for how Jack's life is a series of routine catastrophes, his assistant at the clinic come out while he's on the ground, stunned and with blood pouring down his face, and she says all impatient-like, Jack, come on, the lady's here who has the appointment for them two dogs to be vaccinated.

She says it like it's just another day of Jack fooling around in the corral, bleeding to death.

Jack says, I'll be there in just a minute. He manages to corral that bull and then goes over to the kid, who's also picking himself up off the ground. Jacks says, See, that's what happens when you be whooping and hollering like that. Jack settled down a bit and says, What exactly happened? Kids says, I don't know. Last thing I remember, you were ten feet in the air. I never seen anything like it, except in the circus. That's when I passed out.

Jack got some paper towels and cleaned himself up, muttering about good help these days. Then he slapped some clean towels on the wound and put his cowboy hat back on over the mess. He gone in to see the woman, and while he's examining the first dog, blood starts trickling down his temple. She seen it and asked him what for. He explained and she says, Heck, my husband's a medical doctor, and he's sitting out in the car. So Jack fixed up the second dog, and then the doc come in and sewed up Jack. Settled on a swap of services; no bills or checks traded hands that day.

Jack done a lot of surgeries on bulls, and he done quite a few on the most sensitive part of a bull. Sometimes, if they try to leap a fence or just leap a cow, they can injure their peter. We're talking about bulls that cost tens of thousands of dollars potentially, maybe even hundreds of thousands, and they cost that much because they're used for breeding. Consequently, to put it plain, all them hundreds of thousands of dollars pretty much get funneled right through that peter, and ranchers'll do whatever they can to make sure it remains in good working order.

Well, feller heard about Jack's reputation and give him a call and explained that his bull's thing ain't working. Feller said he took him to one vet who told him he might as well sell the bull for hamburger.

Jack listened and figured what was wrong, and he tells the feller to bring him in, but that it'll require two surgeries two months apart, and he'd have to leave the bull with Jack for that spell.

This is one of them cases where it was a feller's prize bull, had a lot of money into him, so he agreed. Trailered that bull down four hundred miles from somewheres, South Dakota I reckon, and left him with Jack. Jack done the first surgery and it gone well enough, but you never know with these things. Waited the two months and then Jack done the second surgery. That's about all Jack could do. Time would tell. Feller comes by and picks up the bull and takes him home.

About two weeks later, the feller that owned the bull was back home on his spread. Been no sign of life from the bull's peter. A couple of fellers come to visit the bull's owner and they brung their wives and young daughters with them. The two fellers, both ranchers, wandered out into the pasture. Owner takes the women and girls over to the corral and starts bragging on his prize bull.

All of a sudden, that bull's tool come out twixt his legs. This bull was a big one—real big. Consequently, his peter was as big as the business end of a Louisville slugger. That ol' rancher was hoping against hope that bull would come back far enough so it could be used for artificial insemination. It was beyond his wildest dreams that it might start breeding natural again. When he seen that peter—and them women and girls seen it big as day too—he tossed off his hat, threw up his arms to the heavens, hollered like he was calling the hogs home to supper, and spun around while doing a jig.

He carried on like that for a minute or so, just whooping it up. Then he seen them women and girls looking at him like he's the world's biggest pervert. He stopped—froze—and then went and collected his hat real quiet-like. Then he spent a good half hour calmly explaining himself before setting the record mostly straight. Good thing they were ranch women, or he might still be standing there talking it out.

With all the running around he done, cops all know Jack. He gets going on his calls, which are often emergencies, but he also has ten other things running through his mind. He'll be talking on the cell phone, and next thing you know, that big ol' club inside his shoe has laid the gas pedal about flat, and Jack is roaring across the fruited plain at eighty or eighty-five mile an hour.

Once, he was going to a festival of some kind, and he's got his whole family in the rig. He's late, and they're flying. The cops have a checkpoint set up, and they pull Jack over. It's a highway patrol officer he recognizes. Jack gets to talking and says, 'Last time you stopped me, wasn't I on my way to the Jenkins,' they had a goat was having kids. Cop pulls down his sunglasses a bit so he's looking at Jack with his bare eyes and says, No, Jack, that was *five* times ago. There was the time you was speeding south of Dunning, and the time you was speeding west of Anselmo, and the time you was speeding north of Burwell. The cop gone on like that around the compass. Finally he says, I'm beginning to think you're a habitual criminal.

Jack got his share of tickets, all right. There's a place in the local paper where they list them, too. Folks on the street in Broken Bow started asking Jack if he was running for office they seen his name in the paper so much.

Another highway patrolman that pulled him over a lot pulled him over again. He come up to Jack's window and tells him to get out his license and read off the number. As Jack fetches it out of his wallet, the cop says, 1-5-2-9-7 while he's also writing them same numbers down. Then he says to Jack,

Just read off the last four digits. I ain't got them memorized yet.

Another time, a highway patrolman stopped him and come up to the window. He's a bit hot on this occasion, and he says, Jack, what in tarnation are you doing? You're going too fast, and you're weaving like crazy. You about run that woman off the road back there.

Jack says, Gosh, was I that bad? I didn't even think I was over the white stripe.

Over the stripe? the cop says. Hell, you put her car on the shoulder and her right tires on the prairie. What are you doing, anyways?

Jack says, I was reading my mail. Pile was getting out of hand at home.

Cop was fit to be tied. He says, Jack, if you don't leave the mail for the office and driving for the road, I'm going to run you in.

Jack still ain't that old, really, but he may be one of the longest practicing vets in the state. Vets only last an average of fifteen years before they bail and do something else. Jack been doing it for thirty-three years. He figures he's semen-tested nearly forty-six thousand bulls. He don't think anyone else in the state done more than a few thousand. Involves sticking a probe in their back end to start with. Some of them bulls can tighten it up and make a chore of things. Jacks says, To lift their tail and get the probe in there on a two-thousand-pound bull … it takes a real man to do that all day.

Then he laughs that belly laugh of his.

The Rebel

CAN'T tell stories about folks around here without mentioning the Eggleston and Birnie clans. Way back, Mitt Eggleston and his brother were born in Danville, Iowa—1880s, I reckon. His real name was Milton, but everybody called him Mitt. When the two boys were fifteen or sixteen, they were pretty wild and run away from home. Went west. Walked from Danville to Julesburg, Colorado, which is just over the Nebraska border. Back in those days, folks didn't talk much about where they been and who they were and what they done. Fact, asking a man where he's from and what he done for a living might be a conversation starter these days, but back then it was a major breach of etiquette, even get a few men reaching for their pearl handle.

Point is, family was never quite sure they pieced together what Mitt done in his early years. They do know he done some buffalo hunting because his grandson John still has the horns his grandpa give him. Mitt hooked up with Buffalo Bill for a spell but didn't like him. Grandma called Buffalo Bill a stew bum, and Mitt called him worse than that.

Wasn't easy back then. Mitt tried homesteading up in the Sand Hills, near Gordon. Like I been telling you, them Sand Hills are tough on folks. Farming is about impossible, and ranching ain't easy, neither. Mitt come down and found a half section on Ryno Table around the turn of the century. Left his

pregnant wife and their firstborn on the homestead up near
the South Dakota border and lived in a tent while he farmed
the tableland. Weren't nothing here back then but bluestem
and prairie—no farms, no trees. Anyway, Mitt got up a soddy
after a time and moved the family down in a covered wagon.
Following spring, a tornado ripped the roof off the soddy. But
they lived through it. Years after, Mitt told his grandson John
that them Sand Hills are okay for men and cattle, but they're
hell on women and horses. Mitt and his wife had four kids,
including Dan and Grace.

That reminds me of Jim Boblits's younger sister, Harriet.
She was almost as spirited as Jim. She married Frank Tierney.
An uncle left them a fourteen thousand acre place back up in
the Sand Hills. They had a spread down towards Broken Bow
as well. Don't know the whole story, but Frank had Harriet set
up on the Sand Hills ranch while he worked the one south of
Broken Bow. She weren't too happy up there. Pretty woman,
maybe a bit spoiled, and a Boblits, like I said. One day she
burned down the ranch house and come home to the Seven
Valleys. She was done living up there.

Annnnnnnyway, let me cross on over to the Birnie side of
things. Robert Birnie come over from Ireland when he was a
boy. He married Grace Eggleston when she was nineteen and
he was forty. Caused a bit of a stir in these parts. Their firstborn
was John. Born in a soddy. John says his father was a good man,
but he was fifty by the time John was half-grown, and he didn't
know nothing or talk about nothing but cattle. Never talked
about baseball or school, never played with the boy or went
hunting with him. Grandpa Mitt done that with John.

Grandpa Mitt was old school. He give John a .22 rifle
for his tenth birthday one autumn. John practiced shooting

targets all winter, but it wasn't until spring the two got out in the field. That's when Grandpa Mitt taught grandson John gun safety—all in one easy lesson. You know how a ten-year-old boy sometimes be waving a gun around like a fan? On their outing, young John got a regular breeze going with his .22, and on one go-round he give Grandpa Mitt a quick glimpse down the barrel. Next thing you know, young John got a boot in his ass that sent him tumbling into the canyon they were standing beside. When Grandpa got down to the bottom and got it all explained to John, well, the boy practiced good gun safety after that.

Grace Eggleston Birnie, John's mother, was a stern woman. Very religious. Anything fun was sinful. Music and dancing was the devil's temptation. But that doesn't mean a teenage boy ain't going to be a teenage boy. One night John was driving an old car he'd bought, and for some reason known only to the sixteen-year-old mind, he got to steering it down the sidewalks of Callaway. When he got to the end of one, the town marshal was standing there waiting on him. John got thrown in jail, but they didn't take his matches away. He lit his bedding on fire, figuring he could escape in the ruckus. Fire truck come, and they stuck the hose through the barred window. They put out the fire, and soaked John down pretty good, too. Then they left—which made for an unpleasant night for John. But that was nothing compared to the next morning when his mother come to pick him up.

John got thrown in jail another time. He was with a large group of kids on Halloween night. The lot of them got to pranking, mostly backhouse tipping—that's knocking over privies—and got thrown in jail. The real jail was too small, so they got put in a big ol' heavy cage outdoors that wasn't bolted down. Rig managed to hold the overflow of drunks on Saturday night well enough, but it was no match for a pack of teenagers, especially one that had to answer to a mother like Grace. Kids were able to lift up that jail, crawl under it, and go home. John's mother never did hear about that particular brush with the law.

Lack of proper jails was often a problem back in them days. Heck, up in Dunning, they used to chain disorderly drunks to tree trunks on Main Street on Saturday nights and then let them go in the morning after they'd slept it off.

Annnnnnnyway, whole point is to tell you about John's son, Dave. I'm telling you all about ranchers and cowboys, but not everyone gone that route, and plenty that didn't done just fine. Dave's one of them.

When Dave was a kid, he'd go out to the Eggleston place on Ryno Table. His Grandpa Bob and Grandma Grace lived on Eggleston land with Dan and another brother, neither of whom ever married. Not only was Grandma Grace not into giggly fun of any sort, she wasn't into electricity, neither. When power finally came to the Seven Valleys in the early '50s, she wanted nothing to do with it. Dave would go out there as a kid in the '60s, and they still had horse-drawn plows, a pump instead of running water, and kerosene lamps.

Uncle Dan lived in a bungalow not far from the main house. He was a bit of a strange one. Like I said, never married. Never paid income tax, neither. Never drank or smoked. Nice feller in his way, but he read the encyclopedia way too much. Day in, day out. A to Z. Dave and his siblings would go out there on a weekend, and Uncle Dan would sit on a stump and whittle—played a mean fiddle, too—and tell the kids all about agamogenesis or Zoroastrianism. Wasn't information Dave was going to use the next day, but I suppose it kept the conversation going.

Uncle Dan read about plants a lot. Dave would go out there pheasant hunting, and his father would say they were taking Uncle Dan along. The kids would groan because they knew they'd be stopping every few yards to hear about prairie cordgrass's unique overlapping spikelet arrangement or some such.

Uncle Dan wasn't much of a farmer, neither. Caught his hand in a corn picker and lost a few fingers. Six or seven years later, he caught the other hand in a wood chipper and lost a few more. Thing he knew best was horses. Used to make a good part of his living taking a stallion around to service mares. All cash, too. And Uncle Dan could ride. Sure could. Hardly used a saddle. He'd just swing a leg over and go. He'd stand on a horse's back and ride like he was in the circus. Lived in his own world. Time meant nothing to him. Light or dark, neither. He'd wake up in the middle of the night and go to work. Or he could sleep for a whole day.

Like I said, Dave's another one wasn't cut out to be a farmer or a rancher. Rebelled against that way of life. 'Course, Dave rebelled against everything. Got married before his seventeenth birthday. About '70, it was. Folks said it would never work … the wild protestant Birnie kid, and Joan, the smart catholic girl. They had a baby right away.

Dave worked as a grocery bagger in Broken Bow, and they lived in an apartment. He was making $1.35 an hour. All he could think about most days—as he put the cans in the bottom of the grocery bags and the bread on top—was being voted a future leader of America in high school.

Dave knocked around for a while. A printer named Emerson

hired him. He owned a small print shop. Wasn't real progressive in his business operations. Had an offset printer in the back of his store, but mostly he relied on an old press with lead type, which Dave hand-fed with paper a sheet at a time. Every day for a year and a half, the two of them would knock off at three o'clock and head over to Emerson's house and drink beer with his wife, Gladys.

Dave kept moving. Worked as a printer at the newspaper in town, had a factory job down in Lexington, even worked for his Dad for a while at the feed store he owned. Back then, the only radio station in Broken Bow was still operated by the family that begun it in '49. Dave's uncle got involved with the station and hired Dave in '82. Dave had always wanted to work in radio but hadn't done nothing about it. Twenty-nine when he started his morning show. He's a talker, a natural in front of the mic. Weren't long before he had the little old ladies in town listening to the Doors.

Remember, Dave got that rebel streak in him. Drove his uncle crazy with the music he played, but folks liked the show. Dave would tell small-town stories. He poked fun but paid respect, too. Built a pretty good following. Then some guys come passing through Broken Bow in the late '70s, maybe early '80s. Long hair. Stayed at a hotel in town. Only here one night, but the cops picked them up as they were walking from their hotel over to dinner. Took them down to the station for questioning. Didn't hurt them none, but made their evening an unpleasant one. Harassed them is what they done, might as well say it. Turns out they weren't a couple of drifters, but a couple of professors on their way to an academic conference in Omaha or Lincoln or somewheres.

Dave's uncle knew about what had happened, and so did

the chamber of commerce, but in a small town, that kind of stuff has a tendency to get shoved under the rug. 'Course, them professors weren't part of the code of silence, and the story made the front page of the *Omaha World-Herald*. That was the first Dave heard about it. He added some breeze to the dustup— maybe more than a bit—on his show. His uncle told him the story was off-limits. If it weren't positive, it weren't to be talked about. Dave marched into his uncle's office and said, If that's the way you want to run your radio station, I'm not sure I want to be a part of it. His uncle said, That's it then. Dave left to go clean out his desk, not quite sure if he'd quit or been fired after three years on the air.

Dave had started his own photo studio on the side and switched to it full-time. But money dried up for everyone in the mid-'80s, and he ended up driving a hay truck out of South Dakota for a while. He did some weekend radio work in Ord. Few years later, his uncle softened up and asked if he wanted to work part-time on-air. Not long after he started up again, his uncle got fired. Ownership and management got to shuffling around there for a while, but when the dust settled in 1990, Dave not only had his morning show back every weekday, but he was the general manager, too.

Still a bit of a rebel, though. One year the budget in Broken Bow got a bit tight, and in late fall, the mayor declared the town couldn't afford to plow the streets for every little snowfall that might come along that winter. Had to be five inches or more before the plows would roll, he said.

Well, sure enough, one of the first storms of the season blowed through and left a blanket of snow that come halfway up your boot. Don't know if it was a little less than five inches or a little more, but the mayor saw a golden opportunity to make his point, and them plows didn't budge from the city garage.

Well, right quick the streets were looking like Fairbanks in February, with cars slipping and sliding when they weren't getting stuck. So Dave and another feller gone out in the station's van … on a remote, they call it. They begun measuring snow all over town and reporting on conditions to the good folks of little ol' Broken Bow. Four inches and frost heaves on Industrial Drive, he'd say. Then, Helen Dunwiddy is spinning her tires over here on Seventh Avenue, where we're measuring a full five and a half inches.

Well, by the time they got back to the radio station, the mayor was waiting for them in the parking lot. He give Dave the what for. Told him the reasons for the policy: the trucks is all broke down, the cupboards are bare, they're being intelligently frugal and all that. Mayor went away fuming. 'Course, despite the what for, streets were plowed by the next morning.

Dave is still doing his show to this day, still managing the station, and still married to Joan. If you're driving through Broken Bow some morning, tune him in. It's the kind of station where he does the talking, and then, when they go to a commercial, it's his voice in the jewelry store ad, imitating an old lady buying a brooch. Then when he comes back on the air, he'll talk for ten minutes about writing the commercial and recording it. He's even got Davey Davis on for a few minutes every morning.

John Hardy

FOLKS that live in New York and Los Angeles think places like Lincoln and Omaha are the middle of nowhere. Folks that live in Lincoln and Omaha think that places like Broken Bow are the middle of nowhere. And folks that live in Broken Bow think the Sand Hills are the middle of nowhere. And they're right.

Ever catch a Sand Hiller out of state and ask him where the Sand Hills are, and he's likely to say, Just west of the corn.

It's a remark needs some enlarging on. See, they start growing corn in Ohio, Illinois is covered in the stuff, Iowa's one big field of it, and they don't call Nebraska the Cornhusker State for nothing. But all of that changes when you hit the central part of Nebraska. That's where the Sand Hills start, and sand ain't much for growing corn. So the Sand Hills aren't about farming, they're about ranching.

Places like Thedford and Seneca and Mullen and Hyannis: it's all hilly, rolling grassland. No trees except along the river bottoms. Towns are spread out. Not many folks. But there are some real cowboys up there. Yes, there are.

I got to tell you about two ranchers from up that way run together some: John Sibbitt and John Hardy. The Hardys are a famous clan up around Seneca. Their spread is just east of town, hard by the Middle Loup River. John Hardy had three brothers all told. Father's name was Clint. Grandfather was Walter. And there was grandaunt Matt, Walt's sister. Woman, but her name was Matt. Aunt Matt was a tough ol' bird. She and her husband, Uncle Bill, were among the first homesteaders in them parts in the 1890s.

Aunt Matt and Uncle Bill only been on the place a short spell when Aunt Matt begun thinking the neighbor to their west was moving the fence line on her. Weren't no surveyors in them days, but a man—or a woman—knows his ground, and Aunt Matt knew the feller was moving fence on her. One day she was out riding the fence and come across him. She says, If you move the fence again, I'll shoot you. About three months later, they found the rancher shot dead along a new fence line. Aunt Matt denied shooting him. She denied it for years after, right up until she was on her deathbed. That's when she come clean and said she pulled the trigger.

The house that served as headquarters for their ranch is on the outer edge of the river bottom, about a quarter mile from the Middle Loup. Gorgeous stretch of ground, shaded by cottonwoods and hardwoods. One day in the 1890s, a young feller rode up about noon leading a couple of extra horses. Aunt Matt fed him a hearty supper. Remember, out here the big meal is at lunchtime. Turns out it was the young cowboy's *last* meal. Just as they were putting their napkins down, a posse from Broken Bow rode up. Kid was a horse thief.

After a short trial, Aunt Matt helped string him up from an oak tree not far from the house. Tree only toppled a few years ago. They buried the horse thief up a draw east of the house.

That ain't all the blood on Aunt Matt's hands, neither. Well, maybe not. A while later, Uncle Bill up and disappeared. Ain't likely he left Aunt Matt and left the country without no word being said and no forwarding address. No one knows what happened. Never seen again. Maybe it was payback by a neighbor for one of Aunt Matt's transgressions—or maybe it *was* an Aunt Matt transgression. Whatever, she didn't make no mention of Uncle Bill on her deathbed.

Walter Hardy, Aunt Matt's brother and John's grandfather, was quite a horsebreaker, but one day a colt took off on him when he was in his fifties. Went through a fence and a stand of trees. Threw him, but his boot got hung up in a stirrup. Colt kicked him all to hell and then dragged him between two trees. Walter managed to jab a spur into a trunk and jerked himself free of the saddle, but he was beat up real bad and only lasted a couple of hours.

Walter's son and John's father was Clint. He was born down around Sargent and moved up to Seneca later. He was one of ten kids in the family. That's actually on the small side. Most Sand Hills ranch families in them days had twelve to fifteen kids. Clint's wife was born in Virginia in 1897 and come out as a three-year-old on a wagon train bound for California. Bunch of families they were with decided they liked the looks of the country north of Seneca and homesteaded there.

Oldest of John's brothers was Burton. Known as the best horsebreaker in that country. He broke horses other men picked themselves up off the ground and walked away from. One time, about 1943, he and John gone up to the Triple L Bar. Owned by a feller named LeGrand who lived in Iowa. Brothers found a whole slug of horses unbroke. They had to rope and brand them and eventually break them. There was a bunch of mares they broke quick enough, but there was also one big ol' Belgian stallion that was having none of it. Back then, you didn't see horses like that in the Sand Hills.

Now, John is a topflight cowboy in his own right, but after

he been thrown half a dozen times by that ornery Belgian, he knew it was one Burton would have to notch. But that stallion didn't know one Hardy from another and threw Burton off half a dozen times, too. Well, days gone by, and the boss was coming out from Iowa to visit the ranch. John didn't see him leave, but Burton gone off to pick up the boss in Thedford or somewheres and fetch him back. When they come over a hill by the Triple L Bar, the boss was seated next to Burton, and he was driving that big ol' Belgian hitched to the wagon. That stallion was calmer than a petting zoo pony. Weren't many horses beat Burton.

Accidents happened all the time in ranch country. Back then, remote as the Sand Hills are, a serious accident was dangerous business. Could be a day or more lying in a buckboard before you could get an injured feller to the railroad or a paved road and on to a hospital. On New Year's Day one year, Burton was moving cattle for a neighbor up to the stockyard. Colder than heck, ice and snow all around. Cattle broke back on him. Burton run ahead of them, but his horse flip-flopped, and Burton broke his leg in five places. A few years later, a horse buckled on him again. Broke the other leg in three places. That time he had to crawl two miles on his hands and good leg through snow to get back to the house for help.

Burton was a good ol' boy. Always laughing and talking. When he went into town, he'd go looking for some of the little old ladies lived there. If he caught them outside in their yard, why, he'd rope them. They'd protest and tell Burton to get the heck away from them and stay out of their yard, but he didn't listen. He'd lasso them and tighten up, pinning their arms to their sides. Got so's when Burton would ride into town and them little old ladies would be out gardening, they'd see him and squeal and try to run for their houses, but he'd catch them and rope them. Then he'd go have coffee with them. They loved Burton.

Couple of them Hardy boys were fighters, which I'll get to, but Burton wasn't one of them. Never had a fight in his life. But he got a job up at the Harris place, and there was a feller there, a large bully of a man, and he was bound to fight Burton. Bound to fight him. Don't know if maybe it's 'cause Burton was well known as the best bronc buster and he wanted to fight the best, or maybe Burton was just next on his list.

Annnnnnnyway, this feller come after Burton one day near the bunkhouse. Bunch of chickens round there been scratching holes. Burton starts backing away and steps in one of them holes and goes down. The big feller jumped on Burton and begun raining blows on him. Burton fixed on guerilla warfare. He spread the middle and index fingers on his right hand and poked the feller in his eyes. Weren't necessarily a moment of glory for Burton or the Hardy clan, but it did stop the fight.

One day in '68, Burton's luck run out. He was riding a colt down south of Thedford. Wasn't breaking it, just running cattle. He was chasing down a yearling when it tripped and went down. His colt somersaulted over the yearling with Burton in the saddle. Busted him up real bad. He only lasted a couple more days. Nebraska can be tough country.

Third-youngest brother was Bob. Besides ranching, there's three things a young feller could do in the Sand Hills in them days – rodeo, boxing, and baseball. Seneca had fifteen hundred people back then, so there was a fair amount of activity. Give you an idea of what's happened to western Nebraska, there's less than a hundred people in town today. Annnnnnnyway, Bob went off to the marine corps and become the light heavyweight champion at Parris Island. He was in Okinawa during

World War II when the marines were trying to take the island. A new lieutenant come in and wanted to make his mark, so he put together two hundred of the best men he could find and charged them up a hill. The Japanese were waiting on them. Only seven, including Bob, come back in one piece.

John's the other brother I'll be telling you about in a minute. He did a lot of boxing as a kid and could handle his younger brother Bobby without much trouble. Handled him all their growing up years. That'll catch in the craw of a younger brother.

John was a Golden Gloves champ. But when Bobby first come back from the marines and the war—hell, before he'd barely kissed his mama and dropped his bag—he told John to lace up the gloves. It was a helluva row, and Bobby did come away with a black eye, but it didn't last too long, and Bobby was the one left standing.

Years later Bob was walking a cow down the road from town on another January day. Bitter cold and icy. John come by and told him to get in the truck and let his son do the walking. But Bob said, Go on now, I'm enjoying this. John let him be. Bob had had surgery and was on blood thinning medicine. He fell on the ice a short time later, hit his head, and bled to death.

Then there's ol' John. He was a dandy. He could dance and brawl as well as he could cowboy and play baseball. Ol' John didn't stop sowing his wild oats until he was forty-nine. Bachelor until then. That's when he met Marge. She was a nurse tending to his father, who'd had a stroke. They been married since '69.

Back when John was a boy, the Middle Loup run higher than it does now. Just seemed to be more rain and snow and less folks sucking water out for irrigation. There'd be heavy rain and gully washers, even change the course of the river, sending it one way around a big sandbar rather than the other way. Well, John and his brother Bob were swimming in the river one day when they were eleven or twelve, and they come on a human skull stuck in the sand. They were scared of it, so John put a stick through an eye socket and flung it into the middle of the river so the current would carry it away. Regrets that to this day, thinking if he'd saved it, maybe someone could have figured out if it was the horse thief or maybe even Uncle Bill, what got washed out of a shallow grave up one of the canyons.

John is a big practical joker. Do the same tricks over and over. Sit drinking coffee with him, and while he's talking away—he's so smooth, got a voice entrances you almost—he's pouring salt in your drink. But you never notice because he never looks down, never takes no note of it, just keeps looking at you with that twinkle in his eye. He loves to put something in his hand before he shakes. Hell, he'll hide anything in his palm: mashed potatoes, jelly, yams. One time down at the Elks Club in Broken Bow, the U.S. congresswoman for the district come by to talk, and when she was done, all the town notables were lined up to shake her hand and then all the ranchers from all around. John was at the end. She shakes a few dozen hands, and when she gets to John, he sticks out his paw and they shake. She didn't know what to make of it when she come away with a pat of butter spread all over her hand, but them ranchers sure got a hoot out of it.

Ol' John was just ornery to be ornery. When he and Marge were getting married, her Uncle Bill come out to give her away. 'Course, this ain't the same Uncle Bill as got disappeared by Aunt Matt. That was seventy years before.

Annnnnnnyway, Uncle Bill was a kindly man and the

favorite person in Marge's life. John was washing his car when Uncle Bill arrived at the ranch. He stepped out of his car and walked right over to John to meet him. John turned to face him, still holding the hose turned full on, and shook hands with Uncle Bill and talked to him real kindly. Never met him before, but as they talked, that nice warm water was gushing all over Uncle Bill's shirt and running down his trousers.

One time, there was a young couple, new at the time, managing Larry Cleveland's ranch. Larry brought them over to John Sibbitt's place for branding one spring, and John Hardy was there. The wife was real pretty and more or less just a spectator that day. Hardy couldn't hardly wait to get over there to talk her up. Larry don't think much on it, but on the way home, the woman asks who the handsome cowboy was that was talking to her. Larry says, You mean John?

She says, Yes, that was his name, John. Did you know he just got out of the penitentiary for killing a man?

Hardy had spent a couple of hours pumping her full of all kind of bull crap. By the end of the afternoon, he was the baddest hombre these parts seen in some time—a touch of Jesse James, a smidgen of the Sundance Kid.

Baseball was big out here in those days. Most towns had a softball team, but their pride and joy was their hardball team. Even the smallest town would field nine and go play other towns. John was the best pitcher in them parts. Everyone knew he was good, but with just a bunch a fellers in small-town Nebraska playing each other, hard to tell how good a good player really was. One day the Seneca team went up to play Valentine. It wasn't just a town team, Valentine was a low minor league team for the St. Louis Cardinals in those days.

John pitched against the Valentine team and won 2–1. A

legendary scout for the Cardinals happened to be there, name of Runt Moore. He come over to talk to John, who was in his early twenties, and sounded him out about playing big league ball. John had figured on a life of ranching, which he loved, but the idea of having a shot at the majors was something that started kicking around in his brain. John got a call from Runt soon after. He told John he was following his progress and should pitch in an upcoming game against Alliance. John did and threw a shutout against them.

Few weeks later, Seneca headed down to play Broken Bow. Runt was there with another scout, and the feller had a newfangled radar machine. It was before they had radar guns. You had to throw a ball through an opening, and the radar measured the speed as the ball passed through. Whole thing was boxed in by a big frame. First time John threw, he missed the opening and hit the frame. Shattered it. Took Runt and the other feller a spell to put it back together. Next time, John threw the ball right through the opening, and the machine clocked it at ninety-four miles per hour.

Remember, he played for a town team. Never had proper training. Played catch a lot as a kid, and all the roping he done must have counted for something, but he was busy working all day on the ranch. Hell, once he fell off a windmill he was fixing and still pitched that night.

Annnnnnnyway, Runt come around and talked to John before the game that night in Broken Bow. He says, I got a contract for you to sign. We'll take care of business right after the game. Deal was for thirty thousand dollars. That was a huge number back in them days.

John had his stuff that night. He struck out the first eight batters he faced. He threw a curve to the ninth batter, the opposing pitcher. Later, several of the infielders told John they could hear his elbow crack as he released the pitch. Everyone rushed to the mound as John dropped to his knees in agony. After a while, he was on his feet and being helped to the dugout. He looked up and saw Runt Moore in the parking lot, head down, walking away towards his car. Later, at the hospital, they took twelve pieces of bone out of John's arm. After a year of recovery, he pitched again, but he wasn't ever the same.

John Sibbitt

JOHN Hardy is friends with John Sibbitt. He's another rancher, from Hyannis. Wild one. An original, too. Run with the choke open his whole life. Weren't nothing he couldn't do and nothing he wouldn't try. He done rodeo. As tough a bronc rider as you ever seen. Was one of the best pilots in that country. Flew until he was eighty. He also drank, fought, and raced horses, motorcycles, and hot rods. He was a crack shot, too. Great boss with a crew. They put up a lot of hay on his ranch over the years. He worked on a dead run. But then Sibbitt would up and say, We done a day's work. And they'd knock off early and have some fun. He's a rare breed: a man's man and a ladies' man both.

The Sibbitts' ranch was huge back in the 1930s and needed about fifteen hands to run it. Once, when John was sixteen or so, he rode out with the foreman and a half dozen hands. They were pushing cattle up to grassland near the edge of their ground. The old cows know the pasture pretty well, and sometimes they'll wander off to good grass and leave their calves behind. After the cowboys had lunch, the foreman told them to stay where they were, at the back of the herd, and just hold them. He was going to go south a bit and slowly move the cattle there back to the main herd. They'd mate up heifers and calves and then drive them all home.

Well, them hands were mostly eighteen, nineteen, maybe

twenty years old, and of course they're going to pick on the youngest one, even if he was the ranch owner's son. So as soon as the foreman disappeared over a small hill, why, they all dismounted and laid down in the grass. Guess it's time for you to do a little day herding, Sibbitt, they says. And then they all gone to sleep.

Ol' John got a fiery nature, but he just nodded his head, rode off a bit, and let them fellers fall fast asleep. Then he come back and lined their horses up, and one by one he tied the bridle reins around the ranch hands' legs. Then he took off his slicker, mounted up, and rode down that line of horses waving his slicker like mad and whooping and hollering. Them horses took off like they were shot from a cannon. The foreman come back over the hill just in time to see the horses running in all directions and his ranch hands being drug behind them across the prairie.

That's when fellers first started getting the notion that when John Sibbitt was around, you didn't shut your eyes.

John might have got his wild streak from his mother. She was a character. In them days, a woman didn't show herself much, but it come through every now and again.

For a while, John had a hot rod. Had a plank for a seat. Cut the top off. He was only fifteen or sixteen then. One time he come roaring up in front of the cookhouse on the ranch, where his mother was. He was revving that hot rod something fierce, and he says, Come on, Ma, let's go for a ride!

So she gets in, and oh, he give her a time. He spins them tires and roars out of the yard and up through the hills and over the soapweeds and down in the draws and back up and down and all around and finally skids to a stop back in front of the cookhouse. By this time, his mother's stomach is in her throat, her hair's stuck back permanent, like there's a constant fifty-mile-an-hour wind, and she's coated in a layer of dust. How'd you like that ride, Ma?

She got out of the car gingerlike, smiled a bit, said she liked it just fine, and went inside.

Well, about two weeks later, he was coming into town riding the hot rod, and it broke down. First car that come by out of town was his mom in their big ol' Buick. John flagged her down and says, Ma, you'll have to tow me to the garage in town.

So she pulled out in front of the hot rod so John could attach the chain, and then they headed for town. After you cross the railroad tracks, you come to Route 2 on the edge of Hyannis. Turn left and you're in town. Mrs. Sibbitt didn't turn left. She turned right—and cranked her up, too.

Road is wide open to Ashby. There are a few turns but hardly any cars out there, especially in them days. She takes that Buick up to fifty, sixty, seventy miles an hour. With that long chain, the hot rod was like the last one in line in the kids' game Snap the Whip. Hot rod starts snaking from side to side. It was all John could do to keep it out of the grass on either side of the highway. She whipped that Buick around after a few miles and raced all the way back to Hyannis, finally coming to a stop in front of the garage.

She leans out the window and looks back. John's breathing hard, eyes wide as saucers, bugs splattered on his face, hands frozen on the wheel, trying to smile, and she says, How'd you like that ride, John? Oh yeah, he got it from her all right.

Do enough pranking and your orneriness is liable to catch up with you. John always seemed to escape consequences, but he had some close calls. One time, when he was a teenager, the foreman and the ranch hands were riding near the house, and John and some kids his age were trailing along behind. One of them was a gal named Babe, lived on the ranch over the hill. Foreman hears a scream—a girlish scream—and looks around.

John had roped Babe. He'd caught her around the leg but also got the stirrup. None of that's too unusual, except John's horse starts bucking. Finally, it throws him. Still no problem, except the other end of his rope is tied to the saddle horn. Once John's horse gets him out of the saddle, it bolts. *Now* there's a problem. If Babe's horse don't bolt, too, Babe could get turned into a wishbone with mighty unpleasant results. But Babe's a good horsewoman and keeps her wits. She spurs her horse with her free leg and reins it onto a parallel path with John's horse, keeping up with it and keeping a bit of slack in the rope joining the two horses. Foreman sees what's happening and gallops ahead, catches John's horse, and settles her down. Believe Babe's father had a few choice words for John that evening. Think he mended his ways for a couple of days.

One time, when John was young, he had his motorcycle over in Alliance. Sibbitt was hell on wheels on that bike. He was with Jake Prindle, a hand on the ranch who was only a few years older than John. Rodeo was going on. It was a big deal in them days. Big deal. John and Jake were watching the action through a hole in a fence. Setting up for a wild horse race. What that was, they brung a bunch of mustangs—fresh caught on the high plains—out on the track, each with a halter rope. Teams of three cowboys went after them. Had to mug them down, saddle them up, and race them around the track. Big crowd in the grandstand.

'Course, them mustangs didn't like any part of the oper-ation. Didn't like the saddles, didn't like the cowboys *in* the saddles, didn't like the crowd, and didn't understand the whole circular track thing, neither. But mostly they were just wild. Some of them ol' broncs would try to kill ya.

Annnnnnnyway, just as they got them all saddled up, John turns to Prindle and says, Hey, Jake, watch this. Sibbitt gunned that motorbike through the hole in the fence and raced it down the track to where them horses and spectators was. He spooked about all them mustangs and separated them from the two fellers in the three-person teams trying to hold them steady. Horses bolted to every point of the compass, nostrils flared. Riders weren't just bucked, they were turned into projectiles. Cowboys everywhere were running for their lives.

Sibbitt snaked and skidded through them all, tossing up a rooster tail of dirt and scattering the lot of them. Crowd in the stands was drop-jawed. Sibbitt gunned the cycle back down the track and through the hole in the fence, and he skids to a stop next to Jake. He's smiling big, his back to the track, and says, What do you think of that, Jake?

Jake was looking over the fence at the carnage downtrack and says, I think we best get out of town.

For all his wildness, John had to get serious pretty young. His parents died within a year of each other, the last one going when John was only twenty-one. That's young to be taking over a ranching operation the size the Sibbitts had going. Couple of other ranchers in town were just waiting for him to stumble, figuring they'd gobble up his ground. One of them fellers never did grow his ranch. But John not only survived, he tripled the size of his spread, and he's still running it sixty years later. He ain't just a smart operator, neither. Ask anyone who knows him, they'll tell you he's the most loyal friend ever was. Lived his life honest. If he told you something, that's the way it was.

Sibbitt started flying in the late 1930s. Had one of the first planes in the area. Once, when he was still young, before he got married, he landed his Piper Cub over in Ashby and taxied right up to his girlfriend's house. There was a field there, and along the edge were telephone poles and a single wire. Poles were in rough shape. They were half fell over.

When John was done seeing his girl, he rolled across that field and got her airborne, but the wheels didn't clear the phone line. Got stuck in the landing gear while the plane's trying to climb. Wire stretches and stretches, and them telephone poles start jerking out of the ground. But then they don't no more and the wire stretches taut. That plane almost comes to a stand-still in midair.

Finally the wire snaps. It's just like a rubber band firing a little wooden plane. Whoosh! The Piper Cub rockets ahead like it's been launched off an aircraft carrier. Only problem is that big ol' rubber band gives the flight plan a little too much arc, and the plane noses over a hill and crashes.

The foreman gets word and races over from the Sibbitt ranch in his truck. He comes over the hill and sees the wreck below. John is all cockeyed in the cockpit. His leg is hanging out of the plane through a hole that got punched in the fuse-lage, but the boy is grinning from ear to ear. Weren't busted up at all.

Sibbitt loved to buzz stuff. He couldn't hardly be flying when he was young and not come down on the deck looking for trouble. There's a dance hall in Ashby with a tin roof, like a Quonset hut. Looks like a huge, overgrown thirty-gallon drum half-buried in the ground. One Saturday night there was a dance going on, and everyone was having a good time, including Sibbitt. No one noticed when he stepped out. Drove home, got in his plane, and come in low over the dance hall. When I say low, I mean like he's seconds from landing the thing. He did a touch-and-go on that tin roof, popped it with one of his tires. Inside the hall, it sounded like the end of the world. Like a bomb gone off. Women screamed, the band dove off the stage, and everyone run for the exits.

Ranchers in them parts all knew Sibbitt. If he was flying and caught you out on the open range, he'd put you off your horse. If you heard his plane, you looked for the nearest windmill and made a run for it. Anything to save your life. Sibbitt wouldn't tangle with a windmill, but if he caught you before you made it, you better duck and watch out for the landing gear. You'd get a breeze from his prop wash and prove yourself a horseman if you could stay up on your spooked mount.

One time a neighbor of Sibbitt was flying and buzzed one of the hands on his ranch. I'm telling you, them fellers got close. A wheel hit the horse and sent the cowboy flying. Killed the horse and put the hand in the hospital. That weren't too good.

If a raw hand from back east got hired on a nearby ranch, John would fly over and catch him alone on horseback on the grass. He'd pull out his rifle and take a couple of shots into the ground about ten foot away from the feller, kick up some sand. Scare the hell out of him. Welcome to the neighborhood. Welcome to Sibbitt's neighborhood.

John was sure ornery in his day. He'd carry little sacks of flour in his plane. Come over town flying real low, downwind so he couldn't be heard, and dive-bomb a feller walking in the street. Got so good at dropping them sacks he could hit a feller square in the back from two hundred foot up. Turn him into a walking ghost.

Them old-timers that got hit would get so damn mad.

You'd hear ol' Sibbitt laughing over the roar of his engine as them old fellers were shaking their fists at him and cursing even as they were shaking that flour off.

Got to be sport for the merchants in Hyannis, too. They'd hear a muffled plane engine, low and close, and then they'd hear someone yell out, Sibbitt! They'd all race to their front doors and windows to see who was out in the street caked in flour. They'd catch the eye of the feller and shake their heads in anger and sympathy at that durn Sibbitt, and then they'd turn away and go back into their stores and laugh until their bellies ached.

He just loved to rattle the townfolks in Hyannis. One time he gone up in his little Piper Cub in a stiff wind, snuck in over town, and cut the power to where he just barely maintained level flight. Well, with that strong breeze, the plane ended up going backwards over town. Folks looking up from the sidewalk weren't sure if they were in a time warp or if maybe the world had stopped and started spinning the other way.

One thing he done a few times is take the plane over town with Jake. The plane had an overhead wing with a strut that anchored it to the fuselage. With John flying, Jake would climb out of the cockpit and hang from the strut. As they come over the main street of Hyannis, Jake would kick his legs and cry, Help! Help!

Got the men down on the street gasping for air and the women screaming for divine intervention. Like I said, they done that a few times. Then once, when Jake is hanging out on the strut, he hears some screaming over the engine that ain't his. He looks over at the cockpit, but John ain't in it. Jake does a chin-up on that strut and looks over the fuselage and past the cockpit and sees John hanging off the left strut, kicking his legs and screaming for help. John had put the plane on autopilot so he could join in on the fun. Jake didn't do the hanging thing no more after that.

It was just crazy what they done sometimes. One time when they were flying, they got another feller to drive a pickup along a straight stretch of the highway to Ashby. They brung a rope ladder and lowered it out of the cockpit. John settled that plane down right over the moving truck. Jake climbs down the ladder into the truck bed and releases hold of the ladder, and then he grabs it again and climbs back up and into the plane. They'd seen it in a movie.

One time, just a few years back, when John was in his late seventies, Joe Minor caught Sibbitt outside his truck on the dirt road leading to Sibbitt's place. Like Sibbitt himself done, Joe flew into the wind to hide the engine noise and then come in low over top of Sibbitt, missing him by only a couple of feet. As Joe finished his pass and gained some altitude, he was grinning from ear-to-ear—someone finally got one on Sibbitt. He glanced back at the road, and Sibbitt is laid out flat on his back and not moving. Joe is terror-struck, figuring he give the old man a heart attack.

The airport in Hyannis is a single narrow asphalt strip that runs nearly right up to Sibbitt's road. Joe landed the plane, taxied fast to the end of the runway and the edge of the cut grass, and jumped out of the cockpit. He run as hard as he could, and when he reached Sibbitt, John was still flat on his back in the road, out cold. Joe is starting to panic. Then, eyes closed, otherwise not moving, John's arm rises up in the air, slowly but steadily, and then his middle finger stretches out. Ol' John got the last laugh again.

John got a little showman in him, no question. Always

looking to entertain. One time at the county fair, he decides to saddle up a bucking bronc with a washtub instead of a saddle. Plan is for him to ride in the tub and for Jake Prindle to ride a scoop shovel attached to the horse's tail with a twenty-five-foot rope, like he's waterskiing on land.

First time they lined up to do it, John Hardy was working as head gate man. Usually, when the chute gate opens in a rodeo, the bronc and rider have a clear path out to the arena. But Hardy run Prindle's rope through the bars of the gate chute when he ain't looking. When the gate swung open, of course the horse with the washtub on it and Sibbitt in it bolted. But when the slack in the rope run out, Jake was jerked smack into the metal gate and stuck there like a bug on a windshield. That set things back a day while Jake recovered.

Next night at the fair, after Jake checked his rope, the gate swung open and away they went. Jake slides this way and that on the scoop shovel, barely holding on, and finally gets thrown. Meanwhile, that washtub is heaving this way and that on the bucking bronc's back, and John's riding her out, just his hat sticking up above the rim of that tub. The crowd is whooping and hollering. Finally Sibbitt bails, but a snap on his chaps gets stuck on something, and he ends up riding for another thirty seconds half upside down and falling out of that tub before the rodeo clowns rescue him.

I won't even tell you about the time at a fair John decided to have a chariot race, Ben-Hur–style. Managed to construct a two-wheeled cart, and hitched it to a team of bucking horses. Fortunately, no one was killed that day.

One time this feller about John's age—quite a bronc rider but drank too much—was out in front of the horse barn on the Sibbitt place with some other fellers. John was up in the bunkhouse. This group of fellers had a bow and arrows, and they were bragging like fellers will do about how good they could shoot and how high they could shoot. So one of the fellers shoots an arrow, and the thing goes a mile high and then lands on the roof of the barn, right along the front edge. The bronc rider figures if he climbs up into the barn and opens the door of the hay mount, he can stretch over and maybe fetch that arrow. So he done it. He got himself up into the open door on the front of the barn, thirty feet above the ground. He steadies himself by holding onto the frame of the mount door with his right hand. Then he stretches his left arm and hand as far as he can and reaches a shingle jutting out along the front edge of the roof right next to the arrow.

He no sooner gets himself in that precarious position than a shot rings out and the shingle the feller's holding onto shatters in a bunch of pieces. Sibbitt had come out of the bunkhouse with his rifle to show them fellers who the real best shot was. 'Course, the proof of his prowess had some immediate consequences for the bronc rider up in the barn. He falls and starts swinging on his right arm like a monkey changing trees.

Bronc rider reaches desperately with his left hand for the frame of the hayloft and secures himself. He pulls himself up and in and escapes injury. He was mad, real mad. Ready to fight John on the spot, except he knew he couldn't take him.

John wasn't one to go picking fights, but he wouldn't back away from one, neither. Being athletic, nimble, and tough, he won most he got into. But once there was a railroad work gang fixing the main line that run through Hyannis and Ashby. Them crews would do a fair amount of drinking at night. One night this gang was in a bar in Ashby, the one that John's girlfriend's father owned. Words got said and next thing you know, four of them work crew fellers jumped John. They give it to him pretty good before he escaped and got out of there.

About twenty minutes later, some of John's friends seen him skidding to a stop in the parking lot. They gone out to see what he was doing coming back. He was making a beeline for the front door with a pistol in his hand, and he says, I'm going to get it down to one.

He was going to shoot three of them so he could fight the one that was left! 'Course, he'd been drinking himself—that's a plan got some liquor mixed in it—so his friends wrassled him to the ground and disarmed him.

I ain't even told you about all the times Sibbitt and Hardy run together. Done it for decades. One time at a wedding in Hyannis, Sibbitt and Hardy decided to entertain the guests by riding a bronc in the sky. They saddled up the fuselage of Sibbitt's plane, and Hardy mounted up. Sibbitt taxied down the runway with Hardy holding onto the saddle horn with one hand. That fuselage bucked like a bronc weren't broke to ride and nearly throwed Hardy before they even got airborne. Believe that was one prank never quite got off the ground.

Heck, you could tell stories on them two cowboys all day. They're both in their eighties now and both still ranching.

The Goat Herder

IF you were to drive your pickup from Broken Bow northeast a stretch to Comstock, you'd cross a lot of windswept grassland—prime cattle country. Only a few trees, and most of them shelter belts planted a hundred years ago by homesteaders. But just before you arrive in Comstock, the road drops down into the Middle Loup River valley. Ain't very wide, but when you cross the bridge and enter town, you're in a different world. Lots of trees along the bottomland, and also a bunch of trees in and around town, which ain't much more than Main Street and a few blocks of houses on either side.

A feller lived there a few years back was the last of his breed. Georgie Fretz was a trapper. As a grown man, he used to walk around barefoot all summer. Looked a bit different than most. Had one eye went up to the northwest and another that headed down to the southeast, which tended to get your own peepers to meandering when you talked to him. He had short, stubby arms and long legs and was very hairy. His friends called him the Missing Link. Not sure what his enemies called him.

Georgie never had a job his whole life. Never really had an address, neither. Seen a feller on TV talking about living 'off the grid.' Ain't a better description of how Georgie lived his life. In the winter, his home was a dugout built into a hillside just outside of town. Threw a wood roof across the bottom of a V in a narrow draw and lived there with his dogs. More like a cave than anything. If you ever went there late at night and called out to him, you'd see half a dozen heads pop up: Georgie's and all them dogs packed around him. In summer, he'd camp out or live in his bait shop, a tar paper shack where he'd sell minnows and worms. He'd sleep there sometimes. No running water or power or nothing, of course.

Georgie was always surrounded by his dogs. They were always hassling one another, trying to be top dog, so to speak. Georgie played favorites. His favorite dogs of the moment would get to ride in the cab of his pickup with him, and the rest would have to ride in the truck bed. Them dogs were like kids, only worse; if they didn't get to ride in the front seat, they'd mope and whine and carry on. Georgie used to have an old furry cap with earflaps, and he'd wear it with them flaps hanging down. When his truck come along the street in Comstock with two or three of them dogs in the cab, you was never quite sure which of them was Georgie and which was the dogs.

Sometimes, he'd just have the one dog, Pooch, his all-time favorite, up front with him. As he drove by, you'd see Georgie talking to Pooch and the dog nodding.

One time Georgie had his old pickup truck parked on Main Street in front of the general store. It was so old there was a hand crank in front, down around where the license plate is on today's cars. Had to crank it to get the engine going. Well, Georgie is bent over working that crank, and Pooch is sitting in the driver's seat, apparently working the choke. Georgie calls out, Now.

Engine did something, sputtered and whatnot, but it didn't kick on. Georgie was fit to be tied. He ordered Pooch out of the cab and booted the dog in the butt, and he says, Dammit, I told you to push it in, not pull it out!

To eat, he fished and hunted and trapped up and down the river. Lived off the land. Didn't need much cash, except to buy a bit of gas for his pickup and a few groceries on occasion. Money he got come from selling bait he caught himself in the summer or pelts—coon and beaver mostly—in the wintertime. Oh, and he'd dig a grave now and then. Got twenty-five dollars per grave.

He had an old steam engine down by the river. In the summertime, when he mostly lived along the Middle Loup, he hooked an old washing machine up to it. Done his clothes that way. He'd do his dishes in the river, too. Put them all in a sack with a bit of soap, dropped the sack in the water, and shook it.

You might think fellers like Georgie Fretz are part of a bygone era, that there ain't folks no more don't have a real home and just live off the land. But I know of one. She ain't a trapper, and she ain't exactly living off the land, and she ain't a semi-bum like Georgie was. She chose the life. But she's sure enough living back up in the hills in a tent year round. She tends goats.

When she was twelve, Jo Ellen Wiese told her parents she wanted to raise sheep. A year out of high school, she got married and had kids right away. She was a homemaker. Marriage didn't work, but while it wasn't working, she took vet classes. Raised her kids mostly on her own. About six years ago, she got her first sheep. Just a few head. She was living on a farm rent-free in exchange for doing chores around the place. When her last child graduated from high school, that was about the time the farmer decided to start charging her rent. That's when Wayne Jenkins come along. He says to her, I got some sheep. Why don't you run yours with mine on my place. You look after them all. I'll provide the feed.

She done it. Wayne only kept his sheep a year, but it give Jo

Ellen a start, and she kept running hers on his land. Then she added a few goats. Not unusual for baby lambs to be orphaned. They're called bummers. Other sheep don't want them, but the goats ain't particular as moms, so she got the goats to raise the bummers.

Last year, a ranch owner next to the Jenkinses' place offered Jo Ellen a deal. Partners. Fifty-fifty on a goat herd. Both own half of each goat. Got themselves thirteen hundred head. Feller don't even live in Nebraska no more. Lives in California. She tends the herd full-time on his ground. Sheep are gone. Shepherding was her childhood dream, but full-grown sheep and goats don't go together. She's fine with goats and goatherding. Just shifted the dream a bit.

Ranchers out here are always looking for ways to make money or save money, and goats are another way. Them goats do a couple of things. Like I told you before, prairie fires used to keep this country clear of trees up until a hundred years ago. Without them fires, trees have come back in a big way in places like river valleys. Mostly cedars. They can get so dense they start shrinking your grass. You can clear them by hand or even bull-doze them out, but if your cabbage patch is a few thousand acres, them cedars can run ahead of you. Point is goats will eat the saplings. They also eat a lot of weeds and other plants cattle won't touch. So you can work the same pasture with cattle and goats, and them goats ain't taking the grass from the cattle, least not for the most part. But you don't run goats just to eat your weeds, you raise them for slaughter. Pretty big ethnic market for goat meat, and getting bigger.

Annnnnnnyway, Jo Ellen remarried. Her husband drives a truck by day and stays with her at night. Living in a tent in the middle of Nebraska and tending goats twenty-four hours a day probably ain't gonna get profiled on *Lifestyles of the Rich and Famous*. In winter, after dinner cooked over the woodstove, they'll listen to the radio—no TV of course—read some, actually talk to one another, and then go to bed. That'd be about eight o'clock. They're up at four. That ain't so bad in the summer, but in the dead of winter, out here on the western edge of the central time zone, they're beating sunup by about three and a half hours.

Each morning Jo Ellen drives her husband from the tent to his truck, which he parks out by the road and the fence line. There's a broad, level pasture out by the road. That's where the goats spend the day grazing. The back of the pasture, to the east, is framed by low hills. There's a gap in the hills, a draw with a flat path twenty foot wide that winds back into the hills for nearly a half mile. Goats use it as a highway, going out to the pasture in the morning and coming home up the draw at night. It broadens out a bit at the back end before curling like a fishhook and disappearing into the hills.

At the end of the fishhook is where Jo Ellen has her campsite. She has a living tent and a storage tent. The storage tent is really just a large tent fly, shaped like a small Quonset hut and wide open on one end, about the size of a one-and-a-half-car garage.

Life in the living tent is an exercise in creativity. Cooking ain't easy. They use the woodstove or a grill set up in the storage tent. Cooler for a refrigerator. Well water for cleaning up.

The space inside the tent is about the size of a kid's bedroom in a regular house. Bunch of old carpets on the floor and not much more than the stove, a twin bed, and couple of dressers. Also, there's a combination air lock and small mudroom leading into the main room. No power except for batteries. She figures her battery bill is probably a higher percentage of her monthly expenses than just about any other household in America. They have a generator, but they ain't never used it.

Dogs and goats wander in and out of the open storage tent. Three brats hang out there regular. Those are goats that wouldn't nurse for whatever reason so they were bottle-fed as babies. Jo Ellen puts them with the herd, but the brats always wander back to the tent site. It's more home than the herd.

She and her husband cheat a little. Jo Ellen's daughter and son-in-law have a place outside of Callaway, and a few times a week, they head over there for showers and laundry. But she still misses having a hot bubble bath every night. And she don't just miss it like she works in an office and goes home to a house and for some reason can't take a bath there in her nice, warm house. No, she misses it like someone who works outside sixteen hours a day in mud and blizzards and goes home to a cold tent. Now that's missing a hot bath.

Dogs are a big part of her life and work. She got two kinds. Don't mean breeds—she got a bunch of *them*. I mean she got guard dogs that guard the goats, and she got sheepdogs that manage the herd. There's five guard dogs. Different breeds: Anatolian, Pyrenees. They set among the herd or patrol the perimeter and run off any threats, mostly coyotes, although she come out one morning and seen one with a quill sticking out of his nose after a tangle with a porcupine. Them guard dogs work together, too. Like when the herd is coming up the draw for the night. They'll stand up on a sloped ridge, about fifteen foot away from the goats and five or six foot above them, guarding their flanks. Dogs'll spread themselves out, one every fifty yards or so along the strung-out herd. As the herd moves up, the dog bringing up the rear will run to where the next dog is and take up that position, and that one will then move up to the next dog's position and so forth, just like soldiers rotating guard posts. They do all that on their own—no commands from Jo Ellen.

Those dogs are smart, all right. Too smart sometimes. Once, Jo Ellen come into the living tent, and one of her border collies was lying on the bed, and three goats were standing on the carpet next to him. She figured out he learned to bite hold of the string attached to the zipper on the outside of the tent and pull it up. Let himself in. Then did the same thing to the inner flap. Them dogs just have an instinct to herd, so he drove those three bottle brats into the tent with him for no apparent reason except for maybe showing off.

That was Seth done that. One time Jo Ellen come around the curve of the draw to the tent site, and she seen Seth leap into the dog pen and freeze in place. Then he starts looking around casual, like he been there the whole time and what's the problem? She knew something was up. She parked and went in, and sure enough, them three bummers were inside again. Seth had heard her coming and hightailed it out of the tent, but the goats didn't quite understand the getaway plan.

Them border collies are something. Jo Ellen got half a dozen of them. Two are pups just getting started on their training. She trains her dogs for ranch work and competition both. If you ain't from the country, you may not have heard about this before. During a competition, a handler gets out on a wide-open pasture with their dog, and they head over to a post. Anywheres from three hundred to eight hundred yards out, there's about five head of sheep. Handler sends the dog with a command, either 'away' or 'come by.' If the handler says away, the dog kicks out wide counterclockwise. If the handler says come by, the dog's out run is clockwise. Whole point is dog takes a round-about route so the sheep don't see him coming up on them from behind. Then he's got to creep up on them and drive them in a straight line toward the post, but without running them. Then the dog has to drive them through a couple of panels this way and that and finally into a pen. 'Course, herding come natural to them dogs, but creeping and driving them in a straight line and driving *away* don't, so there's a lot of training involved. Jo Ellen done well for herself in small competitions. Probably do even better if she had time to devote to it.

Ranch work is different from competition, but same principles apply: teaching them to respond to commands. If Jo Ellen's standing by the mouth of the draw, it's getting toward sundown and the herd is grazing out on the plain near the road, all she has to do is say, 'bring them.' Just them two words, even whispered, and the dogs will sprint out and round up all thirteen hundred of them goats and drive them up the draw to where they bed down.

Whit is her lead border collie, but that don't mean he ain't above smarting off. Been trained for competition. Remember, come by means the dog heads out to the left, and away means the dog is supposed to kick out to the right. Sometimes, in competition, Jo Ellen will get out there in front of everyone, and she'll say to Whit, 'away,' and he'll head out to the left. She'll say, 'come by,' and he'll head to the right. He ain't forgot nothing. Just being ornery. They get either first place or last, depending on whether Whit wants to get with the program that day or stick it to Jo Ellen.

Whit is the only dog she ever give the command 'get ahold' to, only she doesn't do it anymore. When she says 'get ahold,' he's trained to secure a goat and hold it for her for doctoring or tagging or whatever. With a kid, Whit throws a paw over its back and takes it down like a wrestler and then sits on it until Jo Ellen gets there. When she was telling me about this, Whit was standing at her feet. She had to spell get ahold, otherwise Whit would have taken off for the nearest goat, looking for a takedown. With a full-grown goat, Whit clomps down on the soft skin right behind the front legs and usually just slows them until Jo Ellen gets there. Whit's the only dog she's ever had done it right. Some dogs are too rough—bite too hard—and others just don't get it. They never quite figure out it's about holding, not biting.

Once, they were having trouble getting a full-grown goat into a pen. She sent Whit after him while she blocked one side of the opening. When Whit brought him close, Jo Ellen would try to haze him through, but goats don't like being penned in general, and this one in particular. As soon as he got close, he'd blast right past her back into the field. Went on like that for a while, but it's getting dark, so next time Whit brung him close, Jo Ellen grabbed for him and at the same time shouted the command, 'get ahold.' Whit come at that goat with teeth flashing. Only problem is he chomped down on Jo Ellen's thumb instead of the goat's leg. Real gusher. She didn't lose the finger or nothing, but she don't give the command anymore, neither.

Goatherding means doing different things in different seasons. Goats ain't easy to keep alive. Don't take sudden changes in weather so well. Don't live on barbed wire and tin cans, neither, like some folks think. Got high nutritional needs. Heck, they can get polio if you switch suddenly from a low-grade alfalfa to a high-grade. In winter, it's getting them bred and watching out for sickness. About one buck for fifty she-goats. Almost all-natural breeding. Biggest thing with that is making sure the bucks don't kill each other. At the height of kidding season in late spring, a couple of dozen baby goats are born every day. If a she-goat is open at the end of kidding season, meaning she ain't pregnant, Jo Ellen will record her number and try to breed her for a fall kid. If that doesn't work, the she-goat will go to town.

Goats got to be hayed and grained and watered every day, but the water tanks freeze in winter, of course. Even when Jo Ellen gets them thawed, if it's too cold, those goats won't go up to the tank to drink. They ain't the brightest beasts in creation. Too cold to walk to the water tank? They'll dehydrate and die where they refuse to budge. So she's got to get the border collies on them and drive them to water.

There's every problem you can imagine. One goat fell and broke its shoulder. Jo Ellen got down in the mud and snow and wrestled with it, yanking on its leg, trying to set that shoulder. 'Course, the goat thinks it's being tortured by the Mad Goatherder rather than fixed, and it don't exactly cooperate. Too high on the shoulder to splint. Critter limps to this day.

At least they're trainable. Like I said, when they come out of Texas, the herd was wild. Jo Ellen couldn't get within a hundred yards of any of them before they'd turn tail and take off at a dead run. Pasture wasn't fenced to start, so her dogs got a workout. Once the goats got the lay of the land, they became more cooperative. Now she can call out and the goats'll come running to her.

First winter in the field, Jo Ellen came through the worst blizzard central Nebraska seen in a decade. Only a foot of snow, but winds were up to seventy miles an hour. Now, you need to understand that out here, after a blizzard like that, you can stand on the edge of a field and see hundreds of acres before you, and they all look like they got one inch of snow on them. That means the other eleven inches of snow, multiplied by hundreds of acres, has blown off some place. When you drive to town, you find out where it went. You come to cuts in the road, and the snow is piled in there ten foot deep.

That's what Jo Ellen come through. Her tent site is set down a bit. Top of the tent is below the table, which helps. Wind blows over the top mostly, but it still piled up snow all around the tent during the blizzard. Wind was howling something fierce, and the side of the tent started to bulge in where the snow was piling. Wind wouldn't stop, neither. Like a train coming through the front flap. All night it roared and all day. Jo Ellen sat tight for a while, feeding the woodstove, but them goats is her living, so she braved the storm. Got to twenty degrees below zero. Whiteout conditions, so she couldn't ride horse or jeep. Lot of acres out there and a lot of goats, and as well as she knows that land, she knows even better you don't want to get lost in a storm like that.

Blew out after twenty-four hours, but they were snowed in for three days. They were able to spread some hay after the storm itself, but not all of the goats come through it. Lost half a dozen to pneumonia. Another twelve went missing. Found them several days later. They'd huddled together to stay warm, but the snow drifted over them. Froze to death.

It ain't a life for everyone, but when you're out where Jo Ellen is, on top of the table, you can see from horizon to horizon. No man-made structures in sight, no sound but the wind and the goats bleating. That's how some folks define freedom. When the night comes, that big sky fades away and there are stars, lots and lots of them, from horizon to horizon—three hundred and sixty degrees all around. Those stars slide right into the ground, like the universe is a big dome been set down right on top of you. Like I said, it ain't for everyone, but it's enough for some.

The Crop Dusters

I'VE been telling you all about cowboys, the kind that work cattle, but there's another kind of cowboy around here—the flyboys. Bill Williams is a crop duster been flying out of Broken Bow for years. Back when he was just starting out, second year I think, he went to help out another duster who was spraying pasture for thistle. Bill loaded his plane with fuel in Broken Bow and headed about twenty-five miles east. Met the other pilot where he was loading out in a pasture up on a ridge. Bill asks the feller how much spray he's taking on, and the duster says sixty pounds. Well, Bill eyes a fence at the end of the pasture and it ain't far away, but he figures if the other feller is loading sixty pounds, he'll do the same.

Bill says, Why don't you go first so I can see how far you roll and know what to expect.

Well, the other feller was wheels up no more than two-thirds of the way down the pasture. Bunch of farmers were standing around watching the air show. So now Bill starts his roll, but he ain't getting no lift—plane won't come off. He rolls and rolls, takes it right to the end of the pasture, and there still ain't no lift. He jerks the stick back anyway and hops up. Barely gets as high as the fence, about four feet in the air. Tail wheel catches the top wire. Instead of snapping, it stretches like a rubber band and starts to slow the plane. Lucky for Bill, the plane was more powerful. Ripped out a dozen fence posts before the wire snapped.

There was a big ol' canyon just past the fence. Plane nosed down in it. Farmers started running across the field, heading toward the crash site, just waiting for a fireball to come up. Except Bill used that canyon to gain airspeed and then pulled up. Plane rose out of the valley into view. Farmers cheered and waved their hats.

After they dropped their load and were back on the ground, Bill finds out that when they were talking about taking off and clearance and all, the other duster forgot to mention he only had a quarter tank of gas. Bill was almost full, so his plane was a lot heavier.

Crop dusting goes back to the '20s in the south. Cotton. Spraying for boll weevil.

In Nebraska, it didn't really start until after the war. Bill learned to fly first and then learned to crop dust. Used to go down to Oklahoma, and then later, Kansas. Sprayed wheat for weed. There's more ranching than farming in Nebraska these days, so instead of spraying crops, dusters that are still in the business, like Bill, they're spraying pasture for weeds.

Once, when Bill's brother-in-law Bud was dying, he asked Bill if he'd spread his cremated ashes from the air around some bluffs and canyons east of Myrna, where he was born. Bill said sure, and after Bud was gone, his wife, Bill's sister, come around and they set it up. Now, an Ag Cat is a dusting plane—ain't built for dumping ashes—so Bill ended up taking the whole door off to make the plan work.

Well, morning of the event, whole family was gathered. They wanted to take a portion of the ashes and bury them next to where Bud's parents got plots in a cemetery near Broken Bow.

Couldn't get the ash bag open, so one of the nephews takes a knife and cuts it at the top, but he also nicks it at the bottom. They pour out some ashes and done their thing at the cemetery. Soon enough, Bill's got them ashes and he's airborne. He holds up the bag, and right off, them ashes start leaking from that knick and getting all over Bill's pant leg.

Bill flies up to Myrna, and the family is all on the ground there waiting to see what's left of Bud float down to the Nebraska plains. They want to take pictures, so Bill told them he'd circle once and then come by a second time and dump the ashes. Now, if you was to dump ashes out of a little bitty window of a Piper Cub, wouldn't be nowheres for them to go except to disperse. But with that whole door taken off the Ag Cat, when Bill stuck his arm out into the air stream and turned that bag upside down, couple of things happened. From the ground, a nice white puff of ashes appeared in the sky. But up in the sky, it was a different story. Them ashes followed Bill's arm right back into the cockpit, and in one second flat, Bill was covered with Bud. Fact, he looked like the ghost of Bud, all white with them ashes.

Bill got back to Broken Bow airport well before the family got back from Myrna in their cars. Soon as he was done taxiing, Bill jumped out of the plane and did his darndest to brush Bud off his shirt and pants. Then he gone home. His wife met him there, coming out of the shower, and she asks what he's doing taking a shower in the middle of the day with relatives in town.

He said he had to wash that Bud right out of his hair.

By now, the relatives were kind of getting wise to what had happened. Bill's mother-in-law was ninety-four but still sharp as a tack. Not much got by her. She quietly turned to Bill's wife and says, Don't let Bill do me.

That reminds me of another crop duster works these parts. John Witthuhn has used up all but two of his nine lives. He's had seven emergency landings in his day, two of them crash landings. All seven been fuel problems. Line come loose or got clogged. He even run out of gas once. One time he was spraying a field and was most of the way across on a pass when the engine died on him. There was a shelter belt at the end of the field. Remember, that's a line of trees a farmer planted way back when to help block the wind. Ol' John knew he didn't have the power to either turn or pull up and jump the trees, so he puts the plane on the ground and jams the brakes as hard as he can. But he has too much speed, so he's going into them woods for sure. Not a lot of give in those full-grown trees, so he lines up between two big trunks even though the gap betwixt them ain't more than five foot or so. The plane roars in. Nose of the aircraft slides between the two trees just fine, but the wings don't follow so well. John says he ain't never been on a carnival ride quite like that one. Sheared the wings right off. He skidded to a stop in a plane now looked more like a missile. Come out without a scratch.

Plane wasn't insured. Most dusters don't insure their planes. Costs too much—about 10 percent of the purchase price of the aircraft every year. So if you got a fifty-thousand-dollar plane, after ten years you've paid as much in insurance as you done for the plane itself. Ain't many crop dusters can afford that. Fact, most dusters don't bother praying not to crash. They know that's going to happen sooner or later. Without insurance, they pray not to crash until they've owned their plane seven to ten years, so they ain't out of pocket too much when they do crash.

When John come out of high school, he started as a mechanic. Done that for about seven years and then figured flying might be more lucrative—and fun. Started crop dusting in '78 or '79. Bummed an airplane. Flew anywhere he could get jobs. Followed the bugs. But John quit the crop dusting business last year. With all them genetic-altered crops farmers been planting lately, ain't many bugs to spray. Least there ain't enough bugs to go around for all the dusters. So John is working on contract for the government, fighting fires. They got him in the mountains and even down in Kansas fighting prairie fires that blow up in the national grasslands.

Last year, he was fighting a fire in Colorado. Had taken off ten minutes before and was reaching the fire when a fuel line come loose on him. Airport was out on the plain about seven or eight miles from the mountain. Went like this: there was the airport, then a wide and long boulder field, and then heavy forest that stretched up a hill to the first line of mountains. He was just crossing the first line of mountains when the engine started to sputter. He turned around right away and got off the mountain, but right below him were thick woods with a few houses cut out of the trees. Landing in the treetops didn't appeal, but neither was the boulder field beyond the trees an inviting runway. There was a road, but the traffic on it was stopped dead and bumper to bumper. Mostly fire trucks and a few cars that got caught in the jam and a couple of TV trucks.

When Witthuhn got clear of the houses and the people, he dumped his full load of retardant. By then, he was over flat land. His engine all but quit, and he was losing altitude. He passed over the last of the trees, but there's nothing below but rocky ground. Then he spots an alfalfa field cleared out of them boulders. By now folks on the road paralleling his flight path are out of their cars. They know there's trouble. Then the engine catches fire. Flames are coming out everywhere. Thick smoke, too. The flames start licking at his windshield, and the smoke blocks his view. It gets so hot, he starts worrying the heat might melt the windshield. He can feel fire in the floor under his feet.

Ol' John goes into a sideslip, tilting the plane left but giving her hard right rudder. Kept the plane flying straight, and it also made the flame and smoke blow back over the wing so he could see the alfalfa field. He come in that way, the plane all knotted up like a big burning pretzel, and smacked down in the field. Ripped the crop to shreds before coming to a stop. He got out and ran, afraid she's going to blow. After a spell, nothing happens, so now he's worried about the plane. He grabs a fire extinguisher and puts out the fire.

It gone out over the radio his plane was on fire, and of course there's firefighters everywhere, and what firefighters do is put out fires. So next thing you know, they're all ignoring the forest fire, and Witthuhn's got about a dozen trucks surrounding him in that alfalfa field ready to put out the fire that's already been put out, and helicopters and planes are circling overhead. It's a wonder in all that excitement one of them pilots didn't dump his load of retardant on John's plane and John and the whole bunch of them.

Witthuhn done all kinds of piloting. One time, he was flying a couple of business fellers home to Nebraska and they were over Kansas. Late fall. Blue sky all around, but north of them there was a big ol' black cloud on the horizon. First winter storm of the season.

As they get closer, that cloud gets bigger. Rises from the ground right up into outer space almost. It's hanging right over the Kansas–Nebraska border, but they need to get on up to

Kearney, fifty miles north of the border. The closer they get to that big, black apocalypse, the lower Witthuhn starts sinking that plane. By the time they reach the edge of the clouds, Witthuhn is down to two hundred feet, trying to sneak under the ceiling. The sleet starts to hit, and it's suddenly dark as a new moon night. Can't hardly see nothing. Witthuhn says, We ain't going make Kearney. Best head for Holdrege.

His passengers say, Can't see a thing. How you going to get there?

Witthuhn says he done a lot of crop dusting in those parts, and if they can just find Route 34, they can ride it into Holdrege and get to the airport from there.

No sooner than the words are out of his mouth, they pick up Route 34. But the ceiling has dropped so low you can't tell the ceiling from the floor, and the sleet and snow are starting to pound them. They got so low they were reading the traffic signs for directions. Holdrege, five miles. Hell, they couldn't have come closer to the cars on the road below if the plane were a roof rack. Come up on an eighteen-wheeler from behind and had to *pull up* to get over it.

Next thing you know, Witthuhn's saying, We're downtown.

Passenger says, I know we're downtown. Hell, we're practically landing on the roof of the five and dime. Other passenger is praying and mumbling and playing with beads. Folks on the ground thought they were under attack from the air.

When Witthuhn finds Main Street, he lets out a little whoop, banks hard down a side street, and says, The airport's about three miles due east of here.

With ice starting to form up on the wings, it was a long three miles. They lost the road, but Witthuhn kept saying, It's right around here. It's right around here.

They just about flew through the windsock at the end of the runway. In a little plane like that, you usually turn onto your final approach at a thousand feet or more and a couple of miles from the front end of the runway. Then it's a couple of minutes before you're on the ground. Witthuhn turned final about fifty feet over the runway, and they were on the ground before you could swallow hard and tighten your cheeks.

They didn't have a tower there, only a guy with a radio in a Quonset hut, and he come on the air and says, Who the hell is out there?

Witthuhn says, This here is John Witthuhn from Callaway.

Guy says, Oh hell, Witthuhn. I should have known if there was someone flying in a storm like this it would be you, you crazy son of a bitch.

The Land Steward

IT doesn't happen near enough, but sometimes, by the grace of God, the right person comes along at the right time, in the right place, and does the right thing. That's Cleve Trimble.

Cleve may just own the prettiest piece of Nebraska. He lives in the north-central part of the state, in the middle of the Sand Hills. When you come on his place, it looks like any other ranch up there: miles and miles of nearly treeless rolling grassland, a harsh prairie environment with hardly any wildlife. Then you come to the rim of the Snake River Canyon on his ground, and you're transported to a different world.

The canyon is only a couple of hundred yards wide and three hundred feet deep and maybe twenty miles long. But when you're down in it, all of a sudden you're not sure where you are anymore—Colorado, Wyoming, Montana—but you're pretty sure it isn't Nebraska. There are ponderosa pine all around, wildlife everywhere, two hundred kinds of bird species, and a cool, aquifer-fed river that's the best trout stream in the state.

Cleve's accomplished a lot in his life, but he might never have had more of a mission than he has right now—to save the canyon. And his time might be running out.

Cleve was born in Lincoln, Nebraska. It was his home base growing up, but the family moved a lot. His dad was a lawyer by training, but after the war there wasn't much lawyering to be done, so he went into business. Revived struggling branches of the company he worked for. Family lived in North Dakota, South Dakota, Iowa, Missouri, and then came home to McCook, Nebraska, where Cleve's dad flattened the tires and said he wasn't moving again. Cleve graduated from high school in McCook, went to college in Lincoln, medical school in Omaha, and did his surgical training at Denver General.

Cleve's career in medicine arced high and fast. He tipped to the academic side, mainly focused on the development of emergency medicine and trauma surgery. He developed emergency trauma centers around the country. Flat brought them out of the ground. But actually operating them once they were up and running wasn't enough of a challenge, so he'd move on and start another one somewhere else. Today, the residency he founded at Denver General Hospital and the training program he chaired at University Hospital in Jacksonville are both considered the premiere emergency medicine training programs in the country, if not the world.

He not only had the smarts to create the model for those programs, but he's a powerful personality, too. Had to work through all the political opposition—lot of powerful doctors would battle him—but he thought it was the right thing for those communities, and ain't much going to stop Cleve when he's of a mind to do the right thing.

Cleve's worn a lot of hats. Even though he run for office once, probably wouldn't call him a politician. But he's an expert political scientist. He knows where the political fault lines lie, and he understands the application of power, but in the end, Cleve got more bulldozer in him than coalition builder. He got done at those hospitals what few other fellers could have got done.

Only problem for Cleve was he gone too far too fast.

Achieved all his goals by his mid-forties while he was in Florida. Remember, his doctoring and all was done in an academic context. He was a working surgeon, but he was also the youngest full professor of surgery at the University of Florida … earned it before the age of forty. Editor of a couple of medical journals, too. Made a lot of money.

Once there didn't seem to be nothing left in medicine for him to accomplish, he retired to run a bed-and-breakfast on a little river full of trophy bass in Florida. He was slightly over-qualified for the position.

This was fine for a while, but he kept hearing the siren call of Nebraska. He longed to be back in surgery and back in Nebraska. His mother always sent him a *Nebraska Life* maga-zine for Christmas, and he seen a ranch for sale up in Cherry County. He'd heard wonderful things about Cherry County from his father, but he never been there himself. So he decided the family vacation that summer was going to go through the Sand Hills of Nebraska.

Come June, he loaded up a rented trailer, and the family come out. His wife at the time was what you might call high maintenance. It was the height of the farm crisis in '85, so land prices were way down and potential buyers were treated like visiting royalty. When the family got to Nebraska, the realtor took them out to the ranch Cleve had seen in the magazine— on a creek off the Niobrara River. The place had been hit by lightning the day before. The house, the barn, the fields: it was all a black, smoking ruin. Cleve thought it was a bad sign. His wife didn't think nothing. She'd already shut down by then. But Cleve kept on and found a ranch that was going through bankruptcy.

When he come out to the place, thirty-two hundred acres,

it looked like any other ranch until he reached the rim of the canyon. He was dumbstruck. It was love at first sight. Must have been some sort of subconsciousness thing happening, too. He's a surgeon, and from the air, the canyon looks just like a deep incision in the vast surrounding epidermis of treeless grassland. Seeing the canyon changed his life. He knew he had to have it. He bought it for sixty bucks an acre and moved to Nebraska. There was a short intermediate stop in Lincoln, where his wife from Florida jumped ship and went home, before he relocated to the ranch for good. Been there twenty years now. He finished his career as a solo surgeon in Valentine, which is seventeen miles up the road from his ranch.

It's easy to remember seventeen miles. That's how far a wagon train or a cavalry company typically traveled in a day over flat ground. There's a one-room schoolhouse on Cleve's property. At the time it shut down, some years back, it was the oldest continuously operated one-room schoolhouse in the nation. But before it was a schoolhouse, it was a way station on an old west trail that runs through Cleve's place. It started as a game trail and then was an Indian trail. Later it was used by the cavalry as it moved between Fort Sidney along the overland trail and Fort Niobrara, just east of Valentine, and, finally, by miners and settlers in wagon trains heading up into the Dakotas. Wagon ruts are still visible across the prairie on his property. That way station was the last overnight on the trail before travelers reached Valentine.

Mentioned Cleve was a solo surgeon. Just to give you a sense of scale, Cherry County is bigger than Connecticut, and he was the only surgeon in the county. 'Course, there are three-and-a-half-million folks in Connecticut and only six thousand in Cherry County. And Cleve ain't really retired. He's a consultant now. Goes into small towns where a local doctor become so big he's about taken over the local hospital. Hospital administrator can't say no to him, and his ego become a black hole that swallows resources and needs glorification. Cleve parachutes in. Sometimes the problem is the hospital administrator, but most times the doctor's head needs to be shrunk. Problem is the town is often lined up behind the doc. They either don't know of his bullying and tantrums or they look the other way.

Cleve says doctors like that often have a psychological grip on a small town and they know it. Folks see that doctor as maybe the only one in a county the size of Connecticut who could save their life if the time ever come. You can imagine Cleve's stature as a doctor and the strength of his character and personality for him to stroll into a hornet's nest like I just described and start kicking tails and taking names. And he's been doing it for six years in small town after small town around Nebraska and stretching into Colorado and Iowa.

Annnnnnnyway, when Cleve bought the ranch, the rangeland was the most valuable part of the deal, since you could graze cattle on it. Canyon didn't hardly come into the equation. Financial models back then said there was no way you could run cattle and make money off the place if you paid more than forty dollars an acre. So that sixty bucks an acre Cleve ended up paying may look like a steal today, but back then he was worried he'd way overpaid. And he wasn't even buying it for the grazing, he was buying it for the canyon. Today, if you could measure proper, the canyon and land along the rim probably worth a hundred times more than the rangeland.

Millions of year ago, a river run through the canyon, but then, because of ice ages and different geologic events, that canyon was buried. Around six thousand years ago, when the land looked pretty much like it does today, the Snake River began running west to east across Nebraska and then turned on an elbow and run northeast up to the Niobrara. At first it had to cut through a surface layer of caprock maybe five to ten feet thick. Then when it hit the sandy soil below the caprock, it began to erode the land quickly, and it uncovered the ancient riverbed. A six-thousand-year-old river revealed a ten-million-year-old river canyon. Upshot is when you drop down into the canyon, you go back in time ten million years. It's full of fossils.

Ain't hardly an ecosystem like it. Most, like Yellowstone, are broad expanses. This one is a few hundred yards wide by twenty miles long. Cleve calls it the tube of life. Among the two hundred bird species Cleve's identified in the canyon are bald eagles, osprey, golden eagles, and all four kinds of soaring hawks. There are white-tailed deer, mule deer, antelope, cougar, bobcats, beaver, skunks, minks, and rattlesnakes.

Nebraska sits on top of an ocean of freshwater, the Oglala aquifer, and its pretty close to the surface. After the Snake River cut through the capstone, it eventually hit the aquifer and unleashed it as well. Today, all along the river at the bottom of the canyon, little rivulets from freshwater springs sneak out of the wooded cut bank and feed the main stream. That's what keeps the river cooler and clearer than any other in Nebraska. It also makes it the best trout stream in the state, rainbow and brown. Water temperature is near constant year round. State record twenty-pound brown trout come out of the Snake. And because it's cattle country and not farm country, there aren't any crops, so there aren't any pesticides leeching into the river. Reach into the clear water and all the way down to the riverbed, and you come up with a handful of fossils—all sorts of bones and petrified ivory from mastodons.

Cleve's ground is magical in a lot of ways. The Niobrara River, near where the Snake empties into it, was Sioux Indian sacred ground, like the Black Hills. But Cleve thinks the Snake might have been holy ground too, since there are a bunch of Indian burial mounds on a stretch of river bottom on his property.

Let me tell you a little story. Back in the 1850s, a cow wandered off from a wagon train and into an Indian camp near Fort Laramie. Sioux been camping there awhile, and they were hungry. Ended up killing the cow and eating it. An Indian leader named Conquering Bear knew it was trouble, so he gone to the fort and offered a prized pony in payment. Commander wouldn't take it. He wanted the feller that killed the cow. Conquering Bear said the feller was from a different band, and he didn't have any authority to turn him over. Next day, they sent a hot-headed lieutenant out to arrest the feller that killed the cow. Conquering Bear offered several horses this time, but the lieutenant broke off negotiations and opened fire. Conquering Bear was mortally wounded. The soldiers were greatly outnumbered, and in the fight that come after, all thirty-one were massacred in short order. Weren't a real thoughtful bit of soldiering.

Annnnnnnyway, point is Crazy Horse, the famous Sioux leader, was a teenager then and most likely got in on the battle. After the massacre, the Indians broke camp and headed north. Crazy Horse split from the group and rode into the Sand Hills, seeking a vision. The vision he had didn't exactly reveal his destiny, but it did foretell the manner of his death, and the vision in general is part of the myth and legend of Crazy Horse.

He was a key figure in the Battle of the Little Bighorn and became a symbol of Sioux freedom and dignity. No one knows where Crazy Horse had his vision, but Cleve thinks it could have been on his ground, maybe on one of the canyon promontories that overlooks the Snake River, right above the Indian burial mounds. From that point, you can see down the canyon to the spot where the Snake joins the Niobrara. And there's an ancient fire ring on that promontory.

Twenty-three years after his vision and fourteen months after Custer's Last Stand, Crazy Horse led nearly a thousand of his hungry people to Fort Robinson, in western Nebraska, and turned himself in. He camped near the fort—which is about a hundred and twenty-five miles from Cleve's place—without causing no trouble. But he was such a powerful symbol of the old way of life and of Sioux resistance that they come to arrest him. He gone freely, more bewildered than anything, but when they got him back to the fort and were about to throw him in a small jail, he balked like the mustang he was and turned to run. A soldier stabbed him, and he died a few hours later.

Several thousand Sioux decamped a while later and headed northeast, including Crazy Horse's parents, who were carrying his body. At one point, his parents broke off from the group and buried his remains. Some folks think his grave is on Wounded Knee Creek, about seventy-five miles from Cleve's ranch, over the border in South Dakota. Cleve thinks he might be buried on the Snake River. No one knows, but Cleve had a couple of Crazy Horse scholars down in the canyon at separate times, and he says when he come around the bend in the river to the glen where the burials mounds are, they both got chills.

I once asked Cleve if he ever thought of excavating those burial mounds. Before I even got the question out of my mouth, he says, No way. I'd be struck dead. And he didn't have no joking in his voice or on his face.

Annnnnnnyway, Cleve didn't graze any cattle on his land for three years after he bought it. During that time, he saw the upland grass come back, the canyon wildlife population explode, and the fishery bloom. He knew he had to preserve the canyon, but he wasn't sure how. He looked at some of them big conservation and environmental groups and thought about giving them the land. But they have a tendency to buy and then later hand the ground over to the feds. Cleve don't want the feds to get it. He seen what they done cutting national park funding. But more than that, he seen what they done in his own backyard to the Niobrara River.

The Niobrara runs the whole length of northern Nebraska before dumping into the Missouri River. It's downright gorgeous—ranked one of the five best canoeing rivers in the country—but it's different from the Snake. Niobrara canyon is much wider and deeper, but because it's wider, the canyon walls don't have the heavy growth of timber along the sides like you see on the Snake. Niobrara's pretty because of the river bottom itself: mess of cottonwoods pinching in on wetlands and sandbars, and that meandering river running through it all. Niobrara used to be a wild and scenic river. Then the feds bought it and made it a National Wild and Scenic River, which means folks come in boozing and smoking dope and blaring their music and dumping their trash.

The Snake River Canyon is small and narrow. It can't take hardly no abuse. And it's the Sand Hills, so the one jeep trail that run along the bottom is sand. If even thirty cars a day went through there, much less five hundred, it would destroy it. Paving the road would be another kind of disaster. The ecosystem might be twenty miles long, but it's only tens of yards wide at the bottom. The animals move up and down it constantly. Put a paved road and hundreds of people in there, and you cut off the *animals'* highway.

Here's a measure of how much Cleve cares about the canyon. In the riparian zone you have hardwoods—ash, cottonwoods, hackberry, box elders—and ponderosa pines. Since settlers have come and the prairie fires have stopped, a mess of cedar bushes, which can grow to tree size, have infiltrated. Prairie fires usually run underneath the pines and leave them be. But the cedars, growing right under the ponderosa pines, serve as ladders that carry fire up to the branches and needles of them pines and ignite them. Over the last five years, Cleve has kept a crew working all through the warm season ripping out cedars. He's spent tens of thousands of dollars of his own money on those crews. If he didn't, one wildfire could wipe out the whole canyon.

So this is what Cleve's left with. He wants to preserve the land, but he doesn't want the feds to get it. He ain't crazy about most conservation groups, yet he knows somehow the public ought to be able to share the beauty of the canyon. And he needs to add value to the land so the feds can't afford it—but add value without doing any harm.

The feller who owned the ranch and the canyon before Cleve got in trouble with some bad cattle loans and tried to save himself by plotting homesites on the canyon rim. He got county approval and sold some plots but then lost the ranch. Part of Cleve's plan to save the canyon was to undevelop the development. There were seventeen lots. He bought them all back. Previous owner had plans for four hundred and fifty units along the rim.

Later, Cleve allowed three or four houses to be built on

the rim by conservation-minded friends as part of his value-add strategy. By building a few houses, he proved the value of the property and could project that value over the four hundred fifty proposed lots. That inflates the price of his ground so it's too expensive for the feds to come in and buy. But once he done what he done with those three or four houses, he slapped conservation easements on the rest of the ground so no more could be built. If he hadn't sold a couple of lots for houses and proven their development value, the feds could have said he was dreaming about the price he could get, and they would have valued the land on the canyon rim as plain old rangeland.

One of the houses he built is for his daughter. It's just below the rim so it's out of sight, about twenty foot down, on a bench, which is a ledge that runs the length of the canyon and acts as a game trail. It's not far from the promontory, above the burial mounds, where Crazy Horse might have had his vision. From the porch of the house, overlooking the canyon, you can see a cliff just upriver, across the next scallop in the canyon wall. That cliff has a real interesting history.

When the Snake River first come through and started to form the canyon six thousand years ago, it ran into a bluff and formed a lake. When the lake overflowed and cut through, it eventually uncovered the bend in an ancient river that was ten *million* years old, like I told you.

When animals are dying, they have a sense of thirst, go to a river, and die on the bank. Then they get washed downriver by the current, get caught in a bend, and get covered with sand and preserved. That happened by the bluff near Cleve's daughter's house, except the Snake River kept on eroding to the present day and deepened the canyon even further. So those fossils in the ancient riverbed were suspended in the cliff walls halfway down the canyon.

Well, in the 1930s, along come a couple of paleontologists, the husband and wife team of Morris and Marie Skinner. Morris was born and raised in Nebraska but developed a national reputation in the field. The two of them got hired by Childs Frick to operate a dig on the site of what later became Cleve's ranch. They dug out thirty-nine hundred specimens over three summers, which they plastered and sent to New York City. It became known as Burge Quarry, named after the town that used to be on Cleve's ranch before it ghosted. Only thing left is the foundation of the post office, which Cleve's ranch house is built on. The Skinners worked on and off for Frick for nearly fifty years, a lot of those years based in New York. In the '60s, the whole Frick collection was donated to the American Museum of Natural History.

Burge Quarry was a world-famous paleontological site. The Skinners come up with some major finds ... more species of ancient horses than ever been found anywhere else on earth. When Cleve first got the place, he heard there'd been a dig on the property, but he didn't know where. Morris Skinner was still alive and back living in Nebraska. Cleve met him. He invited him and Marie out to the ranch. That was around 1989, fifty years after the last of their three digs. Cleve, Morris, and Marie spent all morning one summer day in '89 looking for, but couldn't find, the spot where the quarry had been. What happened was back when they were working the site, it was the middle of the Depression, and folks had cleared every tree in the canyon and floated the logs downriver to Valentine for building or heating. With the trees grown back up, nothing was recognizable.

The three spread their lunch along the rim of the canyon. Maybe every husband and wife who are also a husband-and-wife professional team are very close, but Morris and Marie shared a special bond. Morris had just been diagnosed with diabetes, and whenever he reached for food he shouldn't be eating, Marie would slap his hand and say, Morris, now stop that. He'd look at her and real quick say, Yes, dear. And his lip would quiver. He looks over at Cleve, and he whispers a little too loud, If they don't see the quiver, they don't see fear, and if they don't see fear, they're not happy. Got to make the lip quiver.

Marie rolled her eyes. They done that routine a bunch. At lunch that day, they described camp life back in the '30s. There were half a dozen workers on the crew. Morris and a couple of others would climb down the cliff with ropes. They used a bucket tied to a cable and rigged to a Model A named Maude, parked on the canyon rim, to lift out the fossils. Morris did the digging and knew bones, but it come out later he was dyslexic. Marie did all the writing and maybe a fair bit of the science, too.

Annnnnnnyway, at lunch there in '89, Morris was telling how after meals in the '30s, the rule he made was everyone had to walk fifty paces away from camp and dump any cans they'd opened over the rim and onto the bench—onto the game trail twenty feet down—to keep critters away from camp at night. Cleve suddenly remembered once, when he was exploring the game trail, he'd seen a bunch of rusted cans and wondered where on earth they'd come from.

They all jumped up at once, packed away their lunch right quick, and run for the jeep. Cleve drove over to the spot near the rim. Morris hobbled over to it. Marie was petite, but Morris was built like that cartoon character the Tasmanian Devil: big

upper body and small legs with mushy knees. He got that way
from bending down on his knees all his life while shoveling
heavy loads of rock and gravel with his arms. Annnnnnnyway,
Morris gets to the rim and breaks out into song: It's a helluva
death to starve to death, it's a helluva death to die. Then Marie
sung the same verse back at him. It was the song Morris sung
every evening half a century before when he climbed up over
the canyon rim after a day of digging, hungry as all get up and
smelling her dinner cooking on the campfire.

That might have been the last carefree day they ever spent
together. Morris deteriorated quickly after that, and two months
later, he was on his deathbed, tubed and on a ventilator. His
family was at his side. He grabbed a pad and pencil and wrote,
Tube Out.

Doctors told him if they took the tube out he'd die. He
wrote, *Die Anyway. Talk First. Damn Tube Out.*

There was a bit more discussion, but not much, and they
pulled the tube. Morris said his good-byes. Marie sat close by
his bed, holding his hand in hers, and the last thing she says to
him is, I love you, Morris.

He looks up and says to her, Yes, dear. Then he made his lip
quiver. Then he died.

Cleve put up a plaque to the Skinners a while back on
the canyon rim right above the old quarry. Marie is in her
late nineties now. She and some of their children still live in
the area. Folks who spend their days digging and their nights
around campfires, who have to scrape for scarce funding and
don't get much known for all their backbreaking work, form
a tight fraternity. When Cleve had a dedication ceremony for
the plaque, Marie and the children came, of course, but a who's
who of paleontology also come out to honor Morris. As they

departed, no one left flowers on the plaque. They were all paleontologists. They left small fossils instead. They all rest atop the
plaque to this day.

For all his value-adding and game-planning about how to
save the canyon, I still haven't told you about Cleve's stroke
of genius. About forty miles south of Cleve's place is a town
called Mullen. Back in 1995, some miles southwest of town, a
golf course opened. It ain't just any golf course. It's in the dead
center of the Sand Hills, an isolated stretch of open grassland.
Except for parts of Nevada, it's about as remote and desolate
as a place can get in the lower forty-eight. Fellers who built it
weren't crazy, though, they were smart. It's a private club, and
the $250,000 memberships sold out long ago. Rich fellers fly in
from all over the country. It's a links course, duplicates the best
of that breed in England and Scotland. It fact, the Sand Hills
Golf Course was recently ranked the sixth-best golf course in
the country. In fifth place was Pebble Beach. In third place was
Augusta.

Cleve's going to do the same thing at his ranch as they done
in Mullen, but his course may even be better. The front nine
would be built among the natural contours of the prairie, a
true links course like they got in Scotland—and Mullen. But
the back nine would mostly hug the east rim of the canyon and
have dramatic views. Picture the canyon walls as if you were
looking straight down on them from the air. Look like ocean
waves, with peaks and valleys. At ground level, those peaks
are promontories, or points, that jut into the canyon, though
most are rounded. About four holes would have greens set on
the points, so when you're putting, the canyon will spread out
behind and below you, with ponderosa pines framing the green.
Then, from the tee next to the green, you'd shoot over an abyss

where the canyon wall dips in and land your ball on the green located on the next promontory over.

Cleve invited a half dozen of the top golf architects in the world to come look at the site. All of them said they'd waive their fee for the privilege of designing the course and putting their name on it. Cleve chose one of the top traditional designers in the world. Feller's style is called minimalism. Uses the natural contours of the land to shape the course, rather than moving a lot of earth. There'll be long stretches of what golfers call forced carry space, meaning past the tee there'll be a lot of natural prairie grass before the fairway starts up. Parking lot'll be a mile away, and folks'll play their way to the canyon rim. Should be a thing a beauty.

Here's the genius, if you ain't already figured it. Remember, the whole idea is to add value to the property. Cleve believes it's inevitable the land'll be exploited. His goal is to leverage that inevitability and develop it responsibly, to add value while preserving the canyon—but, at the same time, to share it. If he builds one of the finest golf courses in America, the land is too valuable for the government to come in and buy. He's inoculated it against the feds. And by making it a public course, and on the rim, he can share views of the canyon, but nobody will be setting foot in it.

For anyone who likes and respects nature and natural beauty, Cleve Trimble is a hero. He has cancer, and the charts say he's only got a couple of years left. Still looks healthy and is full of life and thinks as clear as the aquifer-fed Snake. Don't seem like his time should be up. But because of him, at least the canyon's time ain't.

The Ranch Wife

THELMA Reichs was born and raised outside of Paxton, down along the Platte River. Her father was a Danish immigrant. He settled in Paxton because there was already a small community of Danes in town. Come over when he was twenty-three, which was typical. He was the second son. Wasn't going to get any kind of inheritance, so he struck out for America and the plains. That's how Nebraska got filled mostly, with second, third, and fourth sons from the Old World.

Thelma's mother was sixteen when she and her future husband met. Story goes that Thelma's mother vowed she wouldn't get married at sixteen, like her mother done. Good to her word. Thelma's mother married when she was seventeen and two days. Her husband was thirty-four.

Life was good for Thelma growing up in the 1920s. There were four kids in the family. School was two miles from their farm. She didn't start until she was six because she couldn't walk the two miles when she was five.

The '30s were tough on just about everyone out here. In '32, the family had to move off a farm they'd been renting for sixteen years. Only lived on another farm a year when they got hailed out. Flattened the crop. Family moved into town, but Thelma's father didn't have any work. Her mother had been canning chicken and fruits, so at least they were able to eat.

Back in those days, men ran just about everything, but

it doesn't mean they were any good at it. Thelma's father was a hard worker, but he just wasn't no businessman, plain and simple. Her mother was. She started out working for a dollar a day cooking at a restaurant. Later, in the late '40s, she bought the restaurant. Run it for five years before her heart give out.

Annnnnnnyway, Thelma met Lawrence at a dance there in Paxton. Got married in '42. Did it quick because they were worried his number was about to come up and he'd get drafted. It did, but the doctors told him he had flatfeet. Later, when the need was greater, they were going to take him anyway, but then word come down they were 'freezing' the farmers. That's what they called it. Wanted to keep them farm boys down on the farm. More valuable growing food here than carrying a gun over there.

Thelma and Lawrence lived on a rented farm for six years. Then, in '48, they moved to a bigger place six miles south of Sutherland. Still rented, though. Deal was they bought their own equipment and seed and gave the owner one-third of the crop. Rented that place for fifteen years. Lawrence wanted to go into ranching, get out of farming. Thelma was a town girl and really wanted to move into Sutherland, get out of the country. They had six children by then, but the farmhouse they lived in was less than a thousand square feet and dingy. They used to put the bedposts in pots of kerosene so the bed bugs couldn't climb the posts.

Thelma won, and they moved into a nice, big house in Sutherland. First night there, Lawrence says, I don't like this. I'm going to find me a ranch. I won't live in town.

Took three years of looking—might give you a hint about Thelma's gitty-up for the idea—but Lawrence found him a ranch. They bought it and moved in just before Christmas in

'62. Ten miles northwest of Anselmo in the Sand Hills. Oldest daughter was in college then. Rest of the kids didn't want to move out there, and Thelma didn't, neither. It was tough on her. Moving in to town in Sutherland, off the farm, was a dream come true. Now she's no longer in town, and she ain't even on a farm along the lush Platte River near Sutherland. She's in the middle of the Sand Hills. Hardly any neighbors for miles. Hardly any trees. Just drifting in the middle of the Great Plains on a sea of grass.

They got quite a welcome. Nobody been living in the house for several months. Had a floor furnace, which means the furnace itself was under the house. When they turned it on the first time, they disturbed several dozen skunks hibernating there. Couldn't get them out. Worst part, though, was when they got romantic. Like a lot of critters, seems like him's a bit more interested than her. They'd hear a squeal and then the female would take off running and the male would chase her. Then they'd hear a clunk when one or the other gone headfirst into a pipe. When they done that, why, they'd cut loose on the back end, and the house would be unlivable for days.

Folks out here is used to putting up with a lot, but it don't seem like a fair choice when you got to either live with skunk stink in a closed house or open your door and air it out in the dead of winter. Those were real winters back then, too, when it was below zero for long spells. Lawrence would trap and drown them skunks, but when you got three or four dozen, it ain't work that's done in a day.

No question, ranch life can be tough on a woman, especially life in them barren Sand Hills. Feller will go out and do his ranching, don't care if he don't see a lot of folk. And when he gets to town, he can do some jawing while he's picking up grain or fence post or wire. But women back then were stuck on the ranch. They used to say the only reason more home-steaders' wives didn't hang themselves is because there weren't any trees. Thelma remembers the first year she was up in the Sand Hills, driving along empty stretches of road, quiet and alone, a hundred miles from Sutherland. Tears would stream down her face while she was thinking, I just want to go home.

Like I been saying, when the first settlers come out home-steading, wasn't a tree to the horizon because of prairie fires. Lightning strikes would burn huge swaths every year. They'd rage for days and burn up any seedlings that somehow sailed into the country on the wind and took root. Nowadays, the lightning fires are all put out, but there are fires of a different sort.

Whenever a dry wind blew up from the southwest, Thelma and Lawrence and their neighbors knew there could be trouble. The southwest edge of their property is bordered by the main line, which runs parallel to the state road. At least a dozen trains a day come through there, mostly coal trains out of Wyoming and empty hoppers heading west to refill. Only takes one spark coming off a wheel and hitting the weeds by the side of the tracks to bring hell down on them.

Thelma says she'll never forget the feeling in the pit of her stomach the first time she heard that roar and come out of the house to see a wall of flames blowing up toward her from the railroad. Her spread is several thousand acres. In summer, that grazing land is dry as tinder. When you raise cattle, that grass is your feed, or your crop—however you want to look at it. Worst was the haystacks. They had fifty-two of them several miles from the tracks. That was their winter feed. Thelma remem-bers nearly dropping to her knees when the wildfire reached the haystacks and turned them into fifty-two pyres. Most folks live hand-to-mouth out here, and to see your winter feed disappear like that was quite a blow.

They ended up trucking their cattle south and feeding them on cornstalks after the harvest. But Lawrence had to build a ramp to offload the cattle, and when he was standing on the back of his truck, his foot slipped, and he landed face-first on the tailgate. Crushed his cheekbone. Laid him up for months. All because of one little spark. They got burned out several times. House was spared each of them times, but that was about the only good news.

Speaking of fires and furnaces, at least they had one. Generation before had to heat with fire. But there weren't any trees, like I keep saying, so there was no wood to burn, neither. That left cow pies. Parents would send the kids out to collect them. Not all that fun to handle, and it took a lot of them to keep a fire going, but at the least the smell wasn't so bad. Smelled more like grass than what you might think burning bull shit would smell like. 'Course, it wasn't real appetizing setting there at the table at night and thinking about the fuel had cooked your dinner.

Wasn't any air-conditioning, neither. When folks talk about the drought back in the '30s, they picture them dust clouds, which is true enough. But it was terrible hot, too. Didn't get electricity out here until the early '50s, so there weren't even fans. Only relief was to send a child up the windmill with a fruit jar to catch some cool water running off it. You'd drink some and pour the rest on the burlap bags covering your windows. If you were lucky and a breeze come up before the water warmed, you'd get the touch of a cool breeze running through the house.

There's some older folks out here says rural electrification is the highlight of their life.

Speaking of the '30s and hard times makes me think of Ken Stithem's story of growing up. His place is only about ten miles from Thelma's ranch. This could be tough country back in them days. When Ken was twelve, his parents broke up. He was the youngest. Had six brothers and sisters. Three other kids died young. His father was rough, mean, and hot-tempered. He beat all the kids at various times. Girls were no exception. Sometimes if one kid was bad, he'd get a notion and lick them all.

Ken's parents married when his mother was fifteen and his father twenty-seven. As the years went on, his mother decided she wanted out. But she had a plan: hang in until the kids were grown, then leave. Ken's father never hit his wife, but he come close, threatened her a bunch. Then one time he did come after her. Had a club in his hand, out on the porch, and was moving toward her. One of Ken's brothers was home, and he come up behind his father and pinned his arms as he tackled him off the porch. Busted up his father's face pretty good. Just about plowed his nose off, in fact.

That was it for Ken's mother. Took a spell, but she secretly arranged for a job. Problem was, didn't quite square with her original plan. The other kids had moved out or were close, but Ken was a long way from that—or should have been.

On November 11, 1934, a man come to pick up Ken's mother and take her to a ranch further up in the Sand Hills. She was going to work as a cook. She wished Ken well as she moved to the car, but at that point it was every man—or boy, or woman—for himself. Remember, Ken was twelve.

Ken's next oldest brother was only fourteen, but he'd quit

school and got a job as a ranch hand and pretty much already moved out of the house. He only come back on weekends, but now he was moving out for good. It was a Sunday, and he asked Ken what he was going to do. Ken says, I suppose I'll stay here. His brother says, You can't stay here. Dad'll have you up at four in the morning fixing his breakfast and then doing chores all day and fixing his dinner at night. And you won't go to school no more. He'll work you to death.

Ken thought there was some truth in that, but he didn't think he had nowheres to go. The second-oldest brother had given Ken and the fourteen-year-old brother a little gray pony when it was just a colt. The two younger boys raised it, broke it, rode it, and owned it together. Ken's next-oldest brother was worried enough about him that he said if Ken would ride up to his sister's place the next morning, about thirty miles away, he'd give him his share of the horse. Ken's sister was eighteen and married—for the second time—and lived up past Milburn.

Ken thought on it all night. Twelve is pretty young to be abandoned by your mother, all but abandoned by your abusive father, and deciding if you're going to ride thirty miles over unknown terrain to the house of a married sister that don't know you're coming. But he made his decision. The next day, after his father went to work—he walked a mile and a half each way to a farm where he was a hand and made fifteen dollars a month—Ken got on his horse and rode. He didn't have a saddle, and his roll didn't have nothing but a second pair of pants and a second shirt. He rode all morning and into the early afternoon. When he come up to his sister's place, Maddie was in the yard hanging wash. He reined that pony to a halt and says, Do you have room for a bum?

She stopped hanging the wash a minute and says, Depends on who the bum is.

Ken says, Well, the bum happens to be me, along with this gray horse. But if he can't stay, I can't stay.

Maddie says, You're both staying.

Ken said he couldn't promise her their dad wouldn't be coming after him. Well, not after him, after the horse. His father done some farming on weekends on their own place, and even though the pony belonged to Ken and his brother, his father used it as part of a three-horse team.

His sister been beat by their father, even after she'd gotten married, and she says to Ken, If I see him come to that yard gate, that's as far as he's going to get.

He never come for the horse or Ken.

Story had a happy ending, I suppose. Ken lived with his sister for eight months then was reunited with his mother. His mother and the rancher she worked for come and got his stuff on July Fourth and took it up to the feller's ranch, but Ken insisted on riding that same pony up to the place—twenty-eight miles.

Ken worked as a hand on the ranch until he was nineteen. Never saw the inside of a school again after the eighth grade. Had a couple of other jobs before the war. Got engaged just before basic training and married while he was on furlough. That was probably the happiest ending of all. He and his wife had a nice brood of kids and were married almost sixty years before she passed on a few years back.

Annnnnnnyway, back to Thelma. Like I said before, back in those days, men had all the say-so, except they didn't really, if you know what I mean. Like with schooling. Lawrence only had an eighth-grade education, and he thought that was plenty.

He told Thelma right after they got married that if their kids didn't want to go to high school, that'd be okay by him. He didn't see much value in it. Just prolonged getting to work. Thelma was shocked by that. She was a reader and had every intention of her kids graduating from high school and maybe going further.

Thelma liked to sew and crochet. One time, she was reading to the kids while her crocheting was resting on her lap. Suddenly, Lawrence's boots are pounding up the front steps. Not only didn't he like formal education, he didn't have much of a hankering for the informal kind, neither—like his wife reading to the kids. Wasted a lot of time could be spent on chores. So just as she hears the doorknob being grabbed, Thelma flings the book over her shoulder behind the couch without looking. It hits the floor with a thud just as the door bursting open covers the sound. Book slid quietly across the pine floor boards unseen by Lawrence as he stepped into the house. Meantime, Thelma had picked up the yarn real quick, and she was crocheting up a storm while the kids stared at it, wide-eyed. Lawrence was never the wiser, although he did say something about the kids' 'unnatural fascination with her needlework.' In the end, three of her six kids ended up with master's degrees.

Lawrence is gone now, but Thelma's doing just fine. After forty-four years on the place, she's made her peace with the Sand Hills. Found her solace in painting. She's drawn since she was a kid, but she got serious about art after she moved up to the ranch. She has a large studio behind the house. Sold over six hundred paintings, last count.

Wanderings

THERE were a lot of practical jokers and pranksters back in the day—if you ain't figured that yet. Two of the biggest were brothers Pearl and Oli Nutter. The Nutters come out of Washington, Kansas in 1934 and settled up in the Sand Hills. Pearl and Oli done a lot of things, but mostly they were horse traders and also furnished stock for rodeos. Pearl done some pranking with Arlington Vandeventer. Like the time during the war, when the army was paying a subsidy of some sort for goat milk. If you had goats, you'd get a check from the government to supplement whatever the milk was bringing. Well, Pearl and Vandeventer gone down to the barber shop in Broken Bow—probably had a little hooch in them—and told the barber they were buying goats for the government. Take all the goats they could get. Special deal. They'd buy every goat folks could round up, five dollars a head. Told the barber to spread the word. Have them goats brought to the front of the hotel on main street the next morning, and they'd settle up.

By sunrise, there were goats coming out of the hills like water through a busted dam. By eight o'clock, there were over a thousand head in front of the hotel with a bunch of impatient folks looking for their five bucks a critter. Problem was Pearl and Vandeventer already checked out and were long gone. Everybody was pissed off, not to mention all the pissing and crapping them goats were doing right there in the middle of

Main Street. Ain't like there's a lot of traffic jams in these parts, but you couldn't get a car though there until well after noon, and it took a couple of days to clean up the durn mess. Pearl and Vandeventer must have got a laugh wherever they were that morning, but they known what they done caused some ill feelings because they didn't show their faces in town again for a couple of years. That barber never cut their hair again, neither

Once during a big Saturday night dance up in the Sand Hills, very late, Oli and Pearl snuck into the nursery where all the babies were at. Babies and babysitters alike were asleep. They switched them little ones from crib to crib and switched their blankets, too. When the parents come in to collect them, it was past midnight, and they were tired and maybe had a few drinks. Annnnnnnyway, took all of Sunday and wagons crisscrossing most of the Sand Hills before every kid was back in his real mama's arms.

Back in them days, when there were a lot of folks in this country and there was a dance every Saturday night and families had seven, eight, ten kids, there was always a new baby floating around them dance halls. Oli carried a woman's eyeliner, and he'd get in line to hold a new baby. He'd get one and open up that blanket and try to make the little one smile, maybe whirl around a bit and amuse the thing while the mother is talking to another mother. Then with his back turned to the mother, he'd pull out the eyeliner and draw a goatee and some bushy eyebrows on the baby. Then he'd wrap them blankets back up, hand the kid over, tell the mom it's the most beautiful baby he ever seen, and melt back into the crowd. About two or three minutes later, a shriek would go up when the next woman got handed the baby seen Oli's handiwork.

One time when they were boys, Oli found him a fake

thumb that was all black and blue. When they got home, their mother asked Oli how he was. He said he wasn't doing so well, hit his thumb with a hammer real hard. He stuck it out, and she examined it. Don't feel no fever in it, she said. Ouch! he said, and jerked his hand away. Left the thumb with her. She screamed bloody murder just before Oli and Pearl busted out laughing. She was so mad she gone after them with a skillet. That night Oli and Pearl slept in the barn.

Pearl and Oli give it to their wives, too. One time Pearl and his wife were visiting Lincoln and had just finished a nice meal at a restaurant. The bill came, and Pearl excused himself to go to the restroom, except he didn't. He took off, left the restaurant. His wife didn't have her purse or nothing. She had a devil of a time talking her way out of that one.

Another time in Lincoln, Pearl walks up to the counter of a store, buys something, and as he's leaving, he tells the clerk, That woman over there, I seen her shoplifting, put something in her purse. *Talking about his wife.* Then he walked out.

Oli done the same thing, only his wife give it back to him. One time when they were in Omaha, Oli got on a bus and paid for himself, but when his wife got on, he claimed he didn't know her. Later that day, they were walking down the street and Oli was lagging a bit. His wife walks up to a cop, bit shaken and distressed, and says the man behind her been stalking her for blocks. Then she ducked into a store while the cop give it to Oli for a while.

Speaking of the law reminds me of Chuck Blakeman. Chuck done his share of drinking in the bars in Oconto and then driving home. A patrolman was aware of his tendencies, so he followed him out of town one night after the bars closed. Chuck was weaving, just having a terrible time keeping his truck between the ditches. Didn't get far before the cop pulled him over.

Officer reached in and took the keys right out of the ignition. He says, Come on over to my cruiser, Chuck, and I'll take you home.

Then the cop threw the keys into a weed-filled ditch by the side of the road.

Chuck didn't take a fancy to that, but he was too drunk to say nothing or form a thought. He walked back to the cruiser, and they both got in. Finally, his mind gets to working, and Chuck says, Why'd you throw my keys away?

The cops says, You'll find them easy enough in the morning when it's light and you're sober.

Sounds like a right smart way of handling the situation—except to Chuck. He cranked down the window, reached over, pulled the cop's keys out of the ignition, and threw them in the ditch. He says, It'll be even easier with both of us looking.

Chuck was deaf in his left ear for a couple of days after that from the cop yelling at him.

Reminds me of another cop story. There was a new one, not long out of the academy, started working up in the Sand Hills. He was bumping down a little ol' country road about fifteen miles southwest of Mullen when up ahead he seen a pickup cross from one pasture, through a gate, across the road, and into another pasture. Driver was a ranch hand on the Bufink place. Had a couple of his kids in the truck. Hell, it was a ranch truck. Everybody has them. Never leaves the property, so there's no license plate or nothing on it. That new cop put on his flashing lights and chased the truck into the field, and the cop give the driver thirteen tickets. Folks figured he was going for a new Nebraska record the first week on the job. No truck license. No driver's license. No seat belts. Too many kids in the cab. On up to thirteen.

Bufinks had themselves a big place and were upstanding folks, and it didn't set well with them. Bufink come into town and give the police chief the what for. Got to understand how it is out here. If the state of Nebraska was a giant football team, ranchers would be the star quarterbacks. You got a big spread, you get listened to. When the dust had settled, it was down to one ticket.

That incident was the talk of town right up until the same new cop put A.B. Cox on the ground. A.B.'s family has had land north of Mullin since the 1890s. The new cop—he was a short feller but ramrod straight, and big, like he worked out—pulls A.B. over for a busted taillight. Well hell, you ain't a cowboy if one or both taillights on your pickup ain't been kicked in by a bronc or rammed by a bull. Cop walks up to the cab, and A.B. introduces himself, but the cop is cool and starts doing some NYPD thing where he shines his flashlight all over the cab and the truck bed like A.B.'s a Sand Hills terrorist. He asks A.B. if he has any firearms. A.B. says, Well, I got a shotgun because I been dove hunting, and I got a rifle for coyotes, and I got a pistol, plus I always carry a spider knife, but, no, I ain't armed.

Now, all them Coxes is a bit hard of hearing. Apparently, A.B. didn't hear the rookie cop so well as the conversation went on, and the cop don't understand A.B. not understanding and decides he's drunk rather than half-deaf. He asks A.B. for his driver's license. They're on a bit of a hill in town, and when A.B. puts the truck in park to reach for the glove compartment, the pickup rolls back a foot or so. The big ol' sideview mirror A.B. has for dragging a trailer bumps that little cop and spooks him. He orders A.B. out of the car.

Like I said, A.B. ain't hearing so well and isn't understanding where this is headed, except he sees a bunch of kids had stopped their bikes to watch, and he starts to figure out the cop is putting on a show for them. Sure enough, he starts running A.B. through a series of sobriety tests. Now, A.B. isn't one to pick a fight. However, he did get into that brawl with the McNett boy when he was younger—was a Saturday night dance down in Tryon, think there was a girl involved. They mixed it up good. Longest fight in these parts for quite a spell. Went on for forty minutes or more. Most of the fights I'm telling stories on are about as long as a young feller's first kiss. Forty minutes is a marathon. Beat the hell out of each other. Tore up the dance hall. They were brawling inside, and they were brawling outside. Drew quite a crowd. Hell, even the band stopped so they could watch. Best I recall, ended in a draw when neither one could lift his arms no more. They're friends now.

Annnnnnnyway, A.B. ain't drunk and don't take kindly to being made a public spectacle of, and he's getting a lot of attitude from the young cop. So while he's standing there with one leg up in the air taking the drunk test and looking like he's doing one of them Chinese exercises in the park, he says to the cop, Did they waive the height requirement to get you into the academy?

That's when A.B. got cuffed and laid out on the ground for half an hour.

New cop only lasted two months before the local police chief got the feller transferred out of the Sand Hills for his own safety.

A.B. run some with John Wiley. Them two would go back behind the chutes at the county fair, or maybe into a bar, and John would be carrying a big ol' sack. He'd set it down and wouldn't say nothing about it. Of course, fellers asked him what's in the sack. He'd say, Oh, nothing, just Mabel. Mabel is in the sack.

He wouldn't say no more, so fellers were more and more curious. Who is Mabel? they'd be asking. Oh, you don't want to mess with Mabel, John would say.

By now, there's all kinds of folks gathering around the mystery sack. Regular crowd. Finally, John would undo the string tying it, and the sack would fall away around a jar—a big ol' beef jerky jar, thick glass, about a foot high. Top screwed on it. In there would be a big rattlesnake not looking too pleased by events.

Be a commotion and then John would say, You ought to leave ol' Mabel alone. But tell you what I'll do. If you can pick that jar up off the bar and move it over to this here table, I'll buy you a beer. And if you can't, you got to buy me and A.B. a beer.

Well, every young buck in the place scurries to line up by the jar, to show how brave he is, especially with a wall of glass between him and the rattler. First feller picks up the jar and starts to move it, and that snake strikes. Bam! And whoosh! Ol' boy would drop the jar on the bar like he grabbed the wrong end of a branding iron. Every time. I mean *every* time. That snake ain't going to do nothing with the glass in the way, but them fangs snapping at you is like a foul ball coming for the bridge of your nose if you're sitting behind home plate. Don't matter if there's a screen there, you're still going to jump. Wiley and A.B. got more refreshment from that little exhibition.

Hell, them two, John and A.B., they're still going at it in the rodeo senior division. That thing with the snakes was decades ago, but just a year or so back, they were down at a rodeo in

San Angelo, Texas. John got hurt pretty good. Took a real bad wreck in the roping. They drug him off to the hospital. Had a few broken ribs. That can be a real serious deal. They put John under and went to work on him. A.B. and another feller is there with John the day after the rodeo is over, stranded, a thousand miles from home. Nothing more forlorn than a cowboy in a hospital the day after the rodeo has moved on. Finally, John starts to come out of it. There's a doctor and two nurses and A.B. hovering over him.

A.B. explains the situation. He says, John, I know you're just coming to. You're hurt bad. But the Doc's saying there's a good chance you'll pull through. But if you don't, can I have your saddle?

John starts to laugh, except it hurts too much. One of the nurses busts out laughing, but the other two took a grim view of the shenanigans.

Speaking of roping, I should tell you about one of the best ropers in these parts, Sparky Malmberg. He was born in Pender, not far from the Iowa border. It was mainly a farm he grown up on, but his father also bought yearlings and fed them out. Sparky grew up with horses, but it wasn't until his uncle invited him out to his ranch in central Nebraska when he was nine years old, and he spent a summer there in the late '40s, that he knew he wanted to cowboy the rest of his life and not farm.

Developed his roping skills after that and his knowledge of horses. Done a little rodeoing—roping and steer wrassling. Made expense money. Did it for pleasure. Promotion thing, too. When folks at the rodeo seen what he could do with a rope and a horse, they'd hire him. In his prime, if you needed a top-notch roper in the Sand Hills, you called Sparky.

Good ropers have good horses. Two just go together. A lot

are good trainers, too. Don't always happen that way, but it was true of Sparky. Fact, he got hired as much for horse training as he did for roping. One time, a feller was raising quarter horses, and he had a mare out on the track training. After she been run, the jockey stopped to talk with another jockey on the backstretch, and when he went to move, the horse froze up. Plum wouldn't move. They hit her with a buggy whip off and on for a couple of hours. Finally got her to move, but she was unreliable after that. That mare just seen everything; some are like that. What I mean is she seen everything that moved anywheres near her. And if it was something she didn't like—a critter, a passing truck, a low-flying plane—she weren't going nowheres. Just quit right there.

So they brung her to Sparky. He put her in a muzzle, no bit in the mouth. He'd get her to move, but then when she froze, with that muzzle on, he could pull her head around to the right, dally on the saddle horn, throw his weight in the left stirrup, and, as he dismounted, take her down to the ground. Then he'd tie her head to the back cinch and go set a spell nearby. Sounds painful, but it's more uncomfortable than anything— like hogtieing your brother when you were kids.

Annnnnnnyway, that horse would sweat itself into a lather. When she calmed down, Sparky would untie her and let her up. When she froze up again, she got the same treatment. Had to throw her half a dozen times before she got it figured out that freezing up meant going down.

Reining competition is something usually done at a state fair. Have to show how your horse handles at a lope in a set pattern: circles, stop, back-up, pivot, roll back. Show off the dexterity of the horse and the rider's command of him. After

Sparky worked that froze-up mare, she become a champion reining horse.

I got to explain a bit about branding before I can tell you any more about Sparky's roping. A ranch works on an annual cycle. Calves are dropped some time in the winter, haying is done in the warm weather. If ranching was like the regular calendar, Christmas would be the spring roundup. Biggest day of the year in ranching. You get neighbors plus hired hands together and castrate and vaccinate the male calves and brand them all. Depending on how big an operation you have, you might have several branding fires going. The herd is penned a ways away from the fires, and a roper will heel the cattle— lasso their back legs—and drag them over to the fire.

Annnnnnnyway, word of how good Sparky was got around the Sand Hills, but them cowboys didn't especially like the idea of a farm boy from eastern Nebraska coming into the country and showing them up when it come to riding and roping, so just about every new ranch he worked he was tested a bit. One time in '58, he was hired for a branding in Brownlee, and the rancher brung out a horse that had a lump under its belly about the size of an orange. Right under where the skirts of a saddle hang. Rancher had a pad with a hole in it for the lump to stick out of, and he says, Use this pad with your own rig, and there won't be no problem.

What no one told Sparky is the mare come out of North Dakota, where she was used to rope calves at branding time, just like Sparky was doing that day. But one time a calf turned on her and the rider wasn't using a neck rope, which every good cowboy uses to keep the horse from turning away from a calf. Mare spooked, threw the rider, and took off. Drug the calf to death and tried to leap the first fence she come to. Cut herself bad. Recovered, but left the lump there. That had happened about six years before. Since then, she'd been ridden and rode just fine, but she'd never roped again—until that day they give her to Sparky.

Sparky got on that mare not knowing any of the history, and everything was fine when he turned toward a calf and lifted his rope. Everything was still fine when he tossed his lasso and heeled the calf. But that's about when all hell broke loose. Mare took off like a fast freight, reliving her Dakota days. It was all Sparky could do to rein her down to the speed of a thorough-bred turning for the post. That calf was bouncing along behind. When Sparky finally managed to bring the mare to a full stop, the calf had so much momentum it almost skidded over the branding fire and scattered the calf wrasslers gathered around it. They got on him something fierce. Can't you find a lower gear on that horse, cowboy? We're trying to survive until lunch. Another one says, What's the matter with you? Hell, the kids ride that mare to school.

Them cowboys all knew about that horse. Sparky's the only one who didn't. Took him a few runs before he figured out how to channel that mare's nervous energy, but when he did, it worked to his advantage. By the end of the day, he'd drug more calves to the fires quicker than any of them hands had ever seen. He won them fellers over. Cowboy way, though. They didn't tell him the story of that horse until a few years later.

In the spring of '57, he was working for a rancher and roping every newborn calf in the field, castrating the bull calves, burning their horn buttons, and notching their ears with a pocket knife. When it come branding time, Sparky done half the work already. Only thing left to do was brand and vaccinate. One of the fellers that come to help with the branding brought a calf cradle in his pickup. Lots of ranchers seen that as normal, but weren't nothing more insulting to a roper like Sparky than a calf cradle. What you done with a calf cradle is set it on the ground and then run the calf into it. Lock the calf in and turn them and expose a side for branding and vaccinating.

After they got the branding fire going, the feller that brought the calf cradle walks over to his pickup and is reaching for the cradle. But Sparky didn't wait around. He spurred his horse and roped the first calf and drug it over to the fire. When the calf wrasslers took off the rope and Sparky was heading back to the herd, he hears the feller say, We'll let him play with his rope awhile, then we'll get out the calf cradle.

When Sparky was in his prime, his roping was a thing of beauty, artistry on horseback. Fast and smooth. With his rope free, he'd wheel that horse from the fire and head to the herd, lasso a calf on the first throw, and turn in one motion and drag it back to the fire. Like he was born to do it. It was like him, the horse, and the calf was all on the same page, even though the horse was a wild animal and the calf had its own agenda. For a couple of hours that day, Sparky was dragging two calves a minute to the fire. One every thirty seconds. Branders could hardly keep up. Calf cradle never left the truck bed.

Sparky was a real pro. Fellers like him had their way. Handled cattle real quiet, not like these young bucks today. They'll fly into a herd and scatter the calves, try roping one by the back fence and miss half the time, and then go chasing the one they missed and scatter more cattle. Sparky would slip in and then rope and drag off the outside of the herd. Work his way through them critters like he's eating around an apple. Calves by the back fence don't even know it's branding day until late afternoon when their number come up and Sparky heeled them.

Technique is to toss that rope under the back legs, not on the ground, but more like rolling it down the front of their back legs so they step right into it. Tighten her up, dally the horn, and head for the fire. Roping one leg is okay, but the chances of hurting the calf are a bit higher, and the calf wrasslers got a free hoof to worry about, so you want to lasso both legs whenever you can. In his day, Sparky could throw twenty-five loops and never miss—and catch both heels every time.

Here's what kind of roper Sparky is. Eleven days shy of his sixty-third birthday, he roped a coyote off a problem horse he trained. Hardly ever seen that done, and when it is, it's usually two fellers running the coyote, with one of them directing the critter. Sparky was in a calving pasture up in the Sand Hills. Got a good jump on the coyote. Come up on him sunning himself in a cow trail, and the race was on. They went up and down over them choppy Sand Hills turning this way and that, locked in on each other. Them coyotes' heads are pretty small. Imagine riding at full gallop over rough terrain, holding the reins with one hand, and keeping that loop open in the other while trying to throw it over a moving target only six inches wide. His first throw hit the coyote in the snout, but the loop closed and fell off. Second throw caught him around the neck. That was the talk of the crew for quite a few days.

Reminds me of a couple of ranchers own a place south of Valentine tried a new method of roping. Fellers got tired of roping off their horses, so they decided to do it off of their pickup truck. They scratched their heads a spell and then reckoned the best approach was to fix a tractor seat to the front of their Ford. Most of the trucks working them ranches up there

got a cow catcher on the front protecting the grill, since they're
always running into cattle or being charged by a bull.

Well, the plan didn't work so well on the first run. There's
a pole that sticks up out of the grill guard, and they slipped the
tractor seat down over it. I won't be telling you their names, so
let's just say Brother One was driving, and Brother Two got seat
duty when they gone after their first stray with the new invention. They ain't even got near a yearling to rope when the truck
hit a hole in the pasture and the tractor seat come flying off
the pole with Brother Two sitting in it. Launched him. When
he hit the ground, Two gone rolling across the prairie like a
tumbleweed. Brother Two been cowboying for a lot of years,
and there's been a lot of broncs in that time separated him from
his saddle, but that was the first time he ever been throwed by
a Ford.

Well, them ol' boys smarted up and drilled a hole through
the grill guard, dropped the seat back on, and run a pin through
that drilled hole, locking that seat in place. They were proud of
themselves now, outsmarting both the cattle and the Ford. They
headed out again, looking for them strays. Found one. Now
they were flying across the pasture, zeroing in on a cow, looking
like they were auditioning for Mad Max: Prairie Edition.

They come up on the spooked yearling, and Brother Two
tosses his lariat and catches him around the neck. I'm not sure
what kicked in first, the truck's breaks or the considerable
power of that eight-hundred-pound cow, but I can tell you,
while the seat stayed put, Brother Two did not. Holding onto
that rope, he went flying face-first into the short grass and skit-
tered a spell before he let go. He looked like a kid gone tubing
on a lake behind a speed boat—except without the tube and
without the lake. He come up muttering about the need for

further improvements and suggesting to Brother One that they rotate driving and roping duties amongst themselves.

Still, they weren't discouraged yet. Just needed to think on it a bit more. But heck, it didn't take no genius to figure out the next step in the development process. They rigged up a seat belt. They were even more proud of themselves now, being at the forefront of cowboying evolution and all.

They headed out after another stray with Brother Two driving this time and Brother One in the outrigger position. They come up on a stray. Brother One looped it, and Brother Two hit the brakes like he's reining a horse to a stop. The cow kept going like cows do, and when the lasso cinched up, Brother One held onto the other end of the rope. Sure enough, that seat stayed on the pole because of that pin, and Brother One stayed on the seat because of the seat belt. But now the weak link was the power of that cow versus Brother One's gloved hands. Cow was the clear winner. Rope ripped right out of his hands, and the yearling run off, dragging the rope.

'Course it did. When you're roping from a horse and lasso a cow, you tie onto the saddle horn and use the power of the horse to help stop the cow. The brothers were upset they hadn't thought all that through, obvious as it was. But they was pioneering the science of truck roping, and they just needed to keep tweaking the system. Next step was just as clear as the ones before. They tied the end of the rope on to the grill of the truck. Brother One held the rest in his hands. Idea was one would rope the stray and then let the slack run out, truck would brake, rope would come taut, and the cow would flop.

So they gone right back out that same day and run down a steer. Brother One tosses that rope, and the lasso drops around that cow's neck just as soft as if he'd thrown a wedding bouquet, and everything is looking just fine. When the cow run out of rope, Brother Two hit the brakes on that ol' Ford pickup, and it kicks up a cloud of dust while skidding to a stop. The tractor seat stays put. Brother One stays seat-belted in the seat. Rope stays tied to the grill. Only thing that don't stay put is the steer. When it hit the end of that rope it kept right on going.

Brother Two looked affright. The grill was ripped clean off the front end. Brother One was launched like a firecracker. He landed and rolled across the grass with that seat still seat-belted to his backside while the grill separated and gone flying over his head.

Them brothers were a sad-looking pair as they watched the grill bounce across the prairie—getting dragged behind that steer like an anchor and then disappearing over a hill. Them boys don't talk much about Ford roping to this day.

Wayne

TOLD you I'd tell you about Wayne Jenkins, Francis's husband. Wayne grew up on a hardscrabble dirt farm between Broken Bow and Oconto. Wasn't poor, really. Not like he went hungry as a kid. Family just didn't have enough land to make a go of it. His father wanted him to be a farmer, but Wayne wanted to be a rancher as far back as could remember. He left high school and started buying and selling cattle. He'd go on up to Sargent, buy on a Thursday, and write a check. 'Course, he didn't have any money. He'd haul the cattle back to Broken Bow and sell them on Saturday. Have a pickup truck full, maybe four or five head. He was young, but he knew cattle well enough to buy them a little low in Sargent and sell them a little high in Broken Bow. He'd put the money in the bank on Monday, and it would be there when that check of his came floating down from Sargent that day or the next. Didn't make a ton of cash, but it was better than hard labor for a dollar a day.

Except one Saturday it snowed in Broken Bow, and the auction was cancelled. 'Course, this was after Wayne had bought some cattle a few days before in Sargent with a check he didn't have money for. He went into the bank on Monday, hat in hand, and asked the banker if he could have a short-term loan. Banker was tighter than hell. He looked at Wayne a minute and says, I know what you're doing, you're kiting checks. Wayne says, I'll sell them cattle in a few days. Banker says, What if you

245

die between now and then? Wayne says, Well, if I go to heaven, I'll mail you the check, and if I go to hell, I'll hand it to you personal.

Banker kicked him out. Right onto Main Street. He gone across the way to Tom Varney's bank. Ol' Tom sat Wayne down and heard his story, but he said the bank couldn't lend him money. Didn't have any collateral. But he said, I tell what I'll do, I'll lend you my own money. And that's what Tom done.

By the time Wayne was twenty, he was doing farm sales. He was the auctioneer when a farm got sold or took back by the bank. Auctioned everything: cattle, horses, equipment. One time, he was doing a farm sale, and he started a whole herd of cattle at forty dollars a head. In them days, they didn't back you up if you were auctioneer, meaning, if you set the bid price and no one offered up, auctioneer owned whatever he was trying to sell. No one bid on them cattle Wayne was selling that day. He ended up owing eight hundred dollars for the herd. Mind you, this is back when a section—six hundred forty acres—was going for eleven, twelve hundred dollars.

Wayne was wondering how he was going to pay for them cattle, or if maybe he weren't long for starting a new life in Omaha or Lincoln. He gone into the bank that Varney run, but Varney was out of town. He talked to two other fellers that worked there and explained the situation and tried to get a loan until he could sell them cattle down in Lexington or Kearney. They laughed at him. Said, If you didn't get forty bucks for them yesterday, you ain't going get forty bucks for them tomorrow. And they sent him packing.

Well, ol' Wayne knew some fellers and found one that agreed to sell them cattle for him down in Lexington. Wayne had come on two remounts some time before. Those are horses he bought from the army. He got the same feller to agree to sell them horses, too. Well, the cattle did sell, and for forty dollars a head, but even better, them two remounts fetched two hundred dollars total. Like I said, that was some plug back then. So Wayne comes into the bank a few days later and deposits that check. Hands it to them two fellers. With them remounts added in, it looked like Wayne had managed to sell those cows for fifty dollars a head. Them two banker boys could have been blowed over with a feather. Couldn't believe the kid had made a thousand bucks on them cows. Varney was back by then, and he couldn't believe it, neither. Wayne whispered to him what had happened—the whole story—and Tom just busted out laughing. He reached over for a cigar box and pulled out a bunch of blank checks and handed them to Wayne. He said, I'll back you. From now on, you just go ahead and do business. And they did—for decades.

Wayne moved onto the Boblits ranch the day after he married Francis in 1957. Place was a wreck back then. Fence was down, weeds everywhere, barns were in tough shape. Wayne worked 365 days a year for a lot of years before it looked like a proper ranch again.

I told you about them coon hunters coming on the ranch. Well, one time the Jenkinses were coming home from church, everybody dressed up real nice, riding together in the family car, when Wayne spots a half dozen deer hunters out in one of his fields. It's one thing forgiving trespasses in church, but it's another when folks are trespassing on your ground. Out here, you don't mess with a feller's stock or his ground.

Family had a 1969 Pontiac Catalina back in them days with a big ol' four-hundred-cubic-inch engine. One of those 1960s cars that was bigger than a locomotive. When Wayne seen those fellers, he spun the wheel, floored the pedal, left the road, and headed straight for the hunting party. There happened to be a fence in the way, but he crashed right through it, sending barbed wire twanging in all directions. That Pontiac rocketed across an alfalfa field, raising a rooster tail of dust and hay. The car was bouncing over the uneven ground, tossing Wayne and his wife and kids around in their Sunday finest like salt in a shaker. Hunters bolted when they saw the apparition descending on them, but Wayne chased them down. He jumped out and give them hunters an earful about property rights. They gone off with their tails between their legs.

Wayne had a way with words. For a spell, he set up a sale barn next to the regular cattle sale barn in Broken Bow. Did it with permission. In his barn, Wayne sold everything but cattle: goats, chickens, equipment, pets, furniture. He was the eBay of the '50s. One time a feller Ken Stithem was working for says to Ken, I want you to take my dog down to Jenkins and sell him.

He was an old dog. Big dog. But he never been good for much. Wasn't a good hunting dog. Not much of a pet, neither. And by this time, he could hardly move. So Ken takes him on down to Broken Bow, and he says to Wayne, Got me a dog I want you to sell. Wayne looks over the mangy, limping critter and says, What breed is he? Ken says, The feller I brung him for says he's a Russian wolfhound.

Ol' Wayne rubs the stubble on his chin and says, Could be, but it looks like his rushin' days is over.

Wayne ain't one to hide his feelings much, neither. Come out and say it like it is. Seems like everyone out here is something and something. Meaning, you can barely make a living just being a farmer or just being a rancher. So folks is a farmer and a teacher, or a rancher and a vet, or a farmer and a feed salesman. For some folks, it don't work out so well. They ain't particular good at neither. Won't say his name, but a feller in these parts was known as the Gospel Singing Cowboy. Preacher, too. He wasn't much of a cowboy, and once he give Wayne one of his singing tapes. A few weeks later he seen Wayne and asked him what he thought of the tape.

Wayne says, Folks speak kindly of your preaching.

Feller says, Nah, none of that. Give it to me straight. Tell me the truth about my singing, flat out.

Wayne says, Well, sounds like you need to give the calf a little more rope.

They haven't conversed much since.

Wayne done a lot of things for folks over the years that weren't hardly seen by no one else. Just did them. Kind of like what Tom Varney done for him. When Davey Davis come back into the country after Cleveland, he needed a $130,000 cash bond to get back into the sale barn business. Those were the days of the farm crisis. Banks were closing and all. That was a lot of money, and there were folks thought taking a chance on Davey weren't a chance worth taking. Wayne and Francis didn't barely bat an eye and got him the bond. Davey started his climb back up.

One feller Wayne helped out all the time was a neighbor, George Goodyear. He owned a quarter right across the road. Been in the family since homesteading days. 'Course, a hundred and sixty acres might have been fine back then, but as things got mechanized, most folks either added to their holdings— a lot—or sold out. Only way to stay in business. Except for George. He stood pat. And it wasn't like his quarter was the most productive land, neither. The South Loup River flowed right through it, and Spring Creek come in from the side and joined it. His ground looked like that symbol on a Mercedes Benz car. Made everything from plowing to planting to harvesting a considerable chore. That's probably why he didn't do much farming. Raised some corn and some cattle, but the critters were all scrawny things. He was one of the last in these parts to still use horses. You'd see him out on the road pulling a hayrack behind a team. His spread looked like a Great Depression farm museum.

George was so skinny he wore a belt *and* suspenders, just to make sure his pants stayed hitched. Didn't have but a few teeth, and all of them crowding around to the sides and back of his mouth. Hardly a one up front. He'd wear a heavy flannel shirt year round, even on the hottest summer day. Most folks round here wore white or tan cowboy hats. Not George. He always wore a dusty black ten-gallon Stetson. If you were in Callaway at one end of Main Street, and he was way yonder coming toward you, there was no mistaking that Maypole sporting a big black hat.

George also stuttered bad. You could talk to him for ten minutes and hardly get a paragraph of conversation in. One night, George showed up on Wayne's doorstep. Real late, maybe two in the morning. Dark night. Rain coming down in buckets. G-g-g-g-god d-d-d-damn c-c-c-c-cow's st-st-st-st-st-ststuck in th-th-th-the kr-kr-kr-kr-krik.

Wayne woke up his youngest boy, and they got in their truck and followed George. When they got down there, sure enough, he had a cow stuck in Spring Creek right up to its snout. The three of them pushed on her and pulled on her, but it didn't help none, she was stuck good. Couldn't tie a rope round her gut since the bottom of her belly was two foot deep in mud. Instead, they tied one end of a chain around her neck and tied the other end to George's old Ford tractor. Itty-bitty thing it was. Not much more than a lawn mower. When George made the jump from horse-drawn plow to tractor, it weren't a big leap.

Annnnnnnyway, George set up on that tractor while Wayne's boy gone behind the durn cow, and Wayne was in the middle of it all. He says to George, I'll be counting to three. Then you put it in first gear, give it a little gas, and we'll ease her right out.

Words were barely out of Wayne's mouth and George is gunning that Ford like he's blasting off for the moon. Wayne starts to counting, and George starts easing his foot off the clutch. On two, George popped the clutch and floored the gas pedal like he was squashing a venomous bug. The front end of that tractor come off the ground six inches, and away he flew. The cow blew out of that muck like a cork off a champagne bottle and went flopping up onto the bank. Wayne's boy fell face-first into the mudhole where the cow he'd been pushing on weren't at no more.

Wayne was waving his arms and cussing at George—who kept going like he got a day of plowing ahead of him. *Ease* her out, George. I said, Ease her out.

Finally George stops. G-g-g-g-god d-d-d-damn, W-w-w-w-wayne, h-h-how is sh-sh-she?

Wayne rushes over, leans down by the cow, and says to George, I do believe the operation was successful, but the patient is dead.

Ol' George had snapped that cow's neck.

There was another time George showed up late at night. Needed help pulling a calf. Raining like the dickens and dark so you could hardly see the hand in front of your face. Wayne gone over there with his boys and come up on the cow. He lassoed it, and the heifer went down bawling. She was weak but had barely begun labor. Wayne and his boys got down on their knees, ready to go to work. But they can't see nothing. They tell George to go get a flashlight. George goes back to the house and gets one. He come out, runs right past Wayne and the boys, squats down by the cow's head, and shines the light directly in her eyes.

Wayne like to pull his hair out. He says, Goddammit, George, we're working *this* end.

There was another time Wayne helped George out. Dark and rainy night again. Story of George's life. He showed up on the porch soaked and says, G-g-g-god d-d-d-damn, W-w-w-wayne, my c-c-c-car's in the d-d-d-ditch u-u-u-u-up to its a-a-a-axle.

Wayne went up there, and sure enough, George had run off the road in his pickup and stuck it good. Looked like a job that'd best wait until morning. Wayne said so. George scrunches up his face and says, The m-m-m-missus g-g-g-gonna sk-sk-sk-skold me f-f-f-f-for th-th-this.

Any married man would know something about that, so Wayne says, George, how about your shoulder got banged up a bit. Know what I'm saying?

Wayne give George a little wink to help his comprehension. George's eyes brightened. Wayne dropped him at home and went to bed.

Next thing Wayne knows, the phone is jangling off the hook at one a.m. and its George's wife, Wilma. She says, Wayne, I think we're going to have to take George to the hospital in Omaha. He's in trouble ... terrible pain. Going down fast. We had a dog got run over once, she says. Lost a leg, and that dog weren't never in pain like George is.

Omaha's a four-hour drive. Wayne says, Why don't you give him an aspirin and call me in the morning. He'll be all right.

But Wilma kept after Wayne, so he drug himself out of bed, threw on some clothes, and went over there. Wayne gone alone into George's room and closed the door behind him. George was laying in bed with his shirt off and his shoulder wrapped up like an Egyptian mummy headed for burial. Wayne says to him, What in tarnation, George? I said fake it a bit. You don't have to go win no Academy Award.

George says, W-w-w-well, W-w-w-wayne, it d-d-d-does h-h-h-hurt a b-b-b-b-bit, y-y-you know.

Wayne grabbed his head in his hands. He couldn't believe it. Then he froze—'cept for an eyebrow that rose up. Got himself an idea. He says, Let out a loud grunt. Go on, do it.

George grunted real loud and painful-like as Wayne got up and headed for the door. He almost run into Wilma, who come blasting in. She says, What happened?

Wayne says, I popped his shoulder back in. Should be fine now. And Wayne gone home.

Reminds me of another neighbor of Wayne's, Leonard. He was cheaper than a sale at Wal-Mart. When Leonard's left work glove wore out, he'd flip it over and turn it into his right glove, and flip over his right glove and make it his left. When he bought new shoes, he didn't replace the new pair with the old pair. He replaced the one shoe that was so worn out he was feeling the weather through it. So you never seen Leonard wearing matching shoes, except for every five or six pairs when the rate of wore-out happened to synchronize. Tighter than hell. Bought his false teeth out of a catalogue.

There were four grocery stores back then in Broken Bow, and Leonard had four daughters. He took all of them along when he went shopping. He gave each of them a list of groceries and sent them off to the four different stores. They had to report back to him with the price of each item. He seen which store had each item for the cheapest, and then he'd send the girls back to the store to actually buy the stuff. Even had the girls pick the grapes off the stems before they bagged them, since the weight of them stems added to the cost.

Never changed the oil in his vehicles. Because of that, his tractor died in the field one day. Engine blew. Set in the same spot for years. Talked a tractor dealer in Broken Bow into letting him 'demonstrate' the latest model. That's what he said. Needed a demonstration to see if it was good enough to buy. Well, ol' Leonard, he done his spring plowing with that tractor. Dealer kept calling him, and Leonard kept demonstrating and demonstrating, plowing right around his old tractor dead in the field. Finally, after about two months of demonstrating, he got a bill of sale in the mail from the dealer.

Leonard was so cheap, when the brakes gone out on his truck, he didn't fix them. When he drove to town with his wife, Lyla, he'd coast to a stop about a quarter mile out and make Lyla walk in. Couldn't drive into town because he couldn't stop at any stop signs. Leonard wouldn't register his cars, neither. He had two, a green one and a blue one, but he only had one license plate, so he'd move it back and forth between them.

One time, Wayne was riding with Leonard in his truck. They came to a steep hill just outside of Oconto. As they crested it, there was traffic on a cross street at the bottom of the hill by the edge of town. An oil truck was just starting across going one way, and going the other way was Mike Spellbrig driving a team of mules. Next thing you know, Wayne and Leonard are flying down that hill like a crazed bull toward an oil truck and a bunch of mules, engine off to save money, no brakes to save money, and Wayne wondering what was going to save their *lives*.

Leonard swerved and missed the back of the oil truck by a sow's whisker and headed straight for them mules. Spellbrig couldn't do nothing but put them mules in the ditch. And that's what he done. Without any brakes and the engine off, Leonard and Wayne whooshed by Spellbrig and them critters like the close breath of a twister. In the silence, they could hear Spellbrig cussing them out as Leonard's truck rolled all the way through town to Highway 40.

Wayne got out and walked directly home—about five miles. Never rode in one of Leonard's coasters again.

Leonard lived by the Jenkinses' place for years, but then he upped and moved, about forty miles away. A new school was going to be built in Callaway, which meant Leonard's taxes were going to go up. He was steamed about that, real steamed. Fact, he was so mad, for the rest of his life, whenever he was scheduled to pass through Callaway, he wouldn't. What he done when he come near the city limits was to take a couple of turns, detour around town, and then get himself back on the main road. All that just to show his disdain for Callaway and its taxmongering ways.

'Course, it might have had something to do with his brakes, too.

Just lost Wayne a couple of years ago. Hard to grieve too long when thinking on Wayne. Everyone's got to go, and Wayne not only lived past eighty, he lived the life he dreamed of living as a boy—ranching under the big Nebraska sky. He done what he wanted to do and the way he wanted to do it. Grieve, sure, but mostly that's a life worth celebrating.

The Cowboy's Cowboy

I'M telling you mostly about ranchers, but the ranch hands are the real cowboys. They're the backbone of this country. But no question, they're a dying breed. One feller that passed on in 2005 was a cowboy of days gone by. He was one of a kind. Drank Windsor for breakfast and ate grizzly for supper. Tougher than tough. Martin Armstrong was his name. Come up out of New Mexico right after he graduated high school. Passed up a basketball scholarship to be a cowboy. He was pedigreed, too, when it come to cowboying. Couple of uncles were well-known Texas Rangers way back, and his grandfather was a trail boss on the Chisholm Trail. Martin placed second in calf roping in the national high school rodeo in '56. Don't know exactly how he ended up in these parts. Think he had some relations, but his first job was on the Gibbons ranch. Back then, it was the biggest spread in Custer County.

Before cars and tractors, everything was horse-rode or driven. Everything. And the Gibbons supplied it. They had 120 cows but 720 head of horses when Ed Gibbons died in '22. They supplied light teams, heavy teams, harness teams, driving teams, work horses, saddle horses. Think about all the car dealerships, garages, and tire stores around today. The Gibbons ranch was an enormous car and truck dealership, except there weren't no cars and trucks, just horses. Lots and lots of horses.

Walt Gibbons took over for his father and bought a big

spread called the Parmalee ranch in '48. Every day when Walt was growing up, there were eleven men on the ranch did nothing but break horses all day long. Although that world faded away after the war, it was the Parmalee ranch and the remnants of that life Martin rode into when he come up out of New Mexico in '56.

You can tell a cowboy by his hands. Martin's knuckles were all swoll up and misshapen and broken from getting them caught in ropes, in the teeth of horses and cattle, and under hooves—and from brawling. He started by breaking colts for the Gibbons full-time and done that for quite a spell. In his prime, he could ride all day and drink all night. Hardly ate nothing. Could live all day on booze and a brownie. In spring, roundup time, he'd head off on his horse, live out on the range. He'd stay out for three or four days. Live in the saddle. At night, he'd take it off his horse, flip it over on the ground, and sleep on it. Lean and tough. Martin was a cowboy's cowboy. That's what he was.

You look on Martin, you seen cowboy in his face, in the way he walked, way he carried himself, way he talked. If you dressed him in a suit and put him in the middle of a crowd in Times Square in New York and said to someone, tell me who the cowboy is, they might look around a spell, but as soon as their eyes lit on Martin, they wouldn't look no more.

Didn't hardly know fear. Lot of fellers that got to do something dangerous, they figure, How can I do this without getting hurt? Martin looked at it more like, How can I do this without getting killed?

Martin hired out his whole life. Never owned his own ground as far as I know, except for a house on a small lot. Wasn't a loner, no more than any other cowboy. Married for a long spell. Met his wife Sally on the rodeo circuit. She was the world champion college goat tier in '63. Goat is already tied to a stake. You ride down and tie it—the legs, that is. Timed event. She was a champion barrel racer, too. Met one summer when she was in college and Martin was working for Gibbons. She was with another guy, a friend of Martin's who introduced them. Her first impression was he might be all right when he grows up and learns to keep his mouth shut. Although, she says, he usually had things right when he mouthed off.

After they got married, he took a job with a rancher up in the Sand Hills, but after a few months, they moved back to the Broken Bow area. Bought a house in Comstock. Martin worked on and off for the Gibbons forever, other ranchers, too. He was a hand worth hiring. Martin could rope better than most, but he also knew cattle better than most. He was also a better horseman. Add that he was just plain tough, and that's how you get a special cowboy.

Martin liked horses that bucked. He especially liked horses that'd bucked everyone else off. One time, Wendell Hovie seen Martin leading an unbroke horse through Comstock.

Where you headed, Martin?

Down by the river, says Martin.

There's some swampy land down there south of town.

Why you heading to the river, Martin?

This one ain't held a rider yet, he says. Ground around here is hard. I want a soft place to land when he throws me.

Ended up breaking that horse like he done every other one.

He just knew horses. Had a way with them. Had all kind of tricks. He'd saddle up a half-broke horse at night and take him out. Since the horse couldn't see so well, it had to put some trust in Martin. It also had to concentrate so hard on seeing where it was stepping, it would forget it didn't like carrying a rider.

He knew what horses were thinking, what they were fearing. Like when he was driving cattle and come to a river crossing. Lot of cowboys would charge right into the water. Martin would hold his horse on the bank of the river and let him think on it. When the horse started forward, then he'd spur him, but only after it become the *horse's* idea to get on across. Plenty of cowboys get crosswise with their horse in midstream because it ain't the horse's idea to be there.

Wendell lives over in Comstock, and he was friends with Martin a long time. Once, Wendell was out in front of his house with another feller when Martin come along on a horse that was half-broke. Comstock is an itty-bitty town along the Middle Loup—same place Georgie Fretz the trapper was from. There's a park there, about a block square, on the edge of downtown, not far from the river and right across the street from Wendell's place. Martin lived across town, had a paddock for his horse back of his place. Wendell and his friend set to watching.

There's a foot bridge in the park, not much wider than a horse and with railings. Bridge ain't hardly longer than ten foot and ain't but two foot above a creek so narrow a kid could jump across it. Point is, that little bridge ain't a thing any half-broke horse going to want to cross.

So Martin come along and starts the horse toward that bridge. It shied before it got near it. Martin tugged on the reins, guided the horse away, and took five minutes to do a big loop around the park. He slowly come back around and headed toward that bridge. This time the horse went a tad farther— took one step across before it reared. Martin backed her off and did a slow gait around that park again. He come on back and done two steps over that bridge before the horse let him know he wasn't having none of it, and they went touring some more around town. Wendell and this feller were watching the whole time, and the feller starts sounding off, What's he trying to do to that horse? He ought not to treat him like that.

Wendell just chuckled. Feller thought Martin was being cruel to that horse, making him go across that bridge, but that horse couldn't have been in safer hands. Annnnnnnyway, took about five or six false starts and half an hour, but Martin got that horse to walk across that skinny little bridge. Martin could be tough on a horse when they needed tough, but a lot of horsemen is rough all the time. Martin knew when they needed tough and when they needed patient.

He could rope, too. Yes he could. Never seen anyone done with a rope what he done. I suppose there's plenty of other cowboys could do it like he done, just never seen it is all. When he was doctoring sick calves, he'd stand out in a pasture with a rope, holding the hondu overhand. The hondu is the knot on a lariat lets the loop slip open and closed. With a small loop hanging down, he'd hold that rope out in front of him about chest high and walk up slow, frontwise to a calf. He'd reach back and toss the rope overhand like a baseball. The loop would open wide as it arced over the calf's head and would settle around its neck real gentle.

Most other cowboys would swing that lasso over their head, but that'd scare the calf away—or at least scare it. Remember, these are sick calves. Even if the calf ain't spooked and you managed to lasso it, most cowboys jerked that rope taut right away to secure the critter. But again, we're talking sick calves here. The way Martin done it, after he tossed that lasso over-hand and the calf felt it settle around its neck, nine times out of ten it would drop its head and start backing away. Martin would let it go. As the calf backed away, the loop would start to shrink down. Eventually the calf would lift up its head. That's when Martin would back up a few paces and take the slack full out. Easy to take the calf down then and do the doctoring.

There's folks that says if Martin had set his mind to it, he could have been a rodeo world champion. That's pretty big talk, but Don Holliday, his brother-in-law, rodeoed with Martin a bunch and called him an artist. Weren't no calf roper like him. One time, Martin up and says to Don, I need another event. Going to do bulldogging. Don says, Well, Martin, you ought to practice some if you're going to do that. So Martin practiced twice.

Don had some good bulldogging horses, so they gone up to two pro rodeos the next weekend in South Dakota. Martin placed in the bulldogging in both of them. Not sure he ever done it again after that. That was Martin, too. Floated in the wind, mostly.

Don't know how to say this delicate, but Martin had a life-long affair with the bottle. Didn't affect his cowboying ability much, at least not until later, and even then he was good as any man before noon. He'd start early with the drinking. Pull a Coke bottle out of his saddlebag before the sun had cleared the table and take a swig. But only the bottom half of the bottle was dirt-colored like Coke ought to be; the other half was clear liquid. He'd let you in on his secret concoction. Night before, he'd pour in Coke first, then vodka, and then put it in the freezer. Vodka and coke don't mix. The coke would settle on the bottom and freeze, but the vodka wouldn't. Drank vodka because the foreman couldn't smell it on his breath. Next morning, he'd load up his saddlebag and work that cool vodka all morning. He'd get through the clear layer by around noon. By then the sun about thawed the rest and he had himself a nice, cold, refreshing Coca-Cola at lunchtime.

There was nothing Martin liked more than a good bar fight. If he had an acre for every fight he was in, he'd of owned half of Nebraska. Weren't a huge feller, but big enough at six foot two. He was lanky, though. Wiry, like a cowboy, not wide. But he could brawl with the best of them. Wasn't an angry feller, and wasn't a mean one when he was sober, but when he got drink in him, he got some fight in him, too.

Martin wasn't afraid of nothing, and when he got to drinking, he was even braver. One time, Martin gone to a bar in Broken Bow to get him something to sip on. He'd known Hoss Smith for years. For some reason, they just rubbed each other the wrong way. Suspect it was because both of them thought they was tougher than the other. Hoss was a very big man. Strong. Tall. Wide body, thick arms. One night, they got into an argument in the pool room upstairs. One word led to another, which led to a punch being thrown, and before you know it, they were in a knock-down-drag-out like you seen in the movies. Fists were flying, bottles were crashing, bodies were sailing across the pool table. They beat the crud out of one another and mostly fought to a draw when Hoss ended up on a knee with his back turned. Martin picked up a chair and smashed it over his head. That seemed to pretty much end it.

Martin went down to the restroom at the base of the stairs. When he come out after washing the blood off his face and hands, he looked up to see ol' Hoss at the top of the stairs, propped up against the wall and the bannister, looking like a war casualty. Hoss crooked his finger at Martin, beckoning him, and he says, We ain't done yet.

Martin went up and Hoss beat him down the stairs and then up the stairs and then back down before they were all done. Martin looked like ground beef when Hoss finished with him. But you know what? They become best of friends. You'd go in that bar for years after, and they'd be sitting side by side on stools laughing it up. Had a lot of respect for one another after their misunderstanding.

One time Walt Gibbons walked into a bar in Kearney, and Martin was there. By appearances, he'd been there a spell. Walt walks over and kind of shoulders into him in greeting. What are you doing, Martin?

Martin turns, and he's a bit slow to speak but says, Well I'll be damned, Walt. How you doing?

Martin didn't wait for an answer before he turns around, leans his back against the bar, and announces to the crowd, This here man is Mr. Walt Gibbons. He's the toughest son of a bitch in this bar, and if he can't kick your ass, I will.

Fortunately for all concerned, it was midafternoon and the bar was lightly populated. But Walt wasn't necessarily of a mind to find out if there were any takers in the sparse crowd.

Well, I'll see you later, Martin. Got to be getting back.

Another time, think it was his second hitch out at the Gibbons ranch, John Gibbons and his daughter Anne gone out to the barn early one morning. Martin was already there, in the feed bin. John greeted him with a big Good Morning, but he didn't get much back from Martin. John and Anne did a couple of chores and circled back around. Martin was just coming out of the feed bin. He stepped into the dawn light spilling through the open barn door.

He looked like roadkill. Couldn't tell his face from prime

rib. Weren't much to say, so John says, Did Sally get after you last night, Martin?

Martin wasn't in the best of moods, but that started to get a little chuckle out of him, except it hurt too much to laugh, all that movement it caused in his face. Then Anne piped up. She couldn't have been more than ten or eleven back then, but she been speaking her mind ever since her tongue begun working, and she don't miss much, neither. She says, Well, you going to try him again, Martin?

Turned out it was a friend that done it to him. Not sure of the particulars. Up in Sargent somewheres, but it was outside, or ended up outside, on a dirt road. Other feller got Martin down and was pounding his head into the gravel. With friends like that ...

One time, Martin and Larry Younse went at it in a bar in Broken Bow. Brawled for quite a spell, knocking over tables and chairs and breaking bottles and glasses. Larry whipped him. That happened to Martin now and again. Weren't unlike him to bite off more than he could chew. When it was over, Larry went back to the bar for a little pain medicine, and Martin went out to his pickup. Set in there a spell stewing. Just wasn't right. Ten minutes later, here come ol' Martin back into the bar, bloodied and bruised, but they gone at it some more. Larry whipped him again.

Another time, Martin was in a bar playing cards and was having a spell of bad luck. Feller named Raymond was behind him, not even in the game, fooling with a pigging string. That's a rope used in rodeo to tie a calf's legs. Raymond gone and lassoed Martin around the neck—playing, you know. But after losing half of his two-week paycheck, that rope touching Martin's neck was no different than a match touching the fuse on a stick of dynamite. Explosion in both cases. Martin brought out some color in Raymond's face with a few blows before knocking him flat and returning to his game. Don't recall Raymond practicing his roping in bars much after that.

One time, Don Holliday and Martin were coming back from rodeoing, and they had Martin's boys with them. The boys were probably ten and eleven years old back then. They stopped for a bite to eat at a bar in Taylor. Don and the kids went in first and got settled at a table. There were four good ol' boys seated at the bar. Martin walks in and looks over at the bar, and he don't stop looking until he gets to the table. He says, Don, can I borrow your pocket knife? Don says, Sure. What you want it for?

Martin says, I'm fixing to whip one of the sons of bitches at the bar, and if he has a knife, I want one, too.

Well, I guess the feller cheated Martin in a dog trade or a horse trade or some such, or maybe he didn't, but Martin gone over there and spun one of them boys around, and he says, I want you to tell everyone in this bar you're a chickenshit. Feller says, Don't hit me, Martin. But he don't say nothing about himself being a chickenshit. Martin drug him off the barstool and threw him on the floor. Then he straddled him and started bouncing his head off the pine floorboards. Again and again he done it. The feller's eyes start rolling back up in his head, but his tongue's still working, and finally he says, Okay, Martin, I'm a chickenshit, I'm a chickenshit, you know it.

Had a nice quiet meal after that. His boys' eyes were big as full moons right through dessert.

Only time Sally ever remembers Martin being scared was when he come back late one night from Elm Creek. A feller in a bar there had been picking on another feller, and Martin finally told him to knock it off. Feller come at Martin, and Martin put him on his back with one punch. Feller was out cold. I mean, he plain did not move. Martin stuck around for fifteen minutes but then left. When Martin got home, he was pacing the floor. Finally, the bartender called about two thirty and said they'd gotten the feller on his feet. He didn't know what day it was or what state he was in, but otherwise he was fine. Martin was in the rack and asleep in about twenty seconds. A guilt-free conscience does wonders for your shut-eye.

Martin didn't solve every problem with a fight. One time he and Don were at the Snakepit in Broken Bow. They were causing a bit of a ruckus and got asked to leave—so to speak. The way the Snakepit was laid out, up front was the bar, and in the back of the building, there was a large dance floor. After Martin and Don rolled to a stop on the sidewalk, they decided to rejoin the festivities by going around to the rear door. With that big ol' dance floor, they could slip back in like a stray rejoining the herd and never be noticed. Only problem was the back door was padlocked. That was frustrating. So they come around to the front again, and Martin finds a fence post and jams it into the two front doors. After he done it, that padlocked back door had nothing on the front door when it come to not getting in or out. Then Martin leans in a window and yells, Fire. He could be ornery. Alarm goes off. Some got their pulse rate up. There was screaming. Wasn't a pretty evacuation. Fact, folks was diving out the windows there for a spell.

Martin had his share of run-ins with the law. One time, after he been drinking in Sargent, he headed out of town. Don't know if he was weaving or if the cop was coming after him 'cause of something Martin done in the bar, but he got pulled over near the Middle Loup bridge. Martin got out of his car and begun arguing before the cop was even out of his. One thing led to another. They scuffled a bit, and Martin took the cop's gun from him. He commenced firing at will into the air. Poor cop—think he was a young feller—didn't know what to make of the loco cowboy. Martin ended up proposing a deal: cop let him go home to bed in exchange for his gun. Officer was just fine with that arrangement.

That cop might of been fortunate. There was another one stopped Martin once outside of Ansley or somewheres late at night after Martin been drinking a spell. Martin got out of his pickup as the cop come up on him. Martin knew there was no test for sober he was going to pass. He'd already had his license taken away due to a previous unfortunate incident, so he was driving on an empty wallet. Martin was weighing his options when the cop come up to him. Like I said, Martin was a gambler, and knowing he was in a pack of trouble, he chose to go double or nothing, so to speak, and coldcocked the cop. Knocked him clean out. Left him in a snowbank. Called for backup before departing the scene.

Believe it or not, Martin was a gentleman in his own way. Proper as hell to the ladies. He'd ma'am them and tip his cap and not use profanity when they were around. Just wasn't always so kind to men. Yup, Martin would respect you or beat the crap out of you, one of the two.

Although Martin might not have been on the right side of the law on all occasions, cowboy ethic run strong in him. Like the time somebody been rustling Gibbons's cattle. Just a few here and there, but rustling cattle ain't something that's looked on with much favor out here. One day Martin was riding range. He come over a rise, and there was the rustler plain as day. Once before he'd taken two calves off of Gibbons's cows and put them on his own. Now he was grabbing a heifer. It was a local feller had a small ranch.

Martin rode up hard to him and lassoed him around the neck. Conversation went something like this. Martin says, It ain't right to steal another man's cattle, now is it? The feller didn't say nothing, so Martin give a little tug on that rope, and it cinched around his neck. Feller said, No. Then Martin asked if this was the first cow he'd helped himself to. Feller still got a bit too much stuffing in him, and he don't say nothing. Martin tightens her up a bit more while backing up his horse, which yanks the feller to his knees. The feller says, No. Martin says, You're going to go get them calves and bring them back, ain't cha? Martin backs away his horse a bit more. By now the feller's flat on the ground, and his trachea's squeezed so tight it'd make a sipping straw look like the Trans-Alaska Pipeline. He managed a wheezy Yes, but his legs done most of the talking; they were kicking and writhing. Pretty much went on like that until the feller seen the error of his ways, which was simultaneous to him turning blue. Martin released him, and the problem never come up again. I won't tell you the rustler's name. Let's just say it was Smith. Forever after Martin would call them the Thieving Smiths. Even ten years later, driving by them, he might say to Sally, Hey, look, there are the Thieving Smiths out for a walk.

Ol' Martin had a lot of salt-of-the-earth cowboy wisdom in him. One time, he and Frank Stefka got orders at sunup from a ranch boss to re-pair cows. That means remate calves that got separated from their mothers. The foreman was known for having more authority than brains. He'd play mind games with the ranch hands and do a lot of pointing and mumbling and not much explaining what he wanted. They called him the Cow Whisperer, but it wasn't an endearing term.

Annnnnnnyway, none of the calves was bawling or nothing, so there didn't seem to be a problem to begin with, but this ranch boss was determined they were all mixed up. Well, Frank and Martin spent all day at it, rounding up cows and calves to remate them. Even ate their sack lunches in their saddles. By sundown, they'd rounded them all up and got them in the pen, but instead of an even number of cows and calves, they ended up with about twenty head of cows and about five calves. The Cow Whisperer waves his hands and says, Open the gate and let them out. He walks away, leaving Frank standing there stunned and Martin looking about like he always done.

When the boss was in his truck and gone and the cattle were scattering across the field, Frank turns to Martin and says, Martin, can you tell me what we just did out here today?

Clear-eyed, face blank, Martin says, We earned a wage.

After that, every time a boss would tell Frank something dumb, contrary, or backwards to common sense, he'd think of what Martin said, and it'd settle him down.

Feller like Martin, who hired out his whole life, knew how it was between ranchers and cowboys and where he ranked in that pairing. When he worked up on the Gibbons place, he was treated fair, and the place was run right, and he called Walt Mr. Gibbons the way all the boys done—he deserved it. But that don't mean Martin didn't know a few ranch hand tricks. He used to catch a nap out on the range, just lie down right next to his horse. Once, Frank asked him if he wasn't worried about the foreman catching him napping on the job. He said, No, I just tie the reins to one of my belt loops and keep it short. If the boss comes, horse'll perk his ears up and lift his head. Gives a pretty good tug. Wakes you right up.

Ol' Martin, he always talked so definite. Combination of

him being positive and seeing the world in black and white. Thing is done or it ain't done. When he said a thing, he said it like it was going to happen no matter what come along. Like the time he took Wayne Matthern out coon hunting. Middle of winter. Wayne never been.

They left a bar about midnight. Martin had his coon hunting dog with him, and they gone out along an irrigation canal by Matthern's place. Cold night, sky clear as spring water. Martin says, We'll start ol' Tex and have a coon in nothing flat. They parked, and off went the dog. They heard him yelping and yelping, but pretty soon that yelping gets further and further away. Finally, Martin grimaces and he says, Son of a bitch, he's running a deer. Could hear that dog bawling for miles in the winter air. Martin, he starts singing out, Yoooo, Tex. Yoooo, Tex. He was calling out again and again.

Well hell, his voice carried about a hundred yards while ol' Tex was in the next county. But Martin went on, Yoooo, Tex. Yoooo, Tex. Pretty soon Martin and Wayne ain't hearing ol' Tex and pretty soon they ain't heard him for a while. Martin says, I'll just unload this dog box I got here in the pickup, and he'll be right here in the morning. Says it like he's saying the sun'll be up at dawn.

Well, no Tex in the morning, or the next morning, or the next. About two weeks later, Martin hears a feller up Route 2 got a stray coon dog, and Martin gone up there to fetch him. Sure enough, it was ol' Tex. Looked like hell. Gone and tangled with something. Ears were shredded, and he was thin as a fence rail.

Wayne was wanting for the longest spell to get on Martin about that dog being Right Here in the morning, but you had to pick and choose your times careful to be getting on Martin—and the time never quite come.

Martin had a border collie, too. Them's funny dogs. Very trainable, but sometimes real timid. You look at them cross-wise or, heaven help them, raise your voice, and they'll shy or slink away. When he was older, Martin spent a lot of evenings in the barn. He'd sit at a table and drink, and he'd make that border collie sit in a chair opposite him all night. Every once in a while, he'd pour beer into an ashtray for the dog to drink. Like he was on a bad date, the dog every now and then would look to leave—not even take a step in that direction—just start *thinking* about slipping away. But Martin would point a finger at him and say, Don't you get out of that chair. Dog would straighten up and set at attention for another half hour before Martin had to bark at him again.

Martin was always looking to play a joke. You never knew what he got up his sleeve. Way back, Martin and Kenny Houston done some rodeoing together. On the road a lot. Hell, back in them days, there were rodeos five days a week, maybe more. Martin and Kenny did some team roping. That's where you got yourself a header and a heeler. Steer goes out the chute, and the header ropes him around the horns and turns him off, and then the heeler come along and lassos the back two legs. Rules were different for different places, but back then, the heeler would step off his horse and use a tie line to do a hard and fast tie on the back two feet. And that's time … clock stops.

Once, up in South Dakota, they were competing in a three-header, meaning there were three rounds. After two, Martin and Kenny were leading. Kenny was fired up. Purse was five hundred dollars, and they were sitting pretty. Martin was the header and Kenny the heeler. Third round, gate opens, steer charges out. Martin lassos him around the horns in great time, and Kenny heels him quick, too. Kenny's off his horse in a flash and reaches for the tie line tucked into his saddle. But there ain't nothing there.

Kenny's yelling, I ain't got no string.

Martin's yelling back, What do you mean, Houston? You ain't got no string?

Well, the steer is struggling on the ground, dust is billowing, the crowd's cheering. But now folks are beginning to wonder what's happening. For a cowboy, being caught without a tie line is like wandering out into the middle of the arena with no pants on.

Kenny looks up at Martin. A little smile creeps onto Martin's face. He'd lifted the string out of Kenny's saddle when they got into the box and tossed it away. Being funny. Being ornery. Being Martin. That five-hundred-dollar purse didn't mean nothing to Martin compared to seeing the look of horror on Kenny's face when he grabbed for that tie string and come up empty.

Martin liked to tour. That's what he called it. Done it on horseback or in a pickup. Just ride or drive around to see what was happening. 'Course, this is the middle of Nebraska, so it wasn't always much. Martin drove about twenty miles an hour. No one was ever sure why. These are paved roads I'm talking about. Everyone else is going sixty or seventy. Some say it's because he felt more like he was on horseback at that pace. Others say it's cause most times he was just touring and there wasn't no reason to go fast when he wasn't going nowhere. Others say it's because he was rarely in possession of his license and didn't want to tempt the law.

Annnnnnnyway, one time over in Comstock, Martin come

by and says to Wendell, Let's go tour. Martin was in the big ol' white Buick he drove when he wasn't in his pickup. They headed up towards where the music festival is held every summer. Festival has grown like crazy. Now they have big names come play, and you can't believe how many folks head out there to the middle of nowhere for the festival. After Martin had fetched Wendell, they're driving around at twenty mile an hour, and they gone by the festival grounds while it's being set up. There's a big dirt parking lot that's blocked off by cones because they got power and phone lines and all kinds of other lines lying on the ground and crisscrossing while they figure out what to do with them. Well, Martin, just to be ornery, gone around them cones and starts driving in big circles around the lot. Drove all over them power cables, like he's a troublemaking sixteen-year-old.

Wendell says, Go on now, get out of here. What are you doing, Martin?

Martin just laughed. Pretty soon there's folks all over yelling at him and Wendell and having fits. Now oversized security guards are coming, and they're chasing the Buick on foot, and they're almost catching up to it because Martin ain't varied from his touring speed of twenty. Martin got a big ol' smile on his face. Finally, he drives back over them cones, not around them this time. Wendell was about eighty years old then, and he's wondering if he's going to get arrested and handcuffed and get his picture in the paper for being the world's oldest criminal—or at least the oldest hooligan.

They get back on the main road heading south, and in their rearview mirror, they see about a dozen people of all ages and sexes and wearing bright green vests united in a common cause:

shaking their fists and cursing at Martin. Meanwhile, Martin's chuckling under his cowboy hat and having a good ol' time.

Martin just done things his own way. Once, when he was working for Walt Gibbons, Walt had leased a couple of studs from a feller out in Colorado and brung them to his ranch out here and was breeding mares to them. Couldn't put a price on them, but they were real expensive horses.

Happened to be a cold winter, and every morning when they gone out to start the tractors, well, they wouldn't start. But if you could just move them a few feet, they'd jump-start sure enough. So Martin fixed up a harness for them high-priced stud horses, and every morning he'd hitch them up and use them to pull those tractors so he could get them started. One day, the feller from Colorado was out to visit and come up on Martin treating his fancy studs like oxen. He give Martin holy hell. Walt wasn't so pleased, neither.

Martin was a tough bastard. Old kind of tough. Bite-on-leather-while-they-carve-a-bullet-out-of-you-without-anesthesia tough. Tougher than boiled owl. He run around with a ruptured stomach for a while. Come over to see Kenny. Says, I seen you sew up horses and pigs before. You going to sew me up today? He lifted up his shirt and showed Kenny his guts spilling out of his stomach.

Kenny shook his head, spit some tobacco juice, and says, There's people that sews up other people when their guts are hanging out of their bellies. They call them doctors, and you ought to go see one.

Martin just smiled, grit his teeth, and declined the advice. If tough could have got a man through that, then Martin would have got through it, but there's tough and there's guts hanging out of your belly. Don't know exactly how or when or where, but about a week later, they managed to rope him, get him off the range, and into a hospital.

Later, when he was getting on in years, Martin had to have hip replacement surgery. He hated hospitals with a passion. Think he hated rooms and roofs and doors in general. Anyway, two days after the surgery, he told them he needed to get something out of his car. He took off and went home and never went back. 'Course, part of the reason he wanted out was so he could get to some pain medicine, if you know what I mean.

Then there's the emus. Lot of mythology about them emus. Here's how it went, although all the stories been told about them don't exactly lie flush against one another.

One morning, Martin come by Kenny's place. He says, Got to get your trailer. Going for a little tour.

Like I said, Martin was always touring. In a truck. In a car. On horseback. Couldn't sit still.

Kenny says, What we need the trailer for?

Martin says, I got some emus give to me.

Emus? Kenny just shook his head. Going to be another Martin day.

So they got all hooked up and went over to the Grangers'. They had four head of emus on their place. Got tired of their experiment and couldn't sell them.

Hell, you can load just about any kind of critter in a trailer, but neither Kenny nor Martin ever loaded emus. They set it up so they had a little gate and an alleyway leading into the trailer. But them emus weren't cattle. Each had a mind of its own—even if it was the size of a pea. The whole time Martin and Kenny was pushing those big rumps toward the trailer, the emus were pecking and kicking and clawing, and feathers were flying everywhere. Soon as they got them near the trailer, them birds would fly back.

Next thing you know, one of them birds turned on Kenny and took a big bite right out the bill of his Stetson. Automatic-like, Kenny shot his arm out and grabbed that emu around the neck to keep it from going after his eyeballs next. Then, about as quick, Kenny lets go of him. That emu dropped over dead. Just like that.

Everything stopped. Kenny be a bit wide-eyed at what happened so sudden. Martin, he tipped back his hat and says, Them emus don't take much choking, do they?

They got the other three loaded and hauled them back to the ranch. Took the dead one, too. Tried to butcher it. Kind of butchered the butchering, though. Them's tough birds to cut up and even tougher to get down. Ol' Kenny and Martin tried to eat that emu every which way they could, but they give up 'fore they ever made it a meal.

Only had them emus a couple of days when the primary purpose of them birds in Martin's life come clear to him. They were meant for roping practice. If you made a living lassoing big-headed, thick-necked cattle, what better way to practice than on a critter with a little head and a long, scrawny neck.

Martin would let them emus loose in a pen and rope them around the neck, but he got tired of that soon enough. Remember how I told you in team roping a header catches the steer around the neck and the heeler lassos the back two legs to trip him up? Martin got to heeling them emus just to watch them fall on their beaks.

Martin had a bay he was training. Nice little horse. Cutting horse is used to cut cattle out of a herd for whatever reason ... doctoring, branding. Martin decides that bay could get some topflight training cutting emus. See, them emus is quite a bit quicker than a cow, and no cow ever jumped like these birds done.

A week or so after he got them emus, Martin was mounted on that bay ready to get in some emu cutting practice. Kenny opened a gate and let them birds out on the open range. Apparently Martin miscalculated their passion for freedom because them emus absolutely bolted across the prairie. No horse alive was going to catch them birds. Running with them long gangly strides, one emu headed east towards Omaha and was never heard from again. One headed west and run with a buffalo herd for a while. You heard that story. A thirty-aught-six ended that little adventure. The third emu headed south and took up residence in Comstock. Some of the townsfolk liked him, but most didn't. After he'd stole a few too many panties and bras off of clotheslines, Martin gone into town with his rifle and come up on the bird in an alleyway. That ended the entire emu escapade rather sudden.

Martin was a trader. He never bought nothing new his whole life. Traded everything all the time. For being the world's champion college goat tier, Sally won a fancy saddle. He traded that, too.

Few months before he died, Martin called up Don Holliday and says, Don, why don't you come on up here with your trailer and get this ol' buckskin horse of mine, give him a nice home? Been a good horse, getting old now, but the grandkids will get a lot of good out of him yet.

So Don and his son went up and got the horse, and like Martin said, horse was great with the kids. They done a lot of riding on him. About a month later, Martin calls up and he says, Don, ol' Younce over here at the barn says he'll give me twelve hundred and fifty for that buckskin, but for you guys, I'll sell him to you for a thousand dollars.

Don wasn't so pleased, thought that buckskin was a piece of charity on Martin's part. But Martin was Martin, and in Don's case, Martin was family, too, so he wrote the check. After Martin died a few months later, Don was at the funeral, and he hears two fellers talking about a buckskin horse. He slides over and says, You fellers talking about Martin's buckskin horse? They say, Yeah, where's he at? Don says, I got him. They say, Where you get him from? Don says, I paid Martin a thousand dollars for him. One of them says, Hell, he sold us that horse about six years ago and then borrowed him back. Ain't seen him since.

Wasn't like he needed the money. Just Martin being Martin, trading, selling, throw in a pinch of being ornery.

Once, when Martin was getting older, Anne Gibbons come over from work to check on some young hands that were tinning her barn. Like I said, she was a young girl when Martin was in his prime and working her father's ranch. Knew him for many years. By this time, she was in her thirties. Fellers working her barn were cowboy wannabes and talking big that day. Martin drove up in a truck. Touring. Wasn't working for the Gibbonses then. He stopped near the barn, and Anne got in the cab and talked to him for maybe half an hour. When Martin left and she come back into the barn, them young hands asked her who the old-timer was.

She weren't trying to insult them. It just come out. She says, That's more cowboy than any of you'll ever be.

Bottle got him in the end. Don't know exactly what the doctors would say, but I'm guessing his liver just closed up shop one day. Went a lot of years earlier than he should've gone, but

Martin lived life on his own terms. Did it every day until the day he died. Ain't many folks can say that.

At his funeral, his daughter said Martin had been born a hundred years too late. There ain't a more fitting epitaph than that.

Afterword

THE idea for *Nebraska Stories* took root at a dinner party in St. Louis in the year 2000. Stuart Jenkins was there. I'd known Stuart in college, but I knew his older brother, Jim, better; we played football together at the same college. It was well known that Jim was from Nebraska, but we never really talked much about it. At the dinner party, Stuart started telling tales about growing up on the family ranch in the remote central part of the state, and they were some of the funniest stories I'd ever heard. I wondered if enough could be collected to fill a book and discussed the idea with Stuart. He told me I had to talk to *the* storyteller in the family, his father, who was in his late seventies at the time.

I journeyed to Nebraska one weekend. Jim had moved back to the ranch a few years before and built a new log home on one end of their four-thousand-acre spread, but we met in the old farmhouse, the one that had been on the property for seventy-five years. It was where the boys had grown up. Wayne Jenkins got to spinning yarns and didn't stop for well over two hours.

Driving home to St. Louis, I felt an odd combination of exhilaration and dejection. Exhilaration because Wayne's stories were even better than I thought they'd be, but dejection because they were fragmentary and limited. That's no criticism of Wayne or his storytelling. His stories were the rural equivalent of cocktail party chatter—anecdotes of thirty seconds to a few minutes in length when related verbally, but as short as a paragraph when written.

I had never attempted—or ever had occasion to think about—translating oral storytelling into the written word. But as I transcribed the tapes of my interview with Wayne, I immediately saw the challenge: readers were unlikely to respond to an endless series of disconnected fifty-word anecdotes. The same might work well at a dinner party or in a bar, but such anecdotes translated directly to print simply weren't literary. However, as I fussed with the transcribed material, I was pleased to note the anecdotes lent themselves to being grouped around a half dozen neighbors and relatives. I began to piece the material together into roughly two-thousand-word character sketches. It seemed to me this was an ideal solution (since readers naturally respond to people and characters), as opposed to trying to group the stories around events, themes, or perhaps chronology. And the length of the sketches was sufficient to establish character, create narrative critical mass, and generally build and hold reader interest. Creating "narrative critical mass," in particular, seemed to be the missing ingredient in the oral rendering of the stories.

Again, joy and dejection. Joy upon figuring out all of the above, but dejection after fully transcribing the initial Wayne Jenkins interview, fashioning character sketches from the material, and finding they totaled only five or six. I wasn't sure how to proceed. I figured I could wring a few more stories from Wayne, but not nearly enough to assemble a book-length manuscript. I put the project on hold until December 2003. I had finished another writing project by then, and *Nebraska Stories*—as I was already calling the barely written (and even less-so conceived) book—was haunting me. The initial stories were just too good to go untold. I consulted with the Jenkins brothers, and they said I should head back out, said I simply had to talk to Davey Davis.

I did. I made the long drive hoping and praying all the way that his stories about his neighbors were as good as Wayne's. As I began interviewing Davey, I got that awful dichotomous feeling again. I was elated because Davey's stories were as funny as Wayne's, but dejected because he wasn't telling me any stories about his neighbors, like Wayne had. If Davey didn't have any Ralphs, Georges, or Leonards for me, then the project was stalled, perhaps for good. Or so I thought. But within ten or fifteen minutes of the start of the interview, I realized Davey was the character I was looking for, not his neighbors. I knew the character sketch I got out of that interview was going to be Davey himself.

I was sky-high on the drive home to St. Louis. I love stories, and the tapes from Davey were chock-full of classic tales. But I still didn't know what I was going to do with them because the other stories I'd written up were in Wayne's voice. Then I had an epiphany; a model took shape in my mind. I decided the way to give the book some structure and readability was to tell Davey's story in Wayne's voice—and to do the same with everyone else I subsequently interviewed. And that's what happened.

I went on to interview over sixty-five people. For those whose stories merited a character sketch, I held on to the model just described, except that, by the time I finished collecting stories and rewriting them countless times, the voice of the narrator had become a conglomeration of the sixty-five voices I had heard.

Perhaps I should make clear that the voice of the narrator

is *not* Wayne Jenkins and does not reflect his opinions. Wayne never met three-quarters of the people profiled here.

This book is nonfiction. It is certainly a fictitious device to turn around and tell someone's story, as they have related it, in a third-person composite voice, as I have done. But the content of each story is largely true. Yes, I just used a caveat. Where there were gaps in a few of the stories, I filled them in, but only for continuity sake; none of the filler added substance to any of the stories. Very early in the process of writing, back when I had only interviewed Wayne, I tried to write a fictitious anecdote to supplement others in a character sketch based on one of Wayne's neighbors. It didn't work. It felt wrong and it read wrong. Fiction, in this case, was no match for reality, and I permanently abandoned the idea.

Let me add, however, that I am quite aware that I largely went fishing for fish tales in my interviews for the book, and I cannot assure readers that those I spoke with haven't exaggerated. And I won't pretend I cross-examined their accounts with prosecutorial zeal. But for some reason it is important to me that readers understand *I* did not enlarge any of the fish in these tales, even if interviewees may have. And in one case, I unilaterally shrunk a fish that seemed a bit expansive. Additionally, the sketches are completely reordered compared to how they were related by sources, in order to create a sense of continuity that makes for entertaining narrative. Some sketches rely on multiple sources, with material gathered piecemeal over several years. But none of the rearranging constitutes fictionalization; it is simply my value-add as an author.

Aside from the fiction-nonfiction divide, I sometimes had trouble explaining to potential interviewees just what it was I was doing. It isn't journalism. It isn't really history. It isn't straight oral history, either. It may be folklore, but I don't really know what that is. I just know funny and engaging stories when I hear them, and I felt an urge to collect and share these.

While this book is unarguably a commercial venture, it is mostly a labor of love. When I began the project, I had no publisher and no advance. Its success all through the years of interviewing and writing, and even now, as it is being self-published, was and is far from certain. I was and am motivated primarily by a genuine desire to preserve stories that document, in a lighthearted manner, a way of life that is both quintessentially American and also, sadly, fast disappearing. Many of the people portrayed in the book are in their late seventies and eighties, or have even passed on in the time it has taken me to complete the project. They are part of the Greatest Generation, as it has come to be known. Whether forged by war, the Depression, or simply the American experience of their time, I fear their breed will never come this way again. They are some of the finest people I've ever met.

Acknowledgments

THIS book would not have been possible without the help of the Jenkins family. I am first and foremost indebted to Wayne Jenkins. Wayne was the first person I interviewed for the book, and his stories eventually contributed to five profiles and parts of several others. I interviewed Wayne twice and usually paid him a social call on my many subsequent visits. The idea that this book is intended to document the stories and lives of the sources listed here before they pass (and their stories lost to history) was sad prophesy in Wayne's case. He died in 2006, before the manuscript was completed. As mentioned in the afterword, the voice of the narrator started out as Wayne's and then morphed into a conglomeration of voices. But I can still hear the echo of his twang when I reread the sketches, certainly in such words as "Annnnnnnway …" a favorite Wayne segue voiced in a distinctive, arced pitch. Wayne gave the book its heart and soul.

I am also indebted to Wayne's sons. Stuart Jenkins' stories sparked this project. Jim and Juliana Jenkins were incredibly helpful in spotting and assessing potential interviewees and always left the light on for me in the old ranch house.

So many of those I spoke with welcomed me into their homes and readily sat down for an interview with the barest notion of what I was attempting to do—and many did so without much notice. I am very grateful to those who so generously shared their life stories with me: Davey Davis, Dorothy Miller, Dave Birnie, Mike Cox, Thelma Reicks, Ted Hanich, Frank Stefka, Jack Longfellow, Ray Brown, Francis Gschwind, Jo Ellen Wies, Cleve Trimble, Bill Williams, John Witthuhn, John and Marge Hardy, A.B. Cox, and Sparky Malmberg.

I am also thankful to those who added anecdotes about others and those who provided other kinds of assistance: Ira Pitkin, Joel Johnson, Don Douglas, R.P. Smith, John Birnie, Ken Eggleston, George Stewart, Larry Tierney, Loren (Jake) Jacobsen, Anne Gibbons, John Gibbons, Kenny Houston, Wendell Hovie, Sally Armstrong, Larry Cleveland, Don Albion, Bill Zutavern, Ferd and Susan Beshaler, Roy James, Bill Thurston, Don Holliday, Roger Chesley, Glen Nutter, Lester Miles, Wayne Mattern, Pete Bishop, Lorraine Smith, Ron Worm, William Gust, Jimmy Warner, Joe Nutter, Gary Sears, Larry Cleveland, Joe Andrews, Ken Stithem, Daryl Nelson, Chuck Blakeman, Dave Kirkpatrick, Bill Thurston, Myron McGraw, Royce Ferguson, Merle Haywood, Bob Smith, Miller Heller, and Rollie Glaus.

Thanks also to editor Karen Davis for her keen eye and helpful suggestions, and to cover designer, Caitlin Heimerl, for her charming watercolor.

About the Cover

THE origin of the western tradition of putting old cowboy boots on fences and fence posts is apparently lost to history. There are innumerable explanations, some of which make common sense—probably the best judge of their credibility when you're talking about ranchers—and others that don't make much sense at all. Some say the boots are put there because the scent of humans keeps coyotes and other critters away. Problem with that theory is, if you have a spread that's hundreds or even thousands of acres, one boot isn't going to slow the animal traffic much. Others say the boots are the equivalent of a Dear John letter whenever a ranch hand quits. Idea is, he sticks his boot or boots on a fence post as he heads out the gate and on down the road. A corollary theory is that a rancher plops a boot on a fence post to let folks know he's home. Problem with those two theories is pretty obvious. In the first case, you end up with a ranch hand walking down the road in his socks after quitting. In the second case, you have a rancher driving up his driveway in his socks. A theory that makes some sense is that a boot stuck on a fence post is meant as a sign of respect for a rancher who has just passed on. Of course, lately, folks that put boots on fences are maybe just copying other folks they seen doing it—it's gotten popular, even artistic. Like I said, no telling. It could also come down to whimsy. Room for that in the west, too.

About the Author

CRAIG Savoye was born in New Jersey and raised in California and Connecticut. He has had careers in journalism, government, business, public relations and academia. He was a staff writer for the *Christian Science Monitor* in Boston, a corporate relations manager for a mainframe computer company in California's Silicon Valley, a public information officer at a national laboratory, and is currently an assistant professor of mass communication at his alma mater, Principia College, in Elsah, Illinois. He lives in St. Louis with his family.